CLOSE TO ZERO

How Donald Trump fulfilled his apocalyptic vision
and paid his debt to Putin with a devastating
biological warfare attack on America

Jonathan Vankin

Published in the United States by Twilight of the Idols Inc.

Cover design by John Whalen

Front cover photo by Tina Dufour / Trump White House Archived (Public Domain) https://www.flickr.com/photos/whitehouse45/49608880598/in/photostream/

Back cover photo by Shealah Craighead / Trump White House Archived (Public Domain) https://www.flickr.com/photos/whitehouse45/42547210635/in/album-72157697284924301/

Coronavirus SARS-CoV-2 image by Felipe Esquivel Reed / Wikimedia Commons (Creative Commons Attribution-Share Alike 4.0 International License https://creativecommons.org/licenses/by-sa/4.0/legalcode) https://commons.wikimedia.org/wiki/File:Coronavirus_SARS-CoV-2.jpg

ISBN (eBook) 978-1-7369621-0-7
ISBN (paperback)978-1-7369621-1-4
ISBN (hardcover) 978-1-7369621-2-1

Rights inquiries:
Twilight of the Idols Inc.
8 The Green
Suite #8609
Dover, DE 19901
inquiries@twilightoftheidols.net

Media inquiries:
media@twilightoftheidols.net

To the hundreds of thousands of Americans who lost their lives to the COVID-19 pandemic.

May the memory of each and every one be a blessing.

"And again, when you have 15 people, and the 15 within a couple of days is going to be down to close to zero, that's a pretty good job we've done."

— Donald Trump
February 26, 2020

CONTENTS

INTRODUCTION

"If he can in any way profit from your death, he'll facilitate it,
and then he'll ignore the fact that you died."

— *Mary L. Trump, Ph.D.*
re: her uncle, Donald J. Trump,
President of the United States

Donald Trump was relaxing on the golf course in West Palm Beach, Florida, two days before New Year's Eve of 2019 when a call came through that he just had to take. On the other end, Vladimir Putin, the president of Russia.[1] The call was at least the 17th between Trump and Putin,[2] but the first he had taken during one of his 111 golf outings[3] (to that date) since his inauguration on January 20, 2017.

Two days later, on December 31, the Chinese government informed the World Health Organization of a new respiratory illness,[4] infecting 266 people in Wuhan, China's 10th-largest city. But at that time, China did not tell the WHO what it had learned four days earlier — and two days before Putin's call to a golfing Trump. The respiratory illness was caused by a newly discovered coronavirus, SARS-CoV-2.

A coronavirus is a highly specific type of virus that causes severe respiratory ailments.[5] But is distinct from the family of viruses that causes the flu. The SARS pandemic of 2003 was caused by an earlier coronavirus.

The new — or as it was called by medical professionals "novel" — coronavirus quickly spread around the world, slamming the United States especially hard. In the U.S., SARS-CoV-2 infections mowed down more than 80,000 people[6] in the first three months of the pandemic, three times that many six months later, showing few signs of slowing its deadly pace. As early as February, fears of what the virus could do to the U.S. economy triggered a drastic stock market crash.[7]

Those fears proved well-founded. As states and cities attempted to slow the spread of the virus by ordering residents to remain confined at home, and closing down all but "essential" businesses, the country's economy spiraled into an overnight depression, with an astonishing 30 million Americans losing their jobs in a four-week span starting mid-March.[8]

In the second quarter of 2020 — that is, in April, May and June — the United States Gross Domestic Product dropped almost 33 percent.[9] That was four times worse than the worst quarter of the 2008 Great Recession.[10]

But as the pandemic ripped through the country of which he was at least nominally president, Trump responded in a manner that has yet to be explained.

He did nothing.

Strike that. He did worse than nothing. He took active measures to make the pandemic worse. He deliberately, in calculated fashion, caused Americans to die.

Just one month before the world's first case of what would become known as COVID-19 were discovered in Hubei Province, China, the Johns Hopkins Center for Health Security together with the Nuclear Threat Initiative compiled a ranking of 195 countries, rated by their degree of preparation for the next, inevitable global pandemic.[11]

At the very top — U.S.A.! U.S.A! We're Number One!

This book is the story of how one man, his cronies, and the apparatus that supports them, took America from the best in the world to one of the very worst[12] — on purpose. What the evidence and events I'll cite throughout this book showed me was a concerted program of destruction — an attack by means of a biological agent. Donald Trump waged his own, personal, biological warfare attack on the United States.

I know that sounds like a far-out accusation. But this book is primarily a compilation of facts taken from the public record. When I evaluate the totality of the evidence cited in these pages, I can come to no other conclusion. The assumption that Trump in some way attempted at all to guide the country through the crisis with minimal damage, or that he even wanted to, does not hold up.

The assumption that he cared about preventing deaths or suffering of Americans does not hold up either. The assumption that he worked to rescue the economy — or, again, even cares about it beyond what it might mean for his personal fortunes — also collapses quickly when matched with the facts.

The facts do tell me that Donald Trump did all of this because he intended to. He had a plan, and he executed it. Trump himself offered perhaps the most compelling evidence, when he told Bob Woodward[13] — as close to an iconic figure as exists in journalism — that he knew early on that the coronavirus was "deadly stuff," but that he "wanted to always play it down." Which as we will see, in quite some detail, was exactly what he did.

Trump, it should be said, also proffered Woodward an excuse, albeit a lame and implausible one, for his "play it down" approach. "I still like playing it down, because I don't want to create a panic," he said.[14]

It was very much in character for Trump to temper his admission to Woodward with a rationale for his seemingly inexcusable actions. According to his former "fixer" and intimate confidant Michael Cohen, "plausible deniability wasn't just a strategy for Trump — it was his way of life."[15]

Trump's "panic" cover story was absurd on its face. When had he ever cared about preventing panic? He predicated his presidential campaigns, and much of his presidency, on his ability to incite panic.[16]

Whether it was his attempts to stoke fear over MS-13, immigrant "caravans," impending "Civil War," mass "voter fraud," or Joe Biden's secret plan to "abolish the suburbs," Trump never shied away from instilling fear, at least in his own supporters, of one ginned-up imminent existential threat or another.

On the other hand, Republican National Committee Chair Ronna McDaniel may have given the game away when she told NBC's *Meet The Press* on September 13, "Think of what would have happened if he'd have gone out and said, 'This is awful. We should all be afraid. We don't have a plan.'"[17]

Indeed, if Trump had publicly admitted that he *had no plan* to deal with the pandemic, I suppose that may have caused panic. On the other hand, his lack of a plan for doing anything but letting the virus sweep across the United States unabated was evident from the earliest stages of the crisis.

If you think that whole idea is crazy, that accusing Trump of a deliberate attack on the United States, killing hundreds of thousands, is totally beyond the pale, all I can humbly entreat you to do, dear reader, is to read the book and judge the evidence for yourself.

When I started work on this project the idea that Trump was killing people on purpose seemed obvious to me. But not too many others saw it that way. At least, not many who were willing to say it out loud. That was in April of 2020.

By August, even a U.S. senator was scooping me.

"Can we take the gloves off and tell the truth? Trump is deliberately killing people," wrote Connecticut Senator Chris Murphy, after Trump delivered his nomination acceptance speech in front of a tightly packed, maskless crowd in the midst of the pandemic. "His plan is to kill people. Let's just say it."[18]

Even Dr. Deborah Birx, a top medical adviser on Trump's coronavirus task force, finally admitted — albeit more than two months after Trump left office — that the overwhelming majority of American COVID-19 deaths never needed to happen.[19]

"I look at it this way. The first time we have an excuse," Birx told *CNN.* "There were about a hundred thousand deaths that came from that original surge. All of the rest of them, in my mind, could have been mitigated or decreased substantially."

What Murphy was saying six months into the pandemic, and what Birx admitted much later, had been clear since the beginning. As late as the beginning of April, when more than 5,000 Americans were already dead, Trump suggested to his medical advisers that "we let this wash over the country."[20]

The idea that the coronavirus pandemic should be allowed to "wash over" the United States seemed to stick in Trump's head. His aides said that he brought it up on multiple occasions.[21] I don't have any special, psychological insight into why Trump became fixated on the concept of the virus as a cleansing force for America. Perhaps it has something to do with his grandiose, apocalyptic vision of life that we'll explore in Chapter Two.

As the pandemic roared its way through the American summer, indications started to emerge that it was, in actual reality, the case that Trump and his cronies themselves saw the pandemic as not merely a pestilence to "wash over" the country, but a targeted weapon to wound and kill political opponents. Maybe Trump hoped the disease would wash away his political enemies. Who knows?

A rather stunning exposé by *Vanity Fair* magazine reporter Katherine Eban in late July revealed that the Trump "political folks" chose to do nothing to stop the coronavirus because "it was going to be relegated to Democratic states," and letting the pandemic ravage those "blue" states "would be an effective political strategy."[22]

Trump all but copped to that "strategy" at a September 16 "press conference," as he boasted about the "really good job" he had done by holding coronavirus deaths to fewer than 240,000. *240,000!*[23]

He then stated, "we're down in this territory, and that's despite the fact that the blue states had had tremendous death rates. If you take the blue states out, we're at a level that I don't think anybody in the world would be at. We're really at a very low level. But some of the states, they were blue states and blue state-managed."

By the end of August, Trump grew weary of the government's top infectious disease specialist, Dr. Anthony Fauci — who made an annoying habit of openly contradicting Trump's repeated pronouncements in which he waved off the deadly severity of the virus.

Instead, according to a *Washington Post* report, Trump adopted Dr. Scott Atlas, a radiologist with no special knowledge or training in the field of infectious diseases.[24] But Atlas was a frequent Fox News talking head, and "fellow" at the conservative Hoover Institute. Atlas advocated a "herd immunity" approach to the virus — which was a fancy way of saying, "let it wash over the country."

According to an analysis by the *Post*, a "herd immunity" strategy would ultimately result in 2.13 million American coronavirus deaths. And because a disproportionate number of those who died from the virus in the U.S. were people of color and the elderly, the "herd immunity" plan looked a lot like a eugenics program, designed to weed out society's most vulnerable people.[25]

The White House issued an official denial that the administration was considering a "herd immunity" approach to the pandemic. But in an internal email sent on July 4, a top, Trump-appointed science adviser — Paul Alexander — at the Department of Health and Human Services declared that there was "no other way" than to "establish herd."

Alexander, writing to his superior, Trump appointee Michael Caputo, said that supposedly "low risk" groups should be deliberately exposed to the virus.

"Infants, kids, teens, young people, young adults, middle aged with no conditions etc. have zero to little risk …we want them infected," he wrote."[26]

Alexander was no rogue. According to Kyle McGowan, a Trump appointee at the Centers for Disease Control, "It was understood that he spoke for Michael Caputo, who spoke for the White House."

On August 31, Trump himself publicly appeared to endorse exactly the disastrous "herd" notion in an interview with *Fox News* host Laura Ingraham.[27]

"Once you get to a certain number, we use the word herd, right?"

Trump told Ingraham. "Once you get to a certain number, it's going to go away."

Hours after that interview, *CNN.com* published a report stating that Trump's approach to the coronavirus was now guided by "resignation" to the spread of the disease.[28] While Atlas brought the "herd immunity" plan into the administration, his views were "not new inside the White House" and were "echoing Trump's beliefs."

In a televised ABC News "town hall" on September 15, Trump again claimed that the coronavirus would simply "go away," and in his own awkward way, came out in favor of the herd immunity plan.[29]

"You'll develop, like, a herd mentality," he declared. "It's gonna be herd developed."

From Day One, it was clear that Trump was solely focused on doing nothing to stop the deadly virus as it mowed down Americans by the dozens. Then hundreds. Then thousands. Then hundreds of thousands.

In January and February of 2020, Trump repeatedly "played down" the coronavirus threat, as he would phrase it to Woodward. He shrugged off the notion that this virus was a big deal, or even that it would kill anyone in America at all. As late as February 26, three days before the first U.S. coronavirus death was recorded, Trump said that there were only 15 cases in the country and that "within a couple of days," there would be "close to zero."[30]

And yet, on February 7, he told Woodward he was aware not only that the virus was "more deadly than even your strenuous flus," but that it was transmitted through the air, making it extremely contagious.[31]

Just three days later, Trump held a campaign rally in Manchester, New Hampshire, packing more than 11,000 people into a college basketball arena.[32] He held another one nine days later, inside the 14,000-plus seat Arizona Veterans Memorial Coliseum in Phoenix. In all, he held six of his beloved indoor rallies in three weeks[33] before finally being forced to shut it down in early March.

On April 5, Trump bestowed upon Woodward yet more evidence

that he was fully aware of the danger posed by the novel coronavirus.[34]

"If you're the wrong person and if it gets you, your life is pretty much over if you're in the wrong group," Trump said.

On April 10, Trump tweeted, "The Invisible Enemy will soon be in full retreat."[35] On April 13, Trump "privately" told Woodward, "this thing is a killer if it gets you. If you're the wrong person, you don't have a chance."[36]

Trump's "pandemicide," as science journalist Laurie Garrett called it, reached new levels of destruction after November 3, Election Day.[37] On that day, the U.S. had seen a total of 9,751,254 coronavirus infection cases — as reported by the population statistics site Worldometer[38] — and suffered 239,387 deaths from the COVID-19 disease. It had been just over 10 months since the first U.S. case was detected.

Trump lost the election rather decisively, but immediately embarked on a relentless and obsessive campaign to overturn the results and hold on to power by any means necessary. Over the course of the 11 weeks between the election and his departure from the White House on January 20, 2021, the total infection count rocketed to 25,024,986. That's nearly a threefold increase. After accumulating fewer than 1 million infections per month in the first 10 months of the pandemic, the U.S. during the 11 weeks of Trump's self-coup attempt, the country piled up more than 15 million more.

Fatalities saw a similar spike during that span. By January 20, 421,663 were dead, almost double the number (a factor of 1.76 to be exact) from the first 10 months.

A fully detailed — or as fully as I could manage — account of Trump's non-response to the worst health crisis in more than a century appears later in this book. But the most important question, the one that almost never gets asked by the major media covering the crisis, is — why?

Thanks in part to the seeming unwillingness of reporters to investigate that basic question, we simply have no idea why Trump,[39] as media critic Eric Boehlert put it, "essentially ordered the federal government to stand down for the virus invasion."[40]

Though almost no one in the major media showed a willingness to even open up a conversation about why Trump has taken action to make the pandemic worse, not better, there were some widespread assumptions.

Thanks to Trump's palpable mental disorganization, his seeming ineptitude, and rather pathetically insatiable appetite for flattery — and any kind of attention, really — the media and much of the public showed a high tolerance for Trump's nefarious behavior. They treated him as if he had the mind of a child, and not a very bright child. Trump was a comical dummy, incapable of intention, premeditation, or agency of any kind. Just Trump being Trump, a more malevolent version of Chance the Gardener from *Being There*.

This is what former *New Republic* senior editor Brian Beutler calls "the incompetence dodge."[41] Trump simply cannot be the malevolent force he appears to be, this line of "reasoning" goes. It's impossible. He's just too stupid.

The incompetence dodge gifted Trump an endless mulligan for every move he made to subvert and dismantle democracy, whether firing U.S. attorneys and inspectors general who investigate him, commuting prison sentences[42] of his own political cronies, tear-gassing protesters[43] to clear his way for a photo op, or whatever. "Under the incompetence dodge, it is recast as just yet-more self-aggrandizing bluster," Beutler writes.

There have been numerous variations on the incompetence dodge, both from Trump's Republican party, and from the press. News stories and commentary have attributed Trump's bizarre and calamitous coronavirus non-response to his tendency to become "distracted."[44] He was variously described as "slow" to act,[45] because he "missed" warnings about the coming crisis.[46] He relied on his "gut,"[47] according to one account, while another blamed his "impulsiveness."[48]

Really?

In July, at the same time that, with monotonous predictability, he stuck to his plan of doing nothing to slow the pandemic as the U.S. death toll closed in on 150,000, Trump took a separate, malevolent action that could hardly be written off as "incompetence."

Trump ordered a cadre of "secret police"[49] — heavily armed, camouflage-clad federal agents with no apparent identification — first into Portland, Oregon, to confront and brutalize protesters, and then into other American cities,[50] supposedly to handle outbreaks of violent crime, though this paramilitary invasion looked more like fascism.[51]

The following month, Trump made a startling admission, or what should have been a startling one anyway. He stated out loud and for the record that he was blocking funds for the United States Postal Service[52] in order to prevent mail-in voting, a practice he believed would help Democrats.[53]

Perhaps his biggest lie, and worst premeditated attack in the U.S. outside of the pandemic, was Trump's plan to steal the 2020 presidential election by claiming that it was "rigged."[54] An investigative report by *Axios* revealed that Trump had planned "for weeks" to claim victory on November 3, election night, "even if he lost."

He believed, correctly, that the pandemic would keep Democratic voters away from polling places on election day, instead voting by mail — which Trump declared to be fraudulent, a blatant lie he repeated throughout the 2020 campaign.

But his own voters, whom he — also correctly — assumed would believe and internalize his lies not only about ballots but about the deadliness of the pandemic itself, would show up at the polls. And in-person ballots would be counted first, and quickly.

That would produce a "red mirage," the appearance that on election night, Trump was sweeping the election. He not only planned and prepared for this scam months in advance, three weeks before the election, according to the *Axios* reporting, he fully rehearsed his bogus "victory" speech, even visualizing his walk to the podium.

The Trump who ordered federal agents to take over the streets of American cities and attack Americans? The Trump who stated that he was deliberately sabotaging the postal service to benefit his own election chances? The Trump who, in calculating fashion, plotted and rehearsed a cunning plot to steal the election?

That was *the same guy* who was supposedly acting out of distraction, impulsiveness and incompetence as he sat back and watched the coronavirus pandemic "wash over the country," passively viewing like it was just another one of his cherished *Fox News* programs.

Those other three were deliberate acts. So it seems a little naive, or at least inconsistent, to believe his pandemic "strategy" was not an equally intentional attack on Americans. His incompetence is not that selective.

The incompetence dodge also ignores one other salient fact. For better or worse, Trump found a way to become President of the United States. Many have tried, many have failed. But he did it — one of only 45 ever. He can't be quite as dumb as he looks.

So, did the most stunning display of willful negligence[55] by a president in U.S. history come down to his bumbling incompetence? Or maybe to some quirk in his admittedly problematic personality?

Certainly, his inner, psychological motivations are worth exploring, to better understand his actions. But clinical psychology alone cannot fully account for Trump's consistent failures. He has demonstrated that he is quite capable of deliberate, pre-planned actions. The fact that they are heinous, unconscionable actions doesn't make them any less premeditated.

Another generally accepted assumption is that Trump was concerned — freaked out, even — from Day One about his reelection. He believed that hushing up and playing down the danger of the virus would help him stay on track for victory in November. He pushed — with a level of ardor that bordered on desperation — to "reopen" the country because he believed that a strong economy was the key to winning a second term.

While it's difficult to deny that the election was on his mind (when was it not?), the truth is, we simply do not know what Trump was thinking. Did he truly believe that allowing a deadly virus to "wash over" the country was the best move to nail down his reelection?

To describe Trump's series of non-actions, or actively harmful actions, as "failures" is also misleading. "Failure" implies an intention to succeed. If Trump "failed," he must have at least hoped that his actions would slow the tsunami of sickness and death.

In the prevailing media narrative of "failure," Trump *really wanted* to win the game. He just came up short, dammit. He gave it the old college try, but hey, we'll get 'em next time.

If a boxer takes a dive, we don't say he "failed" to win the fight. We say he threw the fight. He lost on purpose.

Faced with the biggest, toughest, most significant fight of his life – the fight to save Americans from mass death and economic destruction — Trump did not fail. He took a dive.

There is simply no evidence that he ever tried to win. I realize how difficult this is to believe, and how badly most of us want *not* to believe it. Nothing on the public record, from which this book is entirely drawn, indicates that Trump expected or hoped that anything he did would protect Americans against the viral onslaught.

Instead, what the public record reveals is that the individual occupying the office of President of the United States waged a biological warfare attack on his own country. On his own people.

Wait. A "biological warfare attack" on America? Am I crazy?

I'll leave the answer to the latter question open. To the former, here is what I am saying, and will say in the subsequent pages of this book — just to spell it out up front, as clearly as possible.

The Great Coronavirus Pandemic of 2020 fits the definition of a biological warfare attack (as explained in Chapter One). The outcomes are consistent with the effects and intentions of previous, though often far less destructive, biological attacks throughout history. So what else do we call it?

A brief digression. Back in the 1990s, I lived in Tokyo, Japan, where I worked as an editor and writer for a major English-language daily newspaper, *The Daily Yomiuri*, a subsidiary of *The Yomiuri Shimbun*, at that time Japan's — and the world's — largest-circulation daily. I commuted every day to the Yomiuri building in the Tokyo business district of Otemachi from my abode in the more residential Ikebukuro, on the Marunouchi subway line.

One day a strange and terrible thing happened.

Members of the Aum Shinrikyo doomsday cult released sarin gas on that line, and several others, poisoning hundreds of commuters and killing a dozen.

Thankfully, I was not on the train at the time. But it sparked in me an ongoing fascination with the case, the cult, and its bizarre but (it would seem, at least to some) charismatic leader, Shoko Asahara.

In 2020, in the midst of the pandemic, my mind went back there. Trump, it occurred to me, was eerily similar to Asahara — who oddly enough also had extensive and shadowy connections to Russia, and an apocalyptic vision of life and society.

To be absolutely clear, I am not claiming that Donald Trump ordered the virus cooked up in a laboratory somewhere, then commanded it to be unleashed on the world, as Asahara manufactured sarin and gave the orders for its release. The virus itself appears to be naturally occurring,[56] and bears no signatures of an artificial agent.[57]

But — Trump's "biological warfare attack" on America? Why use such strong language? You're accusing the president of mass murder against his own people! Outrageous!

Here's why. The record shows that almost every step Trump and the federal government took from the start of the coronavirus crisis appears designed not to end the destruction, but to extend it.

In other words, if biological warfare means employing a biological agent — whether manufactured *or* natural — to carry out a scheme of damage and death, then the coronavirus pandemic in America was exactly that — bio-war.

Trump made a clear choice to unleash — as he so memorably phrased it in his own inauguration speech — "American carnage,"[58] fulfilling an apocalyptic vision that has obsessed him his whole public life. More on Trump's dark vision, and how he appeared to be living it out with his catastrophic pandemic response, in Chapter Two.

Of course, at times, Trump proved unable to contain not just his indifference to but his seeming delight in the American carnage he was causing. In a speech in mid-May, as the U.S. death toll closed in on 90,000, Trump declared that the image of nurses and doctors "running into death just like soldiers run into bullets" was, in his enthusiastic phrasing, "a beautiful thing to see."[59]

Trump was attempting in his own way to acclaim health care workers as heroes, but with at least 27 health care workers dead[60] — and probably many more, according to the Centers for Disease Control — it was difficult not to take Trump's glee as, simply, what it appeared to be: excitement at the thought of other people's suffering.

Is that why Trump caused so many American deaths? In the estimation of psychologist John Gartner, Trump is a "sexual sadist"[61] who was "actively engaging in sabotage" of the government's pandemic response. So, he just gets off on it?

Nobel laureate economist Paul Krugman echoed this psychological theme.

"I might somewhat speculatively add one specific reason why authoritarians don't want to deal with disasters," he wrote. "A punitive mindset. That is, people like Trump get satisfaction from hurting people, not helping them."[62]

Seems like pretty accurate "speculation." But even Trump's twisted psychology does not explain the entire "why."

However — before we can get to the why, let's look at the "what." What did Trump do, or fail to do, that led to thousands of American fatalities?

On more than a dozen occasions, U.S. intelligence agencies warned Trump about the coronavirus outbreak in his "President's Daily Brief,"[63] a classified intelligence summary that according to *The Washington Post*, is "designed to call the president's attention to the most significant global developments and security threats."[64]

The intelligence reports "traced the virus's spread around the globe, made clear that China was suppressing information about the contagion's transmissibility and lethal toll, and raised the prospect of dire political and economic consequences," according to the *Post's* reporting. A week after the *Post* published its report, a White House official claimed that Trump was briefed only twice,[65] both times later in January.

And yet, Trump did nothing, until January 31 when he ordered a partial, and porous, restriction on travel to the U.S. from China. Nearly 40,000 travelers entered the country on flights from China between the date Trump ordered the "ban," and early April.[66]

In March, Trump also at least struck a pose, giving the appearance of wanting to do something to stem the viral spread. He suggested that he might impose a tri-state "quarantine" on the tri-state area[67] — New York, New Jersey, and Connecticut. But he quickly abandoned the thought. Whether he actually ever meant to go through with it seems doubtful.

As states and local hospitals struggled to obtain personal protective gear for their health care workers, allowing them to treat patients and combat the virus without martyring themselves, the federal government intercepted and confiscated PPE shipments.[68]

In February, the Trump administration sent 17.8 million tons of PPE and other medical supplies to China.[69] That shipment came at a time when Trump was consistently and repeatedly denying that the coronavirus would ever become a problem for the United States, referring to the outbreak as "very much under control" and making his February 26 claim that within "a couple of days" the number of cases in the U.S. would drop "close to zero."

At the time, there were 53 known cases in the country,[70] according to World Health Organization data, though Trump asserted that there were only 15, which was the Centers for Disease Control number released that same day.[71] But the CDC definitely did not say that the number would soon be "close to zero."[72]

That Trump spouts nonstop falsehoods about any topic on his mind is not exactly news, but as the coronavirus crisis rolled on, his lies and disinformation took on a more sinister bent than at any point in his term. He claimed on March 6 that "anybody who wants a test will get a test." But kits to test for the deadly virus were rare, and the administration's utter failure to set up a comprehensive testing program[73] has been perhaps the most important single factor[74] in prolonging the pandemic within the U.S.

"When we said there were millions of tests available, there weren't, right?" Trump's testing "czar," Admiral Brett Giroir admitted more than a year later.[75]

On March 13, he cooked up more disinformation about testing. Trump claimed that the administration would bring "1.4 million tests on board next week and 5 million within a month." But even nine weeks later, fewer than 8 million people in the country had been tested.[76]

Let's bullet point it then, shall we? Trump…

- Ignored intelligence reports about the danger of coronavirus, instead fabricating the illusion that the virus was no big deal, encouraging Americans to engage in behaviors that would spread the infection, causing unnecessary deaths.

- Purposely denied life-protecting equipment to hospitals and caregivers, also adding to the death toll.

- Lied about the most important, life-preserving weapon in the anti-pandemic arsenal, diagnostic testing, while doing essentially nothing to create a testing program — again, leading to large numbers of deaths.

- Led a propaganda operation in concert with Fox News and other right-wing media outlets to flood the public with misinformation and diversionary arguments, creating confusion that allowed the pandemic to flourish and cause further deaths.

"What is happening in the US is purposeful, considered negligence, omission, failure to act by our leaders," wrote Yale University epidemiologist Gregg Gonsalves, on May 6 — going on to characterize Trump's actions as "awfully close to genocide by default," and wondering whether he and other "leaders" could be somehow held accountable under international law.[77]

"It's not just that Trump is refusing to provide national leadership in a time of crisis. *He's actively and purposefully making everything worse,*" wrote Eric Boehlert. "That's a helluva story that can no longer be averted."[78]

That's the story we're going to tell in this book: Donald Trump took active measures to cause American deaths. Former President Barack Obama called Trump's coronavirus response an "absolute chaotic disaster."[79] Perhaps it wasn't as chaotic as it seemed.

And one more time, we have to ask — why?

There's no shortage of possible answers to that question. We'll explore as many as we can in this book. For now, let's look at just one, to start. But this possibility — on which we'll elaborate later — tracks with one of the most consistent themes of Trump's time in office dating back to his campaign: his mysterious debt to Putin.

In one respect, the debt is not mysterious at all. As three separate investigations concluded — including one by the Republican-led Senate Intelligence Committee — Putin sabotaged the 2016 presidential election to help Trump win.[80] As we'll explore in Chapter Seven, even before 2016 Trump appeared obsequiously enamored with the Russian autocrat.

As investigative reporter Craig Unger argues in his book *American Kompromat*, Trump's affinity was not merely for Putin — though he was evidently googly-eyed for the KGB operative-turned-president — but for Russia itself, or at least the Russian security apparatus. Unger makes the case that Trump's ascendance to the White House was the culmination of a four-decade operation to groom and cultivate the amoral, narcissistic real estate mogul.[81]

In addition to the December 29 golf course phone call, Trump and Putin spoke four times in two weeks,[82] starting on March 30 — the busiest their hotline had been during his term. They chatted on the phone two more times over the next few weeks as well, making six calls in two months during the thick of the global pandemic, and seven since the virus emerged in China. The phone buddies spoke yet again on July 23.

"That would be a crazy number of calls to any foreign leader," wrote former U.S. Ambassador to Russia Michael McFaul, on his Twitter account.[83] "But to Putin? What on earth were they discussing? So strange."

It was also strange that Trump and Putin were already regular chatty Cathies, speaking to one another at least 16 times prior to December of 2019.[84] As of mid-April 2020, Trump had spoken to Putin an average of once every 60 days for his entire time in the White House.

During the span encompassing Trump and Putin's chattiest period, early to late March of 2020, U.S. intelligence agencies became aware that Russian military intelligence agents had been offering "bounties" — that is, putting out paid hits — on American soldiers in Afghanistan,[85] according to a *New York Times* report that was quickly confirmed by several other major news organizations.

Trump held his two-week phone-a-thon with Putin after he was, according to the *Times* report, "briefed" on the Russian bounties. His response? Nothing.

Well, not exactly nothing. In his June 1 call with Putin, this one reportedly initiated by Trump, he invited Putin to the United States to take part in the 2020 G7 summit.[86] (Russia was expelled from the group in 2014 after Putin's invasion of Ukraine.)

Four days later, Trump ordered the pullout of 9,500 U.S. troops from Germany,[87] in what *The New York Times* called "a further blow to America's weakening European alliances," and one "likely to be welcomed by President Vladimir V. Putin of Russia."

At the end of July, the pullout began, though it would take years to accomplish and cost billions of dollars,[88] according to Trump's own defense secretary, Mark Esper. The move was widely blasted as a "gift to Russia."[89] (On February 4, 2021, new President Joe Biden froze Trump's order to pull U.S. troops out of Germany.[90])

Trump and Putin also talked about "measures taken in both countries to combat coronavirus," according to the Kremlin's own account of the call.[91]

We'll peer into this abyss somewhat more deeply in Chapter Seven, but for now, let's just say Trump's pattern of subservience to Putin has a long history. Here's just one more example.

In the 2016 election, the Russian government secretly intervened to help Trump get elected.[92] Whether Trump knew the full extent of what was going on remains unclear. When it came to accusing Trump or his campaign of conspiracy, Special Counsel Robert Mueller, after his two-year investigation, took a pass.

But Trump appears to have taken part in a cover-up — taking and obeying direct instructions from Putin.

In 2017, the press reported — and Donald Trump Jr. quickly admitted — that Trump's eldest son hosted a meeting in Trump Tower on June 9, 2016, to get some sort of "incriminating information" on Hillary Clinton. When the press reports surfaced a year later, Trump himself appears to have dictated a statement to be issued by his son. In that bogus statement, Trump falsely claimed that the Trump Tower meeting was all about "Russian adoptions."

That was on July 8, on an Air Force One flight back from the G20 summit in Germany. Earlier that same day, at the summit, Trump and Putin held an unscheduled "sideline" meeting where they discussed, according to Trump, "Russian adoptions."

"That is a highly troubling chain of events to put it mildly," wrote journalist Josh Marshall, who noted the possibility that Trump was essentially taking Putin's direction with the "adoptions" cover story.[93]

Did Putin give another direction to Trump in that December 29 golf course chat? Was the call at least partly a heads-up to Trump about the coming coronavirus outbreak — along with some friendly advice to treat the plague as NBD?

In Chapters Seven and Eight we'll wade deeper into the Putin-Trump swamp. Putin's investment, as we'll see, was not in Trump, but in planting a bomb inside America's political system. As the coronavirus approached, ever the opportunist, the Russian strongman perhaps saw the perfect chance to trip the tripwire.

At the same time, Putin and Trump may have believed the fix was in. Trump wasn't going to lose reelection, or so they thought, no matter what havoc he wreaked. If that was indeed their view, they weren't alone. Even as Trump trailed by a whopping 9.5 points in national polls against Joe Biden,[94] one election prognosticator gave him a 91 percent chance of winning anyway,[95] and even polling guru Nate Silver declared that Trump could "absolutely win" the 2020 election.[96]

Trump's nonchalant attitude was, after all, exactly how Putin himself chose to deal with the outbreak in his own country. At least initially. In mid-March, when Moscow hospital records showed a sudden, sharp spike in "pneumonia" cases, Putin dismissed reports that they were actually coronavirus cases as "fake news."[97]

Just nine days later, the mayor of Moscow ordered a citywide shutdown. A doctors' trade union accused the government of deliberately falsifying coronavirus case numbers.[98] But Putin continued to treat the outbreak in such casual fashion that he exchanged a public handshake with Denis Protsenko, the chief doctor at Moscow's busiest hospital.[99]

When Protsenko was diagnosed with coronavirus infection a week later, even Putin could no longer play it cool. Though a Kremlin flak claimed to be "unworried," Putin went into self-isolation for a week.

Even as Russia's reported case total — *reported* — zoomed past 50,000 Russians openly complained that Putin still wasn't doing enough, or much of anything, and that as one Siberian citizen told the BBC, "It feels like a big failure of government right now."[100]

But Putin's own poorly thought-out strategy for bullshitting his way out of the pandemic was emulated by Trump on a grand scale.

In later chapters, we'll detail Trump's consistent pattern of denial that the coronavirus would ever become a real problem in the U.S. — a pattern that could easily be written off as just another series of counterfactual utterances by an individual who resides in an alternate reality of some sort.

The problem with the Trump-as-pathological-fabulist theory, at least in this case, is the fact that Trump knew, *with 100 percent certainty*, that the pandemic was coming and that without quick, decisive action, the disease would wreak havoc.

Not only did U.S. intelligence agencies repeatedly warn Trump of the outbreak in China[101] and its inevitable course stateside, American health officials at the World Health Organization also provided the administration with "real time" updates on the coronavirus situation starting in late 2019, according to a *Washington Post* report.[102]

Awash in information and advance warnings, Trump's steadfast do-nothingism and denial of the gathering viral storm can only have been deliberate.

As we mentioned earlier, the popular explanation for why Trump would do such a thing is, as with all things Trump, psychological. He relies on his "gut."

He has a "preference for following his gut rather than the data,"[103] said *The New York Times*. He is "known to say what's on his mind, to go with his gut and accentuate the positive,"[104] according to National Public Radio. Trump is "short-circuiting the process with his gut feelings,"[105] said one expert quoted by Reuters.

And so on.

But his faith in his "gut," as Boehlert said, "doesn't come anywhere close to explaining what has transpired." Indeed, it defies belief that the magnitude and suddenness of the crisis was inflicted upon the country solely by the unhappy accident of having a president who relies on instinct rather than data.

To kill more Americans in two months than the Vietnam war claimed in 11 years, and to bring the U.S. economy to a crashing halt in less time than that, well, that takes work. A real full-court press.

We may never know what was spoken between Putin and Trump in their pre-New Year golf course cell phone call. Even if the chat was transcribed at all, the administration had a practice — as was established during his impeachment investigation in 2019 — of stashing his most sensitive phone records on a highly classified computer server.[106]

So let's put it this way:

Do we know that Putin gave Trump instructions on how to handle the coming coronavirus crisis, on December 29, 2019?

No, we don't.

Did Trump's response closely mimic Putin's own?

Yes.

Does the massive damage to the United States benefit Putin's Russia?

And yes.

We'll take a deeper dive into those questions as the pages turn, or swipe if this is the Kindle version. For now, one more observation about Putin — he's not an evil genius.

For this sinister theory of a Putin-Trump coronavirus conspiracy to be true, there's no need to think of the Russian neo-czar as some kind of Ernst Stavro Blofeld, a criminal mastermind who carefully plotted every outcome. (And the idea of Trump as Blofeld is simply hilarious.)

But we do know that Putin is a consummate opportunist. As Russia-watcher Mark Galeotti argued in his book *We Need To Talk About Putin: Why the West Gets Him Wrong, and How to Get Him Right*, Putin's state responds to opportunities, but rarely creates them.

When Putin got wind of the coronavirus outbreak in China, as he surely did late in 2019, and knowing how easily he has been able to manipulate Trump over the previous several years, Putin could have spotted an opportunity to plant a thought in Trump's head — an idea that Putin knew would appeal to Trump's preference for talking a lot and doing nothing.

"We in the West define what Putin's state does to us, while he is simply taking advantage of the failures, broken promises and stress points in our systems," Galeotti wrote. "Rather than looking for a grand and complex strategy, we need to accept that Putin, at least abroad, is in effect following the strategy that Mark Zuckerberg encouraged at Facebook – 'move fast and break things.'"[107]

Putin himself probably did not know what he would achieve by implanting Trump with the suggestion to simply do nothing and let the coronavirus "wash over" the United States population. He probably doesn't even care.

"The very act of launching these attacks brings chaos and uncertainty," Galeotti explains. That's all Putin really wants.

Now that we've put that out there, let's steer away from the Russia narrative for a while. The public record as of this writing can only make suggestions as to the "why" question at the center of this book.

The reason we're going to rely on the public record — and *only* the public record — is first of all, to make a point. Not one fact cited in this book was inaccessible to any journalist, legislator, or member of the public. The story we're going to tell has always been there, and continues to be written every day. The pieces just need putting together.

Second, let's not kid ourselves. Calling the coronavirus pandemic a "biological warfare attack on the United States," much less one "waged by the country's own president" is not going to elicit the friendliest of reactions — not from Trump and his supporters.

But more importantly, I fully expect the "mainstream" media (and even much of the non-mainstream media) to reject this argument, and probably me along with it, as well. My thesis in this little volume, I am quite confident, will be swatted away and denied by most of the press, and the famous reporters and pundits who appear on my flat screen every day.

That's all fine. I get it. They missed the story, even though it was all there from the start. They never asked the right questions. All of the facts exist, right in front of them, cited in full in the notes to each chapter of *Close To Zero*.

What the sources in the notes show, this book will argue, is that Trump's response to the pandemic was consistently wrong, so utterly and repeatedly wrong that it cannot be explained by incompetence or stupidity alone. He did this deliberately. His purposeful intention is what makes the coronavirus crisis a bio-war attack, rather than a natural disaster, or "act of God."

One question, however, that needs to be addressed up front — if the 2020 pandemic was a biological warfare attack, why pin it on Trump? Aren't the real culprits in China?

We know that China — specifically Hubei Province — is where the novel coronavirus was first detected. We know that, though China took somewhat tardy but nonetheless strict and even extreme, measures to slow the viral outbreak,[108] the government also appears to have covered up the true extent of the crisis, lowballing both the total number of cases and death toll.[109]

Trump's supporters took to claiming that China should be subject to sanctions or some sort of retribution for unleashing the coronavirus pandemic on the world.[110]

A report by *Washington Post* journalist Josh Rogin even suggested that the virus may have somehow escaped from a Chinese laboratory,[111] and that U.S. State Department cables warned of unsafe conditions in research labs located in Wuhan as far back as 2018. A "senior intelligence official" told *The Post* in late April that the U.S. was examining the possibility of a laboratory origin "very closely," but adding the caveat, "we just don't know."[112]

And on May 5, Secretary of State Mike Pompeo claimed that intelligence agencies had gathered "enormous evidence" that the virus came from a Chinese lab — though he later appeared to walk back the claim.[113]

So why am I not calling the pandemic a Chinese bio-war attack?

Because Trump, or at least his advisers, were fully informed from both intelligence and public sources about the outbreak in China. It wasn't a secret to anyone.

Trump had been warned about the general danger of a pandemic before he even took office. The Obama administration ran a pandemic response exercise with the incoming Trump team in January of 2017.[114]

Though he was repeatedly alerted to the Wuhan outbreak by U.S. intelligence "throughout January and February" of 2020,[115] Trump "played down the threat and failed to take action that might have slowed the spread of the pathogen," anyway, according to a *Washington Post* report that revealed the intelligence warnings.

The World Health Organization also issued repeated warnings as early as January,[116] only to see Trump later vilify the organization and announce that the U.S. would cut off its funding.

Even Joe Biden, the Democrat who would eventually oppose and defeat Trump in the 2020 election, published his own warning, in a January 27 *USA Today* op-ed.[117]

Still Trump took no serious action. In fact, on January 18, Health and Human Services Secretary Alex Azar attempted to personally draw Trump's attention to the looming public health disaster,[118] only for Trump to swerve the conversation to his administration's ban on vaping.

If the conclusion that Trump was killing people on purpose wasn't obvious enough, he left no doubt in late April. He responded to a rash of COVID-19 clusters in meat packing plants with an executive order[119] that not only banned states from closing the facilities, but shielding the corporate plant-owners from legal liability when, as appeared inevitable, workers got sick and died as a direct outcome of their bosses forcing them back to work.

As if the purpose of Trump's order forcing workers into potentially deadly situations were not obvious enough, some Republican governors including Kim Reynolds of Iowa, site of one of the worst meat-plant coronavirus clusters, announced that she would cut off unemployment benefits for those reluctant to risk their health and lives, to coerce workers into returning to their potentially life-threatening jobs.

And even as Trump pushed to "reopen" the country in early May, his own administration projected "a steady rise in the number of cases and deaths from coronavirus over the next several weeks, reaching about 3,000 daily deaths on June 1," according to an internal Centers For Disease Control report.[120] The 3,000 figure was almost double the then-current daily death toll of approximately 1,750.

A few days later, Trump stopped hiding his intention to cause Americans to die altogether. He just gave up. He decided that the American people were now "warriors" apparently drafted into his cause of "reopening" the country — his doublespeak way of saying that Americans would be forced to face the virus head on, unprotected, and fend for themselves.

"We can't keep our country closed. We have to open our country," he said during a May 5 visit to Arizona.[121] "Will some people be badly affected? Yes."

Trump may have felt freed up to speak so frankly because the "reopening," shoving Americans into the viral fire, came after a carefully orchestrated propaganda campaign that began in April, with "protests" in several states against the business closures and social distancing guidelines imposed to slow down the raging spread of the disease — protests organized and funded by an array of right-wing political action groups.[122] Some were linked to the billionaire family of Betsy DeVos, Trump's own education secretary.[123]

Fox News quickly picked up the story, amplifying and promoting the protests which spread across the country.

When the bizarre "protests" against stay-at-home orders popped up in Michigan and several other states — protests that openly violated social distancing guidelines and likely caused further spread of the virus and even more illness and death — Trump urged them on.[124] Once again taking to his ever-trusty Twitter account, he declared, in all caps,

"LIBERATE MICHIGAN," "LIBERATE MINNESOTA," and "LIBER-ATE VIRGINIA."[125]

Bear in mind that Trump's "liberate" tweets came just four days after he told Bob Woodward that the coronavirus was a "scourge" and a "plague" that "rips you apart."[126]

In early May, a group of armed (!) men somehow swarmed inside the Michigan state capitol building, intending to confront Governor Gretchen Whitmer over the stay-at-home restrictions. One was seen with a sign calling Whitmer a "tyrant" who will "get the rope." Others bore images of swastikas and confederate flags.

Trump described the gun-toting mob as "very good people" and urged Whitmer to cut some sort of a deal with them.[127]

The protesters remained a tiny minority, and were comprised to a significant extent of white supremacist[128] and other far-right militants.[129] They received inordinate attention from the non-Fox media, and created an atmosphere of inevitability to Trump's "reopening."

When Trump's "reopening" appeared unstoppable, the CDC created a 17-page plan for safely, gradually lifting restrictions, and imposing new measures to allow business to proceed safely. The plan included such recommendations as requiring restaurants to install "sneeze guards" at cash registers, and to eliminate open buffets and salad bars, as well as such guidelines as promoting "healthy hygiene practices" at children's summer camps.

The Trump administration promptly tossed the CDC plan in the circular file.[130]

What remains clear from these few examples is that even if we accept the premise that the Chinese government was using SARS-CoV-2 as a biological weapon, Trump was demonstrably aware of it, and did nothing significant to stop it. He essentially ordered U.S. defense forces to stand down in the face of a raging, enemy attack.

And one more time for the people in the back, we have to ask the question — why?

Trump himself may have offered an answer as far back as 2014, when he phoned in to his favorite show, *Fox & Friends,* to offer his rather apocalyptic prescription for making America "great" again.

"You know what solves it? When the economy crashes, when the country goes to total hell and everything is a disaster. Then you'll have, you know, you'll have riots to go back to where we used to be when we were great."[131]

Trump, it would appear, subscribes to his own version of the shock doctrine, the belief that everything needs to "go to total hell," and then he'll be there to pick up the pieces.

The third and final of Trump's 2016 campaign chiefs, Steve Bannon — who is perhaps as responsible for Trump's political ascendancy as any other person — once said that his goal in politics was to "destroy the state," adding, "I want to bring everything crashing down, and destroy all of today's establishment."[132]

I know how difficult it is to believe that the President of the United States would actually want the U.S. economy to crash. I get it. But there it is.

He said it. And so did his top political guru.

In a way, Trump's assault on America can be seen as the culmination of his presidency — the crowning, and yet inevitable achievement of his project to dismantle the country. His ultimate crime against America.

In the conclusion to *Close to Zero,* we'll kick around some ideas of what consequences he should face for these transgressions, but the pandemic as the logical, predictable consequence of Trumpism will be a theme of almost every upcoming chapter.

I also know, as I mentioned above, how far it stretches credulity to believe that said president would unleash a biological warfare attack against his own country.

But the public record says, yup, he did. It happened. Donald Trump did not create the coronavirus, but he caused the disaster in the United States of America.

To tell that story, apparently, takes someone like your humble typist here, who has no special powers beyond an ability to spot the obvious. I mean, I've stayed largely outside of that corporate media structure and relatively free of the emotional and career investment in repeating its tropes and guarding its paradigms. So maybe that makes the obvious a little more obvious to me. I don't know.

What I do know is that there *is* an answer to that question I keep asking. Why? Why did Donald Trump allow a deadly virus to assault the United States of America, leaving the country badly weakened and forever changed. He had a reason, or more likely, multiple reasons.

Was he following orders from Vladimir Putin? Does he believe that laying waste to the U.S. economy leaves him in prime position to make a bundle of cash? Was he attempting to build a pretext for cancelling the 2020 presidential election, and seize power permanently? Is he just a sociopath, a "malignant narcissist" whose "mental pathologies inexorably compel him to hurt and kill large numbers of people — including his own supporters," as psychologist John Gartner described him?[133]

Or did Trump allow this lethal virus to sweep through his own country — somehow leaving himself and his family untouched for months despite his own seeming disregard for safety[134] — for *all* of the above reasons. And others?

The facts will tell. I believe they already do.

CHAPTER ONE

. . . .

BIO-WAR, WHAT IS IT GOOD FOR?

*"Biological warfare is inhumane and advocating such a method
of warfare would defile the virtue and benevolence of the
Emperor."*

*— Shiro Ishii, Chief of Japan's World
War II biological warfare program*[1]

Jani Beg had a problem. Just one year into his reign as Khan, or ruler, of the Golden Horde he found his authority challenged by the people of Caffa. An important port city on the Black Sea coast of Ukraine, Caffa was inhabited by Genoese Christians who had offended the Khan by killing a local Muslim in a religiously motivated brawl.[2]

So in the year 1343, Jani Beg, a devoted Muslim, led his massive Crimean Tatar army in an attack on Caffa. He expected an easy victory, figuring the city was populated mainly by merchants — pushovers when it came to a fight, especially against a fearsome Mongol horde. To Jani Beg's great consternation, however, those merchants were not pushovers. In fact, they turned out to be pretty scrappy brawlers.

Instead of an all-out battle, then, Jani Beg opted for a siege. The Khan's fighters took up positions on the hills surrounding the city, slowly strangling Caffa of food, money, and essential supplies. But as greatly as the Genoese suffered, starving in squalor, they held out against the Tatar forces.

Until February of 1344 when, strategically utilizing their access to the sea, the Genoese in Caffa brought in reinforcements from Italy and turned the tables, killing 15,000 Mongol warriors and sending Jani Beg packing back to his northwestern corner of the splintered Mongol Empire.[3]

One year later, Beg was back — for siege part deux. His troops stayed in place for one more year, nearly choking the life out of the port city, until suddenly, in seemingly inexplicable fashion, Jani Beg's men started dropping dead.

The cavalcade of death was particularly horrible and repulsive. As perceived by the Genoese behind Caffa's walls, this surely was the work of God Himself.

Gabriele de Mussis, the Italian lawyer whose manuscript *Historia de Morbo* (*History of the Disease*) is the primary, contemporary source of information on the events at Caffa, wrote:

"It was as though arrows were raining down from heaven to strike and crush the Tatars' arrogance. All medical advice and attention was useless; the Tatars died as soon as the signs of disease appeared on their bodies: swellings in the armpit or groin caused by coagulating humors, followed by a putrid fever."[4]

Jani Beg knew the game was up. He had to retreat yet again. But the "putrid" disease mowing down his soldiers gave him an idea. According to de Mussis's account, the Tatar leader instructed his remaining troops to gather up the noxious corpses of his fallen fighters, and load them on to catapults — contraptions normally used to lob rocks and other projectiles over the walls of enemy cities.

The Khan ordered the corpses catapulted over the Caffa walls, into the city, "in hopes that the intolerable stench would kill everyone inside," according to de Mussis' account, penned in 1348.

For his act of desperate, ghoulish creativity, history has granted Jani Beg the honorific title Father of Biological Warfare.[5]

The Golden Horde head honcho probably didn't have any such grand ambitions. He was simply trying to slaughter as many Genoese as possible, by any means necessary. But at least according to some accounts, it was Jani Beg's horrific stratagem at Caffa (today, the Crimean city of Feodosia) that set off The Black Death, the worst outbreak of plague in history.[6] Plague quickly swept through Caffa, accelerated by the already abysmal sanitation caused by Jani Beg's siege. The Genoese left standing in Caffa poured on to four ships, escaping the devastated city and sailing for Italy — bringing the Great Mortality (as the Black Death was called at the time) with them.

By 1353 the plague had wiped out (depending on the historical estimate you prefer) between 33 and 60 percent of all the people living in 14th-Century Europe.[7]

The Mongol ruler may be the "Father of Biological Warfare," but he obviously was not the creator of *Yersinia pestis*, the bacteria that causes plague. He did not command some Mongol alchemist to cook it up in a cauldron somewhere.

Indeed, *Y. Pestis* was not even discovered until 1894,[8] a full 546 years after Jani Beg first ordered the corpses of his fallen men flung over the walls of Caffa.

No, Jani Beg was an opportunist when it came to bio-war. The plague snuck up on his warriors as they camped in the hills over Caffa, creeping up on them after raging through China for at least 15 years, materializing in the Gobi Desert in the 1330s.[9] Maybe even a bit earlier.

The cascading pestilence was at first a curse for the Mongol horde. But with a little ingenuity and a helping of desperation, their Khan turned it into, if not exactly a blessing, a useful tool. While the plague did not give him his yearned-for victory over Caffa, it unleashed far more destruction on the city and ultimately on all of Europe than he could have, or perhaps would have, ever dreamed.

But the opportunistic, *ad hoc* nature of the Mongol biological warfare attack didn't make it any less a biological warfare attack.

Epidemiologists and historians continue to debate whether it was really the catapulted corpses that caused the *Y. Pestis* outbreak in Caffa,[10] and subsequently Europe from Italy to England and all the way back to Russia. But Jani Beg's intentions were clear. He attempted to gain political control of a territory by making everyone in it sick.

In 2019, Donald Trump did not cause the novel coronavirus, SARS-CoV-2, to appear. The predictable conspiracy theory that the virus was a deliberately engineered bioweapon has been rather definitely debunked.[11] And even if it were true, the notion that Trump, of all people, could possess the creativity and ingenuity to direct its creation seems preposterous. He didn't even appear to have a clue why a person who tests negative for the virus one day could test positive the next.[12]

We don't have to accept that Trump is secretly a mastermind in order to see that what he did with the coronavirus pandemic was, indeed, a biological warfare attack on America. There's no need to look him in the eye to get a sense of his soul, or even to ascertain his political motivations. All we need to do is look at what he actually did.

Every action that he took was designed not to control, contain, or halt the pandemic, but to make it worse. To kill people.

Trump knew that the coronavirus pandemic was coming. U.S. military intelligence, according to reporting by ABC News, warned of an "an out-of-control disease" in China's Hubei province as far back as late November.[13] One source who spoke to ABC said that "analysts concluded it could be a cataclysmic event."

ABC did not specify a date for the first intelligence warning, reporting only that the information did not reach Trump until January when it was finally included in his daily intelligence briefing. Oddly enough, it was November 16 when Trump bolted from the White House, a cache of papers of some kind under his arm — and when was Trump ever seen carrying any sort of work materials on his person?

He made an unexpected visit to Walter Reed medical center in Bethesda, Maryland, that afternoon.[14] According to the official White House line, Trump spontaneously decided to pop in for a few tests as part of his annual 2020 physical exam, several months early.[15] According to the White House, he didn't bother finally knocking off the rest of his tests until early June.

Trump's unexpected and protocol-violating hospital visit took place one day before the Chinese spotted their first case of the novel coronavirus. That was November 17. When Trump went to the hospital, it was already November 17 in Wuhan, China.

Of course, that odd confluence of dates is likely just that, an odd confluence. Whatever took place at Walter Reed may have had nothing to do with anything happening in China, or anywhere outside of Trump's own self. We may never know. We do know, on the other hand, that as the disease percolated in China's Hubei province, Trump received numerous briefings on the incipient pandemic from United States intelligence agencies.

As the U.S. death toll topped 95,000 in mid-May, Trump and his associates looked for a scapegoat, to divert attention from the fact that he was told about the coming wave of disease and, for reasons that are not fully understood (but are the subject of this book, in hopes that they will soon be much better understood), did nothing about it.

The sacrificial burden fell on Beth Sanner,[16] whose title was Deputy Director of National Intelligence for Mission Integration, but whose main responsibility was delivering the "President's Daily Brief,"[17] the summary of red-hot intelligence info presented to Trump every morning, as it was for every previous president since Harry Truman.

But even if Sanner had, as the Trump administration scuttlebutt would have it, "underplayed" the severity of the coronavirus outbreak, according to *The New York Times*, "Trump ignored a host of warnings he received around that time from higher-ranking officials, epidemiologists, scientists, biodefense officials, other national security aides and the news media about the virus's growing threat."[18]

That is, indeed, a "host" of warnings. That Trump somehow remained blissfully oblivious to the coming catastrophe stretches credulity, to say the least.

And knowing that this new, viral plague was creeping up on the country over which he was nominally chief executive, Trump seized the opportunity. Just as Jani Beg hurled infected corpses into Caffa, Trump allowed SARS-CoV-2 to fly into the United States via a modern analog to the Mongol catapults. Jet airliners.

An estimated 1,300 flights, carrying 390,000 people, landed in the U.S. from China[19] before Trump got around to imposing his "ban" on travel from the country where the virus originated.

The coronavirus outbreak was also tearing through Europe, particularly Italy and Spain, in early and mid-March. About 66,000 air travelers from European countries landed in the U.S. every day. In the first week in March, the CDC urged Trump to issue a global travel alert.

Trump sat around for a week before doing anything, finally putting some restrictions in place on travel from Europe on March 13.[20] The intervening days were enough time for nearly 500,000 more people to enter the U.S. from Europe by commercial airlines. And that doesn't count the intervening six weeks before Trump's China travel "ban," and his restrictions on travel from Europe — which exempted travelers from the United Kingdom, site of what would soon become the world's 10th-worst outbreak.[21]

That first week in March was also when Trump sojourned to Atlanta for a visit to the CDC, where he falsely announced that "anybody that wants a test can get a test."[22]

Even as travelers from virus-ridden Europe landed in the U.S. during that week, Trump assured Americans that the virus would "go away," and to "just stay calm."[23]

Jani Beg, at least, did not try to happy-talk his Tatar subjects into believing that the Black Death would simply "go away" — and he did not catapult plague-ridden corpses into the crowd of *his own* people, up on those hills above Caffa in 1347. In 2020, Trump let the coronavirus fly right into his own country.

Let's be clear: domestically targeted, American bio-war is far from being without precedent.

Starting in 1950, and spanning the subsequent two decades, the U.S. military — mostly the Navy — carried out about 200 biological warfare "experiments,"[24] showering San Francisco and other American cities with supposedly "harmless" bacteria, to see how widely disease could be spread, and whether it would blow back on the spreaders and infect them too.

In one such bio-war attack on Americans, Naval personnel contaminated 10 wooden boxes with various pathogens, and shipped them to Norfolk Naval Station in Virginia. According to Robert Harris and Richard Paxman, authors of the book *A Higher Form of Killing: The Secret History of Chemical and Biological Warfare*, one of those pathogens — a toxic fungus named *Aspergillus fumigatus* — was selected specifically because "black workers at the base were thought to be particularly susceptible to it."[25]

Fast forward to 2020, when an orchestrated wave of "protests" swept the United States,[26] which by amazing coincidence commenced shortly after statistics showing a distressing racial divide in coronavirus cases were first made public. While the "protesters" were almost exclusively white — and in some cases actual white supremacists — the stats showed that black Americans died of COVID-19 at approximately three times the rate of whites.[27]

Perhaps it's also just an odd coincidence that black Americans were targeted by domestic bio-war attacks in the 1950s before the 2020 viral attack. But those were not the only two times.

In another biological attack against Americans by Americans that was labeled an "experiment," the government allowed several hundred black men infected with syphilis to be given phony "treatments" while in fact doing nothing to treat or stop the disease. This "Tuskegee Experiment" continued infecting black men for 40 years.[28]

The United States military has cultivated anthrax bacteria as a bioweapon since World War I.[29] But in 2015, the Department of Defense somehow shipped nine containers of live anthrax spores around the country, as well as to South Korea.[30]

The shipments, deemed "accidental" by the DoD, came even after President Barack Obama instructed all agencies of the government to "stand down" on research into bioweapons, until a full safety review could be completed.[31] But the Pentagon had a funny way of standing down.

Of course, other possible bio-war attacks on U.S. soil, carried out by the U.S. government, remain mysterious and to some extent — and in some cases a large extent — in the unverifiable realm of conspiracy theory. In his book *The Belarus Secret*, former federal prosecutor John Loftus documents the post-World War II importation of Nazis, many of them war criminals, into the U.S. military and intelligence apparatus.[32]

Some of those Nazis, Loftus wrote, were scientists specializing in "germ warfare," and who — once ensconced inside the U.S. government scientific research community — "experimented with poison ticks dropped from planes to spread rare diseases."

Some of those "poison ticks," Loftus wrote, may have been dropped "on the Plum Island artillery range off the coast of Connecticut during the early 1950s.

Loftus's intelligence sources also told him that "the poison ticks were the source of the Lyme disease spirochete, and that migrating waterfowl were the vectors that carried the ticks from Plum Island all up and down the Eastern Seaboard."

Loftus cites a "top secret U.S. document" confirming that "clandestine attacks on crops and animals" were carried out during the time the now American-employed Nazi scientists were dousing Plum Island with disease-carrying ticks, and he notes that the U.S. Lyme disease outbreak — which was not identified until 1975 — was "monitored secretly under the cover of a New England health study," by the government.[33]

Lyme disease — named for the town where it was first identified, Old Lyme, Connecticut — infects as many as 476,000 Americans every year, according to the CDC.[34] The infections remain heavily concentrated in the northeast.

In July of 2019, the U.S. House of Representatives passed an amendment to that year's defense authorization bill which ordered the Pentagon's inspector general to investigate whether the military had ever "experimented with ticks and other insects regarding use as a biological weapon between the years of 1950 and 1975."[35]

The unusual piece of legislation came after a book titled *Bitten: The Secret History of Lyme Disease and Biological Weapons*[36] by Kris Newby expanded upon Loftus's almost offhanded assertion in *The Belarus Secret*, 37 years earlier. But the Senate version of the bill did not include the amendment, and Trump eventually fired Glenn Fine,[37] who had been acting inspector general at the Pentagon since 2016.

The House bill, however, set off a new round of debunkings in the press, including one by infectious disease specialist Sam Telford in *The Washington Post*, noting that the bacteria later identified as the cause of Lyme disease, *Borrelia burgdorferi*, had in fact been around for years[38] — centuries even, ruling out the possibility that it was a biologically engineered "weapon."

But Telford's debunking did not address the possibility that ticks carrying the existing bacteria could have been released into the wild on Plum Island as Loftus reported. And in *Bitten*, Newby reports that the scientist who later discovered the Lyme disease bacteria and gave it his own name, William Burgdorfer, specialized in research on tick-borne diseases and was, in fact, the military's "go-to person for special tick requests for bioweapons."[39]

One such utilization of ticks allegedly came in 1962.[40] The CIA at that time was engaged in all sorts of sabotage against Cuba's economy. According to Newby, citing an unnamed CIA source, those covert ops included a tick attack designed to infect Cuban sugar cane workers in Cuba, crippling production of that country's primo crop.

Newby also states in her book that the military released 100,000 ticks in the state of Virginia,[41] and according to a 1979 *Washington Post* report, CIA records suggest that the agency was behind a 1955 outbreak of whooping cough in the Tampa Bay, Florida, area.

In San Francisco circa 1950, the Navy sprayed bacteria into the city for seven days.[42] One of the strains, *Serratia marcescens*, was so rarely detected in the area that when hospital staff saw a patient infected with it, they published a research article with their findings. That patient soon died of the infection.

Domestic bio-warfare has in some incidents been more highly targeted than the (possible) mass dousing of an island with ticks, or spraying clouds of bacteria into major American cities. In one infamous incident way back in 1763, the British colonial military at Fort Pitt — in Pennsylvania, where Pittsburgh lies today — "gifted" several Native American tribes with smallpox-infested blankets.[43]

The U.S. military has been accused of using weaponized smallpox blankets against native tribes as late as 1837.[44] Those claims appear to be based on faulty research, and remain unconfirmed. But the attempt to deploy biological weapons targeted at a specific group that supposedly needs to be "reduced" has certainly happened.

The 2020 coronavirus appears to be less directly targeted, just a nasty disease that "washes," as Trump said, across the country.

In fact, however, the deadly disease did target one specific population. As of Memorial Day, with the U.S. death toll closing on 100,000, the virus was killing black Americans at 2.4 times the rate of whites, according to a study by APM Research Lab.[45] The illness also claimed black lives at 2.2 times the rate of Asian and Latino Americans.

"If they had died of COVID-19 at the same rate as White Americans, about 12,000 Black Americans, 1,300 Latino Americans and 300 Asian Americans would still be alive," the study's authors wrote.

Though the APM researchers could not assemble full data for Native American death rates, it is perhaps not surprising that in Arizona, Native Americans died at five times the rate of all others, and at seven times the rate in New Mexico, according to the study.

There may have been nothing special about the novel coronavirus that made black and Native American people more susceptible. Their higher death rates were certainly attributable to the systemic societal racism that leaves minority communities with poor health facilities, and lacking the resources to pay for better care, as the CDC itself assessed.[46]

Nonetheless, the disease did indeed target those populations. Writing in *The Atlantic* magazine, journalist Adam Serwer tied Trump's zeal for "reopening" the country[47] — despite the fact that the disease was far from under control — directly to the release of statistics showing that black, Native American, and other minority groups were hit hardest by the pandemic.

The first stats suggesting the coronavirus's disproportionate toll on black and Latino people were reported by *The New York Times* on April 7, 2020.[48] Just 11 days later, the first "protests" against the economic shutdowns began.

Trump embraced the protests with giddy enthusiasm. The growing perception that COVID-19 was pretty much a black and Latino disease gave him license, Serwer argues, to simply give up on any pretense of trying to combat the pandemic, and move on.

"What connects the rise of the anti-lockdown protests, the president's dismissal of the carnage predicted by his own administration, and the eagerness of governors all over the country to reopen the economy before developing the capacity to do so safely," Serwer wrote, "is the sense that those they consider 'regular folks' will be fine."

Of course, biological weapons are extremely difficult to target with any precision. Their purpose is mainly to wreak havoc and devastation. But havoc and devastation can serve a political purpose, as the fascination with bioweapons by terrorists makes clear. The Norwegian far-right terrorist Anders Breivik who killed 77 people with guns and a bomb in 2011 also authored a "manifesto" in which he outlined plans[49] — plans he never carried out — for anthrax attacks against the "cultural Marxist/multiculturalist elites."

He may have lacked the "necessary knowledge to culture and weaponize" anthrax spores himself, according to the Federation of American Scientists, but he was much more sophisticated when it came to the theory behind bio-war. His "understanding of the social implications of BW attacks is well grounded," according to an FAS report. Breivik showed a grasp of biological weaponry's potential for "possible high fatality rates (without the loss of infrastructure), massive media coverage, economic damage, and intense psychological effects."

Not an inaccurate description of what the 2020 coronavirus pandemic achieved as it "washed" across the United States, as per Donald Trump's reportedly stated wish.[50] The psychological and social devastation caused by a biological attack could even outlast the physical toll, according to an analysis published by *BMJ*[51] (previously the *British Medical Journal*) in 2001, shortly after a series of anthrax attacks through the U.S. Postal Service followed the September 11 terror attacks.

"The general level of malaise, fear, and anxiety may remain high for years, exacerbating pre-existing psychiatric disorders and further heightening the risk of mass sociogenic illness," wrote the authors of the paper, "Psychological implications of chemical and biological weapons."

Ripping apart the fabric of a society can be even more destructive, in the long run, than the damage done by the pathogen. That's why bioweapons are the ideal instruments to realize an apocalyptic vision, such as the one held by Shoko Asahara, the leader of Japan's Aum Shinrikyo doomsday cult.

Asahara, whose given name was Chizuo Matsumoto, was hanged in Tokyo[52] on July 6, 2018, 23 years after his followers carried out a sarin gas attack on Tokyo's subway system that killed 12 and injured more than 1,000 others.

While the motives for the sarin attack[53] — and a series of earlier, mostly failed biological attacks — remain somewhat mysterious even to the present day, Asahara was undoubtedly committed to an apocalyptic worldview in which he and his followers would stand as the sole survivors of an Armageddon that he would help to bring about.

In the next chapter, we'll look at Trump's own apocalyptic vision, and show how it is perhaps not so different from Asahara's — though it obviously varies in certain specifics. But similar to Trump, as we'll explain in Chapter Two, Ashara appears to have also been motivated by a seething resentment towards society in general, and the political system in particular.

For now, however, the key point is that Asahara believed that biological weapons were one of his best tools for sparking the apocalypse. According to a report by the Nuclear Threat Initiative think tank, the cult operated "the most extensive non-state biological weapons program unearthed to date."[54]

After his cult members were soundly defeated in 1990 Japanese elections — a defeat that looks like the inciting incident in the cult's descent into a violent obsession with the apocalypse — Ashara ordered his acolytes to begin acquiring and cultivating Botulinum neurotoxin, one of the deadliest bacteria known to exist.

Unlike some of its wackier plans, such as building a people-vaporizing ray gun, "the cult's pursuit of chemical and biological weapons was substantially grounded in science."[55] Yet Asahara was never able to cultivate the botulism pathogen. At one point in 1990, cult members drove around Tokyo in a van, spraying a mist containing what they hoped was a deadly botulinum at U.S. Naval bases, the Japanese Diet (aka Parliament) building, and even the emperor's palace. But there were no reports of anyone suffering illness or injury.

After its failure with botulism, the Aum cult in 1992 switched to anthrax. One of Asahara's devotees had connections in a biological lab, and got his hands on a vaccine strain of *Bacillus Anthracis*, the anthrax pathogen.

Vaccine strains are harmless, of course. That's the whole point. But Aum apparently had a half-cocked plan to "use 'genetic engineering' to convert it to a more lethal form," according to the NTI report.

That effort, fortunately, came up short as well. Though his efforts to create and unleash a devastating biological weapon consistently fell flat, Asahara never lost sight of his goal — "that the cult should hasten the apocalypse by launching attacks, including with biological weapons."[56]

Asahara's doomsday vision may have been more bluntly stated, but its echoes in Trump's own statements are eerie. Trump, too, has long held a grim view of humanity and its future. As we'll explore in the next chapter, his own obsession with apocalyptic disasters, and the more explicit end-times vision of his hardcore "base" supporters, found fulfillment in the chaos wrought by the 2020 coronavirus pandemic.

CHAPTER TWO

. . . .

AMERICAN CARNAGE

"When bad times come, then I'll get whatever I want."

— Donald Trump, 1987[1]

When Trump spoke those words in an interview with Barbara Walters, at the age of 41, he was speaking specifically about his dream to build the world's tallest building.[2] Just a pipe dream, really. His 150-story tower on Manhattan's Upper West Side, which would sit midway between 72nd Street and 58th Street amidst a cluster of six 76-story buildings also built by Trump, was never going to happen.

And it never did, and likely never would have under any circumstances, even if Mayor Ed Koch had not denied Trump the lavish tax breaks he was demanding in order to build the imagined complex.[3]

When it became evident that Trump wasn't going to get his tax abatement, Walters asked him what he planned to do, prompting Trump's prediction that he would profit from the misfortune of society as a whole. But that was only one of Trump's public statements to reveal a grim, apocalyptic worldview in which he gleefully prospers as society collapses around him.

To be fair, Trump has at least some reason to believe that he would prosper amid economic collapse. His career as a Manhattan developer launched at a time when New York City stood on the precipice of bankruptcy, in a year when the city erupted into chaos[4] under a massive power blackout, a serial killer stalked the night, raging fires incinerated dozens of decaying buildings,[5] and a record-setting heat wave scorched both New York's streets and psyches.

And indeed, it was also 1977 when 30-year-old Donald J. Trump paid the princely sum of $1 for an option to buy the Commodore Hotel, a decrepit property adjacent to Grand Central Station. He soon converted the aging relic into the majestic Grand Hyatt Hotel. Trump finally sold his stake in the hotel 19 years after paying that single buck, for a tidy $140 million.[6]

So we can see why Trump would view social calamity and crisis as his friend. He may never have become "Donald Trump," and definitely would never have been president, without it. He not only believed in capitalizing on destruction, he had an appetite for causing it, as his onetime closest confidant revealed.[7]

"Trump's theory of life, business and politics revolved around threats and the prospect of destruction — financial, electoral, personal, physical — as a weapon," wrote Trump's former lawyer and "fixer," Michael Cohen, in his memoir. "I knew how he worked because I had frequently been the one screaming threats on his behalf as Trump's fixer and designated thug."

In 2020, Donald Trump would once again turn to his old standby, mass destruction. But this time, things didn't work out as well.

Historians and political scientists have struggled to come up with a comparison for Trump among America's past presidents. Maybe Andrew Jackson, whose face adorns the U.S. $20 bill, though he was a slave owner and trader[8] whose primary policy as president was the "removal" — what today would be called "ethnic cleansing," or perhaps even "genocide" — of indigenous Americans.

Trump himself has claimed Jackson as his own political hero, calling him "the great Andrew Jackson, who actually was a great general, and he was a great president."[9]

Or perhaps there's a parallel in President James Buchanan, who dithered and did nothing as the U.S. plummeted into civil war.[10] Conservative writer Max Boot made that comparison, saying that by his disastrous handling of the coronavirus pandemic, Trump had actually surpassed Buchanan as America's "worst president ever."

I don't compare Trump to any past president, though there are obviously plenty of bad ones to choose from. When I take into account Trump's apocalyptic outlook, fetishization of violence, and seemingly unshakeable hold over his followers,[11] I see a better analogy in a cult leader — particularly in Japanese Aum Shinrikyo leader Shoko Asahara.

In the grandiose visions of Asahara described in the previous chapter, the guru and his cult would emerge as rulers of a world decimated by an Armageddon that they, themselves, provoked with biological and chemical warfare attacks. "Asahara believed that he had to 'liberate' the people by killing them or using poison as a societal purgative,"[12] wrote Karl Umbrasas, author of a study of apocalyptic groups published by the *Journal of Strategic Security* in 2018.

Trump also apparently dreams of himself as the lone, dominant figure to emerge from an inevitable global catastrophe.

It is perhaps no coincidence, as well, that like Trump, Asahara had significant Russian connections and derived much of his money from Russia.[13]

Trump revealed his dream of emerging from a massive catastrophe as the winner in a 2007 interview in which he celebrated the market downturn that would soon degenerate into the 2008 economic collapse and the Great Recession.[14]

"I've always made more money in bad markets than in good markets," Trump said, declaring himself "excited" by the prospect of the housing market collapse.

Trump's deeply-held belief that he personally profits from destruction is not all that different from the underlying ethic of American capitalism, that business success isn't the result of innovation and ingenuity as much as it is of grinding the other guy into the dirt.

Former oilman Samuel M. Jones spelled out capitalism's law of the jungle plainly in his 1899 book, *The New Right: A Plea for Fair Play*

Through a More Just Social Order.[15]

"In the business battle, the extremity of one is the opportunity of the other, and the brother man who is 'down,' or partly so, is considered the legitimate prey of his vigorous, healthy, prosperous rival," Jones, who became the progressive Mayor of Toledo, Ohio, wrote. "It is the rule of our competitive life that the time when the business rival is on the downward road — when creditors are pressing him hard, when banks are clamoring that he shall meet his paper, when the sheriff is threatening to close his doors — this is the opportunity for the other rival to strike the finishing blow and make merchandise out of the misery of his fellow-man."

Trump took the capitalist creed a lengthy step further. He believed that he prospered not merely by crushing individual rivals, but by laying waste to society as a whole.

Of course, what Trump was really doing, it appears, to make his cash in 2007, with his credit still reeling from a series of bankruptcies, was laundering Russian money.[16] He took a $50 million "investment" from a Russian-backed Icelandic firm that one of Trump's own associates described as "close to Putin." But we'll leave the Trump-Russia symbiosis, and how the coronavirus pandemic fits onto that continuum, for later chapters.

The bleak view of "bad times" Trump expressed to Walters in 1987 had only grown more grim and focused 27 years later, just one year before he declared his run for the presidency. In an interview, he described a prototypical version of his plans to "Make America Great Again" — the campaign slogan he would adopt in 2015.

In a February 10, 2014, phone-in to his favorite TV news program, *Fox & Friends*,[17] Trump launched into a monologue about his solutions to whatever he felt was ailing the country at that point — because in Trump's world, something is always a "disaster." But there's nothing an even worse disaster can't fix.

"You know what solves it?" Trump asked the *Fox News* talking heads, rhetorically. "When the economy crashes, when the country goes to total hell and everything is a disaster. Then you'll have a, you know, you'll have riots to go back to where we used to be when we were great."

The collapse of society, "total hell" followed by "riots" were seen by Trump as "what solves it."

When I wrote a little piece about Trump's resurfaced "total hell" quote, for an online news site in early April of 2020 — in an attempt to provide some perspective on the rapid collapse then being brought about by the coronavirus crisis — the editors scolded me for it.

"What you had was not accurate," one told me. "He did not say America would be great after the economy crashed, but that people would riot to get things back to WHEN things were great."

Well, that was one reading, I suppose.

But Trump's claim that riots and "total hell" would be what "solves" the country's problems seemed rather unambiguous to me. Nor was that 2014 statement the first time Trump has expressed his belief that mass societal destruction and rioting was an effective means to create change.

Explaining his idea to force Pakistan into ditching its nuclear weapons program, Trump in 1987 told journalist Ron Rosenbaum, "You do whatever is necessary so these people will have riots in the street, so they can't get water. So they can't get Band-Aids, so they can't get food. Because that's the only thing that's going to do it — the people, the riots."[18]

Trump's attraction to riots and mass violence surfaced again in the midst of the country-wide unrest that erupted in late May — even as the nationwide pandemic raged on and Americans continued to die at rates greater than 1,000 per day.

In a series of tweets that seemed rather inappropriately excited, Trump openly fantasized about unleashing "the most vicious dogs, and most ominous weapons, I have ever seen" on protesters who "would have been really badly hurt, at least."[19]

He celebrated Secret Service agents who would, at least in Trump's vision, "quickly come down on them, hard" when protesters outside the White House "got too frisky or out of line," adding that the demonstrators "didn't know what hit them."

So viscerally, almost erotically excited by violence was Trump that as the 2020 presidential campaign entered its home stretch and he trailed Democrat Joe Biden by a whopping 10.5 points in national polls,[20] Trump made his thrill over an apparently targeted assassination carried out by U.S. Marshals a feature of his campaign rallies.

Michael Reinoehl was an anti-Trump protester who, on August 29, allegedy shot and killed a pro-Trump white supremacist during a violent demonstration ignited by a caravan of Trump fans who rolled through Portland blasting pepper spray and paintballs into crowds from the back of a pickup truck.[21]

I say "allegedly" because Reinoehl never got a trial.[22] He never even got arrested. On September 3 a U.S Marshal "task force" rolled up on him outside his apartment and opened fire, executing him.

"This guy was a violent criminal. And the U.S. Marshals killed him," a visibly delighted Trump said in a *Fox News* interview 10 days later.[23] "I will tell you something, that's the way it has to be. There has to be retribution when you have crime like this."

The following month, Trump started gleefully praising the death-squad killing in his campaign rallies.[24]

"We sent in the U.S. Marshals," Trump told a crowd of supporters in North Carolina on October 15. "Took 15 minutes, it was over."[25]

If there was any doubt that he would actually, publicly praise a summary execution, Trump quickly cleared that up.

"They knew who he was. They didn't want to arrest him. And in 15 minutes that ended," he told the crowd.

Trump's lust for violence became even more pronounced when it came to his *bete noir* — "illegal" immigrants.[26] In Oval Office discussions of the immigration issue, Trump proposed various "sickening" tortures to "pierce the flesh" of immigrants coming across the border from Mexico, according to former Homeland Security official Miles Taylor. Trump also pondered ways to "maim" and gas the immigrants, as well most famously, to tear apart families that dare to attempt a border crossing as a unit.

Other advisers in meetings with Trump about the border heard him propose shooting migrants in the legs to slow their advance toward the border, and building — according to aides who spoke to *The New York Times*, "a water-filled trench, stocked with snakes or alligators."[27] (Trump later denied having considered the "trench" idea.)

"This was a man with no humanity whatsoever," Taylor told *The Daily Beast*.[28]

Trump's extreme pleasure in societal destruction and chaos was never more clear than on January 6, 2021, when a thousands-strong mob of his supporters stormed and took over the U.S. Capitol building. That morning, Trump had joyfully egged them on, speaking to them for two hours at a rally about his bogus and insane claims that he won the 2020 election, which he lost decisively, by "a landslide."

"We're going to walk down to the Capitol and we're going to cheer on our brave senators and congressmen and women and we're probably not going to be cheering so much for some of them," Trump told the angry crowd.[29] "You'll never take back our country with weakness. You have to show strength, and you have to be strong. Something is wrong here, something is really wrong, can't have happened and we fight, we fight like hell, and if you don't fight like hell, you're not going to have a country anymore."

Trump told the crowd he would walk with them the mile or so down the street to the Capitol. Instead, he retreated to the safety of the White House where he watched the insurrection that he set off on TV.

His reaction, reportedly, was very much in character.

"White House officials were shaken by Trump's reaction to a mob of his supporters descending on the Capitol," wrote CNN correspondent Kaitlan Collins.[30] "He was described to me as borderline enthusiastic because it meant the certification was being derailed. It has genuinely freaked people out."

A Republican senator, Nebraska's Ben Sasse, also said that based on his own conversations with White House officials, Trump "wanted chaos on television,"[31] and could not understand why his aides and advisers "weren't as excited as he was as you had rioters pushing against Capitol Police trying to get into the building."

The Trump supporters killed one of those Capitol Police officers, and severely beat two others.[32] During the riot, when Republican House Minority Leader Kevin McCarthy urged Trump to issue a statement denouncing the rioters,[33] Trump adamantly refused — leading to what was described as a "screaming match" between the two.

In fact, according to reporting by *The Washington Post*, Trump resisted pleadings from numerous aides and associates[34] — including his own daughter, Ivanka — to issue a statement denouncing the Capitol mob violence. But Trump wouldn't do it. He was enjoying the apocalyptic spectacle too much, it seems.

Later in the afternoon, Trump recorded a video directed at the rioters, telling them, "We love you, you're very special." He followed that up with a tweet, further endorsing the violent insurrection.

"These are the things and events that happen when a sacred landslide election victory is so unceremoniously & viciously stripped away from great patriots who have been badly & unfairly treated for so long," Trump wrote. "Go home with love & in peace. Remember this day forever!"[35]

Twitter quickly took down the tweet,[36] the first time the company had actually deleted a Trump posting, and subsequently deleted Trump's account, banning him, the company said, "permanently."

Unfortunately, the aggressive soft-pedaling of Trump's grim outlook that I encountered in my own small-scale experience is all too widespread. Willful ignorance and denial of Trump's extreme and bizarre views — which he never kept a secret — was why his apocalyptic vision never received the attention that it should have.

Just one more warning sign missed — especially when, as Trump himself memorably phrased it in an April 18 tweet, "People are dropping off like flies!"[37]

Despite his characteristic inelegance, Trump was not wrong. More than 39,000 Americans had already died due to the pandemic as of April 18,[38] about 13 times as many as were killed by the 9/11 attacks. And the carnage at that point had taken less than two months from the date of the first recorded U.S. coronavirus death.[39]

But even with the massive loss of life, and economy plummeting into the "worst economic downturn since the Great Depression,"[40] according to the International Monetary Fund website — certainly "bad times," and even, one might say, "total hell" — few in the media industry made the connection. They missed the rather clear significance of the fact that the man at the helm of the ship of state viewed calamity and suffering as *good* (at least for him), and even *exciting*.

One of the few who did was Sarah Kendzior, a former academic who specialized in the study of authoritarian regimes — and issued frequent warnings that by electing Trump, that's where America was headed.

Trump, Kendzior wrote on her Twitter feed, "savors the idea of mass death, and especially of being able to cause it and face no repercussions. There are four decades of interviews with him fantasizing about that."[41]

As Kendzior documented, Trump "has been obsessed with nuclear weapons for several decades,"[42] but his "obsession" goes beyond a mere fascination with nuclear armageddon. Trump apparently believes that he, and only he, has the wisdom and capability to start a nuclear war.

"It would take an hour-and-a-half to learn everything there is to learn about missiles. I think I know most of it anyway," he told *The Washington Post* in 1984, for a profile in which the paper described Trump's "fantasy of becoming the U.S. negotiator on nuclear arms limitation talks with the Soviets."[43]

During the 2016 campaign, a report surfaced — which his campaign denied — that Trump had repeatedly prodded his aides to explain to him why, if the United States possesses nuclear weapons, "we can't use them."[44]

Also during the campaign, in public statements, Trump made a point on repeated occasions of saying that he would not take the nuclear option "off the table," though usually being careful to qualify that he would rather not use nukes.[45]

But he also suggested to interviewer Chris Matthews that he would respond to an ISIS terror attack with nuclear weapons.

Once in office, Trump oversaw a new nuclear policy that caused the Bulletin of the Atomic Scientists to push the hands of its "Doomsday Clock" ahead in 2018, to "two minutes to midnight."[46] That was a full minute closer to doomsday than before Trump was elected.

The Trump administration Nuclear Posture Review[47] created a new, aggressive U.S. policy of winnable nuclear war, calling for new, "more usable" nuclear weapons of the "tactical" classification. Tactical nuclear weapons, at least according to the theory, can be used in "limited" battlefield conditions.[48] The more powerful, "strategic" nuclear weapons are basically world-enders.

Trump's policy also reversed the Obama-era rollback of the nuclear arsenal's role in U.S. war policy.[49] Instead, Trump ramped it up, creating a new "first strike" policy that would use nuclear missiles to strike back against non-nuclear threats, such as foreign cyber-attacks.

Trump took further deliberate steps to drive the country, and the world, closer to the nuclear cliff. He simply scrapped the Intermediate-Range Nuclear Forces Treaty with Russia in 2019,[50] and threatened to do the same with the START treaty, another crucial nuclear arms control agreement. He jacked up the budget for revamping the nuclear arsenal to a whopping $2 trillion.

His 2020 interviews with Bob Woodward — the same ones in which he admitted knowing what a "plague" the novel coronavirus would be early on, but deciding to "play it down" anyway — also showed Trump in a state of excitement over a "new" nuclear weapons development.[51]

"I have built a nuclear — a weapons system that nobody's ever had in this country before," Trump gushed to Woodward. "We have stuff that you haven't even seen or heard about. We have stuff that Putin and Xi have never heard about before. There's nobody — what we have is incredible."

Woodward wrote that military sources confirmed that the U.S had developed some sort of a new, secret nuclear system — but that they were "surprised" Trump had pointlessly announced it to a reporter.

(It should also be added that military experts believed Trump may have been referring to the W76-2, a modified version of a nuclear warhead designed for submarine-launched missiles. The new warhead was deployed in 2019.[52])

A *Politico* op-ed in 2019 by nuclear policy experts Tom Z. Collina and William J. Perry called on Congress to "starve Trump's lust for nukes."[53] The authors implored Congress to cut off funding for a new "low-yield" nuclear weapon that would be fired from submarines — a direct result of Trump's "tactical" nuclear war policy.

But as the late Reagan-era Secretary of State George Schulz said, "a nuclear weapon is a nuclear weapon. You use a small one, then you go to a bigger one." Is Trump aware of that likelihood? By his own account, he certainly must be, because it's something he thinks about all the time.

"I've always thought about the issue of nuclear war. It's a very important element in my thought process,"[54] he told *Playboy* magazine in a 1990 interview, in which he teased a future run for president (albeit coyly denying that he wanted to be president).

In that interview, Trump went on to call the belief that nuclear war will never happen "the greatest of all stupidities," and ridiculing the idea that nuclear weapons have not been used since 1945 "because everybody knows how destructive it will be" as "bullshit."

And then, in late May 2020 — again, in the midst of the coronavirus pandemic — Trump reportedly began holding internal administration discussions on "testing" nuclear weapons.[55] If he pulled that off, it would be the first time the U.S. had conducted a nuclear test in 28 years. But at least it would've given him a chance to set off a nuclear explosion or two before leaving office.

His delusions of expertise on nuclear weapons "mirrors Trump's current rejection of expert advice and conviction that his instinct is enough to guide policy," as Kendzior wrote.[56]

From his claims that "I alone can fix it" in his 2016 Republican convention speech,[57] to his assertion that he has no need for foreign policy advisers because "I have a very good brain and I've said a lot of things,"[58] and "my primary consultant is myself and I have a good instinct for this stuff," to his claim in the early stages of the pandemic that "people are really surprised I understand this stuff… Maybe I have a natural ability," Trump has repeatedly declared himself the ultimate authority on pretty much everything, conducting nuclear wars being no exception.[59]

While this type of grandiose narcissism is quite obviously a key element of Trump's personality,[60] according to cult expert Steven Hassan, it traces back to his childhood, where he "was raised by an authoritarian father in what I'd call a cultic church, where you're taught to believe 100 percent in yourself, that magical things are going to happen, and that the only sin is doubting yourself."

As Hassan — author of the book *The Cult of Trump: A Leading Cult Expert Explains How the President Uses Mind Control* — explains, the Trump family was devoted to Norman Vincent Peale,[61] best-known for his 1952 bestselling book *The Power of Positive Thinking*. But Peale was also the pastor at Marble Collegiate Church. The Trump clan would drive in from their stately, 23-room mansion in Jamaica Estates, Queens, to hear Peale deliver his sermons.

Trump himself was married at least once in Peale's church, and both of his parents had their funerals there.[62] Peale "preached a cultish prosperity gospel," according to Hassan, and Trump has often expressed his great enthusiasm for Peale's teachings.

With his "I alone" fixation, and having been reared in a cult, or at least "cultic" environment, it shouldn't be unexpected that Trump views himself as the leader of a cult, or as he describes it a "movement."[63]

His repeated description of any news that contradicts his own self-image as "fake," his instructions to his followers that "what you're seeing and what you're reading is not what's happening,"[64] his condemnation of his opponents as "bad people"[65] — all jibe with Hassan's definition of cult "mind control" techniques.

"It's a black-and-white, all-or-nothing, good-versus-evil, authoritarian view of reality that is mostly fear-based," Hassan said in a 2020 interview. "And there's a deliberate focus on denying facts in order to protect the image of the leader."[66]

The cult of Donald Trump, as you'd expect, reflects — and perhaps encourages — his apocalyptic vision. Wayne Allyn Root, a commentator and right-wing conspiracist for the *Newsmax* site, described Trump by calling him "the best President for Israel in the history of the world... and the Jewish people in Israel love him like he's the King of Israel. They love him like he is the second coming of God."[67]

Trump enthusiastically tweeted out Root's bizarre quote, thanking him for "the very nice words." And around the same time (August of 2019) Trump declared himself "The Chosen One."[68] He later claimed that his "chosen one" comment was "sarcasm." But Trump has on numerous occasions excused his own most outrageous statements by playing the "sarcasm" card.[69]

At the height of the pandemic, for example, Trump with clear sincerity suggested that injecting industrial disinfectant could prevent coronavirus infection. As the ridicule rolled in, Trump backtracked, claiming once again that he was merely using "sarcasm."

But Trump's followers are definitely not being sarcastic when they say that their leader has come to usher in the end times. White evangelical Christians have always supported Trump in high numbers, with 81 percent voting for him in 2016[70] — a higher percentage than cast ballots for Republicans Mitt Romney, John McCain or George W. Bush.

Even three months into the 2020 pandemic, at a point when more than 87,000 Americans had died,[71] 75 percent of evangelicals said that they approved of Trump's handling of the crisis, according to a Pew Research survey.[72]

"For his evangelical supporters, there's a sense that Trump's unlikely election to the presidency proves that he has been chosen by God," religious historian Neil J. Young told *Newsweek* in a 2018 interview.[73] "He shouldn't have won the election, so the thinking goes, so the fact that he did — and that victory came only via the Electoral College, no less — just demonstrates that only God could make it happen."

The headline on that *Newsweek* article explained the evangelicals' thinking: "Trump Will Start the End of the World, Claim Evangelicals Who Support Him."

"Donald Trump is clearly an apocalyptic leader," apocalyptic writer Bob Thiel declared in his apocalyptic 2017 book, *Donald Trump and America's Apocalypse*.[74] "Although he is not the final Antichrist that the Bible warns about, Donald Trump is helping fulfill many aspects of prophecy. Donald Trump is expected to help enable the rise of the final Antichrist — so will any possible successor to him."

It would not be fair or correct to label all of Trump's supporters, even all of his white evangelical supporters, as apocalyptic cultists. But the doomsday element is significant enough that Trump himself fashioned one of his key foreign policy decisions essentially as a signal to the end-times cultists — moving the U.S. Embassy in Israel from Tel Aviv, the country's political capital, to Jerusalem, the Biblical one.[75]

"For many conservative evangelicals, Jerusalem is not about politics. It is not about peace plans or Palestinians or two-state solutions," wrote religious scholar Diana Butler Bass in a 2018 CNN.com column. "It is about prophecy. About the Bible. And, most certainly, it is about the end-times."

Quartz.com White House Correspondent Heather Timmons made the same observation.[76] Moving the embassy to Jerusalem was believed by previous presidents to be a sure catalyst for religious violence. Trump, however, "is listening to a voice they were not: evangelical Christians who appear to believe in the 'Rapture.'"

The "Rapture," of course, is the fundamentalist Christian version of the apocalypse — the final destruction of the world. In this extreme view of Christianity, the end of the world is a good thing, because it means true believers get to zip on upstairs to heaven without even necessarily going through the inconvenience of death.

"Apocalyptic movements are security threats because they are prone to seek catastrophic effects on society," Umbrasas wrote.[77] Failing to understand the nature of apocalyptic groups, he argued, "leaves security to chance that these groups will not be competent in the future to execute a catastrophic attack."

And yet, in 2020, America found itself facing a widespread apocalyptic movement whose adherents look to Donald Trump as their divinely ordained leader. Donald Trump, who has described himself as "The Chosen One" (sorry, "sarcastically"), who believes that he profits when society collapses, who has openly and enthusiastically fantasized about riots and the country going to "total hell," and who — by amazing coincidence — ended up presiding over the deadliest pandemic in more than a century, the most dire economic meltdown in 90 years, and the broadest social unrest in more than 50.

Trump is often accused of a lack of self-awareness, as if he is some kind of savant who despite his many glaring faults and shortcomings somehow stumbled his way, Chauncey Gardiner-like, to the United States presidency. But that characterization is not entirely fair. He knows who he is, and at least in his broad plan for the country and his followers, he knows what he is doing.

"I bring rage out. I do bring rage out. I always have," Trump told Woodward during the 2016 campaign.[78] "I think it was ... I don't know if that's an asset or a liability, but whatever it is, I do."

In one of his typical rhetorical tropes, he followed a startling admission about himself with palliative self-praise, declaring nonsensically in the next sentence, "I also bring great unity."

Throughout his inauguration speech,[79] on January 20, 2017, Trump fixated on a bleak portrait of "American carnage." He vowed to stop this supposed carnage "right here" and "right now." But was it a vow, or an imprecation? Was stopping "carnage" ever really his plan, or creating it?

If you're stuck for an answer on that question, the American carnage of 2020 says hello.

CHAPTER THREE

. . . .

A VERY DIFFERENT THING

"You never really know when something like this is going to strike and what it's going to be. This is different than something else. This is a very different thing than something else."

— *Donald Trump, March 6, 2020*[1]

Sometime during the summertime of 2005, George W. Bush was taking one of what would turn out to be 1,020 vacation days during his eight years as President of the United States,[2] when he picked up a book to pass the time, and started flipping through.

But he found himself riveted, and by the time he had finished the book, he knew that he had to take action. America needed a new national policy — for its own security.

The book was an advance copy of *The Great Influenza* by John M. Barry, a frightening history of the 1918 flu epidemic[3] that wiped out an estimated 675,000 Americans — and 50 million human beings worldwide. Back then, that was one of every 30 people on the planet. Dead.

When Bush returned to Washington, he excitedly called in his homeland security adviser, Fran Townsend, and shoved the book — actually a publisher's galley copy; the hardcover wouldn't come out until October — into her hands.

"You've got to read this," Bush told Townsend. "Look, this happens every 100 years. We need a national strategy."[4]

Townsend pushed back, but Bush was insistent.

"My reaction was — I'm buried," she told *ABC News*. "I'm dealing with counterterrorism. Hurricane season. Wildfires. I'm like, 'What?'"

"It may not happen on our watch," Bush told her.[5] "But the nation needs the plan."

Bush administration Secretary of Health and Human Services Mike Leavitt, a former governor of Utah, was already on the case. Within a few months, working with the Centers for Disease Control, he had a plan ready for Bush to take to the nation.

Which Bush did, on November 1, in a speech outlining three "critical goals" that Bush said must be met to get the country ready for a coming pandemic.[6]

"First, we must detect outbreaks that occur anywhere in the world," Bush said.[7] "Second, we must protect the American people by stockpiling vaccines and antiviral drugs, and improve our ability to rapidly produce new vaccines against a pandemic strain; and, third, we must be ready to respond at the federal, state and local levels in the event that a pandemic reaches our shores."

Leavitt was charged by Bush with bringing together all 50 state governors to coordinate a national plan for responding to what was then believed to be a coming flu pandemic.[8] And under Bush's plan the federal government would allocate $7.1 billion to shore up America's defenses against a deadly pandemic.

Bush's critics, including Senator Ted Kennedy, said it wasn't enough to cover what hospitals and other health care facilities would need to handle a sudden flood of patients. But at least Bush was doing something.[9] It was never even considered that he would simply sit back and do nothing, letting a deadly virus "wash over" the country.

The Bush administration's effort to prepare the country for a pandemic was far from flawless, but at the time it was, as *ABC News* described it, "the nation's most comprehensive pandemic plan."[10]

The strategy covered everything from creating an early warning system for new disease outbreaks, to how to rapidly develop vaccines, to building a national stockpile of face masks, ventilators, and other essential medical equipment.

Bush dealt with his share of crises, many of them created or exacerbated by himself. So who knows how he would have actually dealt with a pandemic, if one hit during his time in office? But ultimately, the one crisis he was best prepared for is the one that never came. Not on his watch.

Bush's successor, Barack Obama, faced the pandemic Bush feared within months after he took office in 2009. Obama moved quickly. On April 26, 2009 — barely three months after his inauguration and with only about 20 cases of H1N1 flu reported in the United States, and no deaths — Obama declared a public health emergency.[11]

In October, when about 1,000 Americans had died from the new strain of flu virus, the new president upped the ante, to a *national* emergency.

The Obama administration got another chance to test itself in the face of a potentially disastrous pandemic five years later, when a sudden outbreak of the Ebola virus struck West Africa, in regions where the gruesome disease had never appeared before.

The United States led the global response to the Ebola outbreak.[12] Obama ordered 3,000 U.S. troops to West Africa to help put measures in place to stamp out the disease. He poured more than $6 billion into the fight against Ebola in Liberia, Guinea, and Sierra Leone, where the outbreak was concentrated.

Meanwhile, the CDC predicted that those three countries would see 550,000 cases of Ebola. If the virus reached Nigeria — Africa's most populous country — the toll would skyrocket far higher. Obama's own ambassador to Nigeria, Jeffrey Hawkins, warned of an "apocalyptic urban outbreak" if the virus reached Lagos, Nigeria's largest city.

But the Obama-led response prevented those grim predictions from coming true. According to CDC estimates, the two-year outbreak concluded with about 28,600 Ebola cases, causing 11,325 deaths.[13] Appalling numbers, to be sure. But nowhere near the original, apocalyptic predictions.

The United States saw only four cases of Ebola. Two of those occurred in people who had traveled back to the U.S. from West Africa. The other two were nurses who treated the first Ebola patient.

Private citizen Donald Trump at that time was busy paving the way for his eventual presidential run with a seemingly relentless assault on Obama, via his Twitter account. Obama's manifestly successful, even miraculous effort to contain the Ebola outbreak got no credit from Trump, who said that he was "starting to think that there is something seriously wrong with President Obama's mental health,"[14] because Obama did not immediately cancel all flights to the U.S. from West Africa.

"Psycho!" Trump added, concluding his tweet.

While Trump was tweeting his signature invective, Obama was busy — and had been since 2009 — creating a governmental "infrastructure" to prepare for, and deal with, the inevitable pandemic.[15] As described by Jason Karlawish, a writer for the health journalism site STAT, Obama's structure included "a top-level White House official devoted to planning and responding to emerging infectious threats and, to guide that person's work, the 'Playbook for early response to high-consequence emerging infectious disease threats and biological incidents.'"

The "Playbook" was a 69-page document that detailed, as the title implied, a game plan for pandemic response and, to the greatest extent possible, prevention.[16] As Karwalish wrote, from the start of his presidency in January of 2009, Obama made pandemic preparation "a priority from Day 1."

Exactly eight years later, Donald Trump took his own oath of office, and immediately created, in Karwalish's words, "a spectacular science-related tragedy. The Trump administration has systematically dismantled the executive branch's science infrastructure and rejected the role of science to inform policy, essentially reversing both Republican and Democrat presidential administrations since World War II."

After this deliberate effort to undo everything the Obama and Bush administrations had accomplished in setting up a system to deal with pandemics, not to mention the entire idea of science-based policymaking (and, perhaps, policymaking at all), Trump on March 19, 2020, when just under 200 Americans had died of coronavirus infection,[17] somehow claimed, "Nobody knew there'd be a pandemic or an epidemic of this proportion. Nobody has ever seen anything like this before."[18]

He also alleged that the Obama administration, which had spent eight years dealing with and preparing for pandemics, "had an obsolete system, and they had a system, simultaneously, that was not meant for this."

Acts of monumental gaslighting were not unusual for Trump, of course. "He uses the avalanche of untruths not just for partisan political gain, but to chip away at our democracy — to undermine the country's faith in shared facts,"[19] wrote Eric Boehlert after Trump unleashed another torrent of dizzying lies at, of all places, West Point's 2020 graduation.

Trump repeated his claim that "Nobody ever expected a thing like this," in a March 24 *Fox News* interview.[20] He had first made the "unexpected" claim on March 10, and on March 16, he said, "This came up — it came up so suddenly. Look, he was surprised; we were all surprised."[21]

It was all lies. Trump knew full well that, as *Wired Magazine's* Garrett Graff wrote, "Over the past quarter century, warnings have been clear and consistent from both US government leaders, scientists, and global health officials: A pandemic was coming — and whenever it arrived, it would be catastrophic to the global economy."

How do we know Trump knew?

It's possible that Trump — who is renowned for his ignorance and was once described by his own former national security adviser as "stunningly uninformed"[22] — remained blissfully unaware of the "quarter century" of warnings. But he most certainly knew what the Obama administration had done to batten down the hatches against a pandemic. His administration was "briefed on the (Obama) playbook's existence in 2017," according to a report by *Politico*.[23]

His own Homeland Security adviser, Tom Bossert, "expressed enthusiasm about (the playbook's) potential as part of the administration's broader strategy to fight pandemics."

Not only that, but during the 2016/2017 presidential transition period, Obama administration officials led Trump's aides through a stunning simulation, according to an earlier *Politico* report — "the rapid, global spread of a dangerous virus in cities like London and Seoul, one serious enough that some countries were imposing travel bans."[24]

The "table-top" simulation was attended by 30 incoming Trump administration officials, and was designed to "hammer home a new, terrifying reality." Namely, that an inevitable global pandemic could cause horrifying death tolls, and massive economic destruction.

And yet, to believe that Trump remained merrily oblivious to the pandemic threat and the extensive preparatory plans put in place by the prior administration, we're asked to believe that not a single one of the 30 officials sitting around the table top watching simulated people die by the thousands — as well as those who saw or knew of the Obama "playbook" — ever breathed a word of it to their boss.

Not a word, though they all knew that as of January 20, 2017, it would become his job to protect the American people from this highly predictable catastrophe.

Trump knew. It bends credulity past the breaking point to claim he did not. And yet, rather than take a single step to protect America, he quickly and efficiently set about demolishing the very "infrastructure" designed to provide that protection.

Obama's team didn't just write a pandemic "playbook." They created an entire sub-agency inside the National Security Council — The Global Health Security and Biodefense unit — specifically to prevent pandemics, and respond when one inevitably got through the defenses. Trump first trashed the playbook, then tore down the defenses.

In 2018, under National Security Adviser John Bolton — Trump's third national security adviser in his first 14 months, and the one who would later call him "stunningly uninformed" — Obama's biodefense unit was consigned to the dustbin of history, just two years after it was officially formed.[25]

Tom Bossert, who led the unit for those first 14 months of the Trump administration, got his pink slip. His job had the title "assistant to the president," perhaps the most influential title among all White House staffers, because such "assistants" are given direct access to the man in the Oval Office himself.

But after Bossert was canned, the job was reduced to "deputy assistant," and filled briefly by two different individuals who were not able to get a meeting with Bolton, much less with Trump. After those two hastily exited, the job was simply abandoned, and remained vacant throughout Trump's term.

On March 13, 2020, as it was becoming apparent that the coronavirus pandemic would soon kill thousands of Americans, Trump was asked by *PBS Newshour* reporter Yamiche Alcindor about his dismantling of the pandemic response team two years earlier.[26]

After first snapping at Alcindor for asking a "nasty question," Trump puzzlingly claimed that he knew nothing about it, and it wasn't his responsibility anyway.

"When you say me, I didn't do it. We have a group of people," Trump said in response to Alcindor's question. He then said that he could ask Anthony Fauci, who at the time was the senior doctor on the White House coronavirus response team — though Fauci was not involved with the decision to dismantle the biodefense unit in any way.

"I don't know anything about it," Trump continued. "I mean, you say we did that. I don't know anything about it."

The cuts, however, were consistent with Trump's overall hostility to pandemic prevention. In February of 2018, Trump announced a devastating 80 percent cut in funding to the CDC's global epidemic-prevention programs.[27] The cuts would have left the U.S. wide open for a biological assault. The CDC said that if the cuts were enacted, it would be forced to end efforts to detect and stop infectious diseases in 39 of the 49 countries where it had such programs.

The massive cuts were avoided, however, when Congress allocated the funds to the CDC anyway.[28]

Writing for the online publication *The Intercept*, former *New York Times* reporter Robert Mackey entertained the possibility that Trump may actually have been telling the truth when he expressed his ignorance of the NSC's pandemic response cuts.[29]

Mackey cited Trump's appearance March 6 at the CDC headquarters in Atlanta, when he "seemed entirely unaware that he had ever had such experts on his staff," in response to a reporter's question.

"The thing is, you never really know when something like this is going to strike and what it's going to be," Trump said at that appearance. "This is different than something else. This is a very different thing than something else."

But as Mackey also acknowledged, in February Trump appeared to be fully cognizant of the cuts. In fact, he seemed to believe that the professionals he fired could simply be rehired in the event of a health emergency.

"Some of the people we cut, they haven't been used for many, many years, and if, if we have a need, we can get them very quickly," Trump said at a February 26 White House coronavirus task force briefing.[30] "And rather than spending the money — and I'm a business person, I don't like having thousands of people around when you don't need them — when we need them, we can get them back very quickly."

The press briefing at which Trump claimed "I don't know anything about" his dismantling of Obama's pandemic response system was also the one where he responded to a question about how his total failure to implement a comprehensive diagnostic coronavirus testing program by declaring, "I don't take responsibility at all."[31]

Not surprisingly, one of the key recommendations in the Obama pandemic "playbook" was to "ensure appropriate diagnostic capacity," according to *Politico*.[32] In other words, testing. But not only did Trump fail to put any type of nationwide testing program in place — to create any capacity at all — he lied about it.

At that same March 6 visit to CDC headquarters, Trump assured the American people, "Anybody that wants a test can get a test. That's what the bottom line is."[33]

It was a lie then, and it was still a lie two months later, when he repeated it.[34] Then a month after that, he dismissed testing altogether as "overrated."[35] (Though in the same *Wall Street Journal* interview, he also ridiculously claimed to have "created the greatest testing machine in history."[36])

As might be expected, after Trump utterly disregarded the Obama warning that guaranteeing testing capacity was crucial, and then lied about it, the United States was barely able to test at all in the early stages of the coronavirus pandemic.

According to a study by the health news site STAT, the U.S. confirmed its 15th coronavirus infection case on February 14.[37] In the three weeks that followed — "a vital early window for action" — the country managed to administer tests to a mere 10,145 people.[38]

The Republic of Korea in the three weeks after its 15th case (which happened on February 2) outstripped the U.S. response, on a per capita basis, by a factor of 17.

Predictably, South Korea also saw far less loss of life from the pandemic. Four months after that 15th case, per STAT, South Korea had taken 272 fatalities. Scaling that number up to match the U.S. population, the South Koreans took the equivalent of 1,758 deaths in four months.

How many Americans died of coronavirus infection in the four months following February 14, 2020?

117,858.

In other words, for every South Korean who died, the United States suffered 67 losses. That adds up to 116,100 deaths that were totally unnecessary, and could have been spared if only the Trump administration had been as well-prepared as the South Korean government.

What magic did the RoK conjure up to achieve this amazing result? Nothing special. The government there did basically what the Obama administration did after the Ebola scare of 2014.

In 2015, South Korea was slammed with a wave of an earlier coronavirus, given the name Middle East Respiratory Syndrome, or MERS.[39] That disease was first reported in, as the name would imply, the Middle East. Specifically, Saudi Arabia.

When MERS reached the RoK, it found a country badly underprepared.[40] According to a report by *ProPublica*, testing was so scarce that patients wandered from hospital to hospital in search of tests to confirm they had the virus. In the process, they infected other patients in those hospitals. A damage assessment published three years later in the *Korean Journal of Internal Medicine* determined that 44 percent of the country's MERS cases were transmitted in hospitals.[41]

South Korea had the worst MERS outbreak outside of the Middle East, and yet its scale was minuscule compared to the 2020 COVID-19 coronavirus. Just 186 cases and 38 deaths in a pandemic that lasted a brief two months. Nonetheless, the RoK government swung into full gear, making sure that the next time a coronavirus or other form of pandemic hit, the country would be ready to deploy testing and other measures quickly.

The South Korean example, and those of several other countries, showed what was achievable by a government committed to controlling the pandemic rather than perpetuating it. On January 27 of 2020, when the RoK had only four confirmed cases, South Korean health officials mobilized what they called an "army" of researchers from top medical firms. Within a week, they had an approved test, ready for use.[42]

But rather than take a cue from the Koreans, Trump simply spat out lies.[43] He blamed the lack of testing in the U.S. on the very Obama administration whose preparations he trashed.

"We inherited a broken test," he complained. "The whole thing was broken."

While it was true that the first COVID-19 tests rolled out by the CDC were defective, those tests were developed under the Trump administration. Obama, who left office almost three years before the novel coronavirus SARS-CoV-2 was known to exist, had nothing to do with them.

Trump not only blew off any form of preparation for COVID-19 testing, he purposefully and systematically took apart the mechanisms that could have allowed him to prepare the country for the pandemic. Then he lied about it, and made no attempt to put those systems back together.

Trump's methodical destruction of America's pandemic defense system did not end in 2018 with his cuts to the National Security Council biological threat unit.

Just four months before China saw its first known cases of the new coronavirus, Trump fired Linda Quick, an epidemiologist with the CDC who was stationed in Beijing, working inside China's own pandemic prevention agencies.

According to a Reuters report, "Quick was in an ideal position to be the eyes and ears on the ground for the United States and other countries on the coronavirus outbreak, and might have alerted them to the growing threat weeks earlier."[44]

Instead, Trump inexplicably removed her from her job, and once the pandemic's approach to U.S. shores became inevitable, blamed the Chinese government for its supposed negligence in failing to warn the world of the viral threat.

So before he even took office, Trump set about systematically tearing down the walls previous American presidents had built to repel new and deadly biological threats.

But why?

That, as throughout the entire pandemic, is the central question about Trump's behavior.

Why did Donald Trump go out of his way to damage America's biological national security — ultimately resulting in a devastating attack by a virus that had killed more than 120,000 Americans in just over four months after the first recorded COVID-19 death on February 6?[45]

We might get at least an inkling of an answer when we understand that Trump's assault on U.S. biological security fits his overall pattern of shredding the country's national security in general.

The threat Trump posed to national security was clear during his presidential campaign when as *Lawfare* editor Benjamin Wittes warned,[46] he deliberately broke with the carefully fashioned policy of both Bush and Obama to separate the "War on Terror" from any concept of a religious war on Islam. Trump campaigned on a pledge to ban Muslims from entering the U.S., a pledge he attempted to fulfill in one of his first official acts as president.[47]

Trump also took a sledgehammer to NATO, the post-World War II alliance, led by the United States, that has effectively prevented a third World War. According to a *New York Times* report, Trump even floated the idea of pulling the U.S. out of NATO altogether.[48]

Most experts doubt that Trump could have unilaterally removed the U.S. from NATO.[49] But the threat itself, along with Trump's hostility toward NATO allied countries whom he accused of somehow not paying enough money into the alliance's coffers, rapidly weakened American relations with the allies.[50]

But Trump's most blatant attempt to undermine U.S. security is clearly his subservient relationship with Putin — though in reality, Trump's business and personal ties to Russia extend back to 1987.[51]

We'll spell out more details of the Trump-Russia story, and how it relates to the pandemic, in Chapters Seven and Eight — though it's not our purpose to relate that whole sordid history here. There are plenty of books and official reports that have done that.

Worth noting here, however, are Trump's repeated denials that Russia attacked the 2016 presidential election and would attack again in

2020. "Denial" is not even the right word. Trump attempted to warp reality itself to cause Putin's operation to simply vanish.

Most famously, Trump stood next to Putin after a one-on-one meeting in Helsinki and before the world's press and a global TV audience, took Putin's side on the election interference issue.[52]

"I will tell you that President Putin was extremely strong and powerful in his denial today," Trump gushed, adding that he "didn't see any reason" that Russian intelligence would have tried to rig an American election.

If Trump's abject and eager surrender to his own country's top geopolitical foe was not a deliberate assault on U.S. security — what is?

In private, according to an account by Bolton, Trump was no less the beta dog. He "repeatedly objected to criticizing Russia and pressed us not to be so critical of Russia publicly," the former National Security Adviser wrote.[53] Of course, Trump's lapdoggery toward the KGB agent who strong-armed his way to become Russia's president-for-life goes at least back to 2013, when Trump brought his Miss Universe pageant there.

"Do you think Putin will be going to The Miss Universe Pageant in November in Moscow," wrote Trump on his Twitter account.[54] "If so, will he become my new best friend?"

Trump was, in fact, penning fan mail to Putin as far back as 2007. We'll get into that odd episode in Chapter Seven.

Trump's preemptive surrender to Putin despite — or perhaps, as we will later see, *because of* — Russia's attack on America, his refusal to so much as admit the attack took place, plays a crucial role in the narrative of Trump's biological warfare attack on his own country.

The Russian attack is often portrayed as "election meddling" or "interference."[55] But the picture starts to come into clearer focus when we understand that Russia was not simply "meddling" or even attacking "the election" in 2016. Trump *was* the attack.

The Russian hacking of DNC servers, and social media propaganda campaign, as spelled out most notably in Special Counsel Robert Mueller's report,[56] were the vehicles that delivered the bomb. But the bomb, the weapon that caused the destruction, was Trump himself.

When we get to Chapters Seven and Eight, we'll explain that premise in greater detail. For now, let's just stipulate that the reason Putin wanted Trump in the White House was not that he thought The Donald would make a good leader and cool pal to chat with over the hotline. He backed Trump for specific reasons, consistent with his other goals for a Russian resurgence.[57]

Russia can never be resurgent, in Putin's mind, as long as a hostile United States remains strong enough to block its ascendance. Trump was a ready-made candidate for the job Putin carved out for his chosen American president.

As we showed in the previous chapter, Trump holds an apocalyptic, doom-and-gloom vision of America in which he comes out the winner in the midst of mass destruction. Trump was never someone who needed convincing to carry out the task Putin had in mind. The Russians simply weaponized Trump's pre-existing destructive impulses.

On December 29, 2019, as we mentioned in the introduction to this book, Putin placed an unexpected phone call to Trump,[58] who answered just as he was about to hit the links at his golf course in West Palm Beach, Florida.

True to form, the Trump administration made no mention of the call. America learned of it from that even more reliable news source, the Kremlin. According to the Russian government account, Putin placed the call just two days prior to New Year's Day while Trump was on one of his numerous vacations simply to thank him for information that "helped thwart terrorist acts in Russia."

Just two days later, the Chinese government reported that it was dealing with, as *The New York Times* put it, "a pneumonia-like illness, the cause of which is unclear."[59] The government of Wuhan, China's 11th-largest city, said that they were dealing with 59 cases of the "mystery" disease.

The Chinese authorities waited until January 9 to reveal that they had a new coronavirus on their hands[60] — but according to reporting by *The South China Morning Post*, they knew it on December 27, two days *before* Putin's unexpected call to Trump. In fact, by January 2, virologists in Wuhan had not only identified the new coronavirus, they had mapped its whole genetic sequence.

Did Putin already know what was going on inside China when he rang up Trump out of the blue, on December 29? So far, there's no public record that he did, so we have to make a probabilistic deduction.

Look at it this way:

Russia shares a 2,600-mile-long border with China, and the two nuclear superpowers have long had a prickly relationship, even when both were ostensibly Communist countries. The tension between the neighboring giants extends at least back to the 17th century,[61] when Russia pushed its way into Chinese territory, necessitating the first-ever Sino-Russian treaty.

Since about 2016, Russia and China have attempted to warm over their chilly relations, but the economic disparity between them means that their new "friendship" is superficial at best.

Russia "does not have the economic wherewithal to pose a gradualist challenge, only the tactical savvy to be an opportunistic disruptor," according to a report by the RAND Corporation think tank. "Moscow seems to have concluded that it can demonstrate its influence more by destabilizing that system than by offering a coherent alternative."[62]

Did Russian intelligence get wind of the novel coronavirus outbreak before Putin phoned Trump? Again, there's no way to know, at least not from public reporting. But given that the "pneumonia-like" outbreak was public knowledge, it seems unlikely that the Kremlin would remain in the dark about the cause of a worrisome disease inside the rival superpower on its border.

Another way we can be reasonably sure that Russian intelligence services were keeping close tabs on the outbreak in China is that we know U.S. intelligence was. American spy agencies were tracking the disease inside China as far back as November, 2019.[63] That their Russian counterparts neglected to do the same seems more than slightly difficult to believe.

And if both countries' spies were keeping close tabs on the outbreak, it also seems like they would have been aware on December 27 or very shortly thereafter that China had identified a brand new coronavirus — and that a deadly pandemic was at hand.

We also know that Trump exhibited little trust in the work of U.S. intelligence agencies.[64] But he appeared to trust Putin implicitly.[65]

We may eventually learn what was actually said in that call between Putin and Trump two days before China publicly confirmed its outbreak of "mystery" illness. We don't know now. And if I had to hazard a guess, I'd say we won't know for years.

But we can say, at minimum, that it would not be far-fetched to imagine that Putin already knew that a new coronavirus was on the loose. If he did, then sure, he possibly *could have* withheld that information from Trump.

But let's be real here, shall we? Putin more than likely would have divulged the coronavirus intel during that golf course call. And he would have done so in a calculating way, one that would serve his goal of destabilizing *both* of his geo-political adversaries, China and the United States.

Why? Simple. Putin knows his word is taken on faith by Trump. Putin knew — it seems safe to assume — that he could dictate Trump's response to the coming plague.

Not the warnings of U.S. intelligence agencies. Not Obama's playbook. Not the CDC, scientific data, or the views of public health experts. He, Vladimir Putin, would tell Trump what to do.

How do we know? Or to be more precise, what else leads us to believe that Putin may have dictated Trump's hyper-destructive response to the virus. Maybe this: Putin's own response to the Russian coronavirus outbreak was nearly identical to Trump's.[66] They followed the same blueprint.

More on the deadly Putin blueprint in Chapter Eight.

CHAPTER FOUR

· ·

TOTALLY UNDER CONTROL

"We have it totally under control. It's one person coming in from China, and we have it under control. It's going to be just fine."

— *Donald Trump, January 22, 2020*[1]

He was a preeminent American political leader, and he was worried. Though there were only five cases of coronavirus infection recorded in the United States,[2] he knew it was time to warn the country. A deadly pandemic that had originated in Hubei Province, China, had landed on our shores. And though it had made little impact as of January 27, 2020, he knew that something wicked this way comes.

America had to act. The leader felt compelled to push the country to move, to stop this potentially disastrous virus.

"The outbreak of a new coronavirus, which has already infected more than 2,700 people and killed over 80 in China, will get worse before it gets better. Cases have been confirmed in a dozen countries, with at least five in the United States. There will likely be more," he wrote.[3] "Here's the truth — the United States must step forward to lead these efforts, because no other nation has the resources, the reach or the relationships to marshal an effective international response."

The American political leader, unfortunately for the country, was not the President of the United States.

The leader was America's former vice president, Joe Biden, who at the time was the frontrunner for the Democratic presidential nomination, to oppose Donald Trump in the election that November.

Biden published his warning in a *USA Today* opinion piece on the 27th. And what was Trump doing on January 27?

Essentially, nothing.

Why not? Why would any United States president who was aware of the threat facing the country simply stand down rather than take some sort of action to stop it? Even if he didn't care whether Americans lived or died, why wouldn't he at least make a political calculation that doing something would be better than doing nothing?

Even an evident narcissist like Trump, who appears to care little for anyone or anything but himself, must understand that playing hero, protecting the country from a deadly biological threat would work in his favor. Sure, we know he craves nothing greater than ceaseless flattery and attention. Doing the right thing *just this once* would give him a sure fire way of getting what he desires.

But he couldn't even manage that.

Maybe Trump is so extraordinarily lazy and stupid that he just couldn't be bothered. Maybe he's so extraordinarily incompetent that he mistook doing nothing for doing something.

Others around him urged him to take action, warning him about the coming calamity, and about the consequences of doing nothing. Those warnings sank in. We know that his radically destructive course of non-action and anti-action was a conscious choice by the simple fact that he lied about it. Over and over.

Trump's ceaseless campaign to create the illusion that he was taking decisive action to protect America, I believe, is solid evidence of his consciousness of guilt over the fact that he was doing nothing.

Another item of evidence showing that Trump was not simply "incompetent" or oblivious to the coronavirus threat: he went out of the way to protect not the country but himself.

In late June Trump was, as *CNN* reported, "ready to move on from a still-raging coronavirus pandemic."[4] He rarely spoke about the pandemic in public anymore, and when he did, it was only to offer his rote fantasies about how the virus would soon "disappear" and the crippled economy would come roaring back to life "in very strong fashion."[5]

Yet, while he was publicly pretending that the virus was no longer an issue, he "scaled up dramatically" the measures to shield himself from infection.[6] (Or so he hoped.)

"When he travels to locations where the virus is surging, every venue the President enters is inspected for potential areas of contagion by advance security and medical teams," *CNN* reported on June 26. "Bathrooms designated for the President's use are scrubbed and sanitized before he arrives. Staff maintain a close accounting of who will come into contact with the President to ensure they receive tests."

Indeed, even as he ordered preventive measures such as mandatory temperature checks and facial masking lifted in the West Wing, he required that any person who came in contact with him must submit to a test.

"Even as Trump attempts to move on, the protective bubble around him has grown thicker," the *CNN* report noted, effectively dispelling the idea that Trump actually lived in the fantasyland he portrayed for the public. He was not deluded, or incompetent.

When Trump gave his speech accepting the Republican 2020 presidential nomination on the White House lawn[7] — the location itself a sizable abnormality and illegality — he packed 1,500 spectators into the crowd sitting shoulder-to-shoulder, almost all without protective face masks.

None of the attendees were tested — except those who came into "close proximity to the president," one White House official told *Politico*. No testing for anyone else — though they were "encouraged" to wear masks.[8] Not very persuasively, apparently. The guidelines issued by the campaign[9] did, in fact, require the Trump devotees to wear masks upon arriving at the White House and in "high traffic" areas — areas where Trump may at some point be likely to pass through — but allowed them to strip off the masks once they took their seats on the lawn, and the TV cameras were rolling.

Once again, Trump — aware of the dangers posed by the virus — took measures to protect himself. But as for everyone else, even his most devoted fans, the pandemic no longer existed. It was over.

Except it wasn't. But a large-scale gaslighting campaign to peer-pressure the country into proceeding as if COVID-19 had already disappeared, as Trump was fond of claiming that it would, was doing its job, and was nowhere on more brazen display than at his acceptance speech.

Trump knew that the pandemic was coming, knew what it meant, and his lethal response to the pandemic was what he wanted to happen. He knew that his actions, or inactions, would kill people. American people. And that's what he did.

"Trump's America stands bare and vulnerable, as the president wages open warfare on the country," wrote Eric Boehlert, in the July 2 edition of his newsletter *Press Run*.[10] There really was no other way to describe it. But in this case, Trump was not simply waging "open" warfare. He was waging biological warfare.

Of course, we can't read Trump's mind. We cannot know with 100 percent certainty what his intentions were when he received his early intelligence reports about the coming coronavirus plague. We have instead, a consistent and, frankly, terrifying pattern of behavior on Trump's part — a pattern of standing down, doing nothing, and even actively obstructing efforts to alleviate the crisis.

In one particularly jarring incident, on April 24, Trump took to the White House podium to suggest that people may be able to cure their own coronavirus infections with an "injection" of household disinfectant.

"I see the disinfectant that knocks it out in a minute, one minute. And is there a way we can do something like that by injection inside or almost a cleaning?" Trump said in what turned out to be, perhaps not surprisingly, his final appearance at one of the daily White House Coronavirus Task Force press briefings. "As you see, it gets in the lungs, it does a tremendous number on the lungs, so it would be interesting to check that."

Together with his lying about the virus, lying about his efforts to do the things any president other than Trump would do, and his extraordinary steps to guard himself from the threat to which he exposed the rest of the country, his pattern adds up to evidence of a clear intention — to increase the damage caused by the pandemic, rather than the other way around.

According to a *Washington Post* report, the day Biden published his op-ed was also the day when a group of top White House aides "huddled" with then-acting Chief of Staff Mick Mulvany to "get senior officials to pay more attention to the virus."[11]

One aide, White House Domestic Policy Council chief Joe Grogan worried — presciently, as it turned out — that if Trump did not start taking the pandemic threat seriously, when November rolled around and it came time for the people to vote on his reelection, he would lose.

Grogan also, according to *The Post*, correctly noted that "dealing with the virus was likely to dominate life in the United States for many months."

Just five days earlier, in his first public comments about the coronavirus outbreak, Trump uttered the words quoted in the epigraph to this chapter. And three days after Biden published his op-ed, Trump imposed a "Suspension of Entry as Immigrants and Nonimmigrants of Persons who Pose a Risk of Transmitting 2019 Novel Coronavirus."[12]

This was his supposed "ban" on travel from China. Trump claimed that this was the first such "ban" in the world,[13] though in reality, 40 countries had already restricted travel from China by the time Trump got around to it.

Also on January 30, Trump repeated his earlier claim that "we have it very well under control," telling his fans at a rally in Iowa, "We have very little problem in this country at this moment. ... We think it's going to have a very good ending for it."[14]

Throughout the crisis, Trump boasted again and again about his China "travel ban," though the so-called "ban" appears in retrospect more like a diversion, to give Trump cover for his plan to stand down the nation's biological defenses.

According to Saad Omer, director of the Yale Institute for Global Health, for any type of travel ban to be effective in stopping the spread of a virus, it must cut off at least 90 percent of travel from an affected area.[15]

Trump's "ban" certainly didn't come close to doing that. The "ban" included a full dozen exceptions, and as we discussed in the introduction, permitted approximately 40,000 travelers to enter the country from China over the subsequent several weeks.[16]

And despite Trump's claim that he "cut off China very early," 430,000 people had already entered the United States from there from the outbreak of the novel coronavirus to the date of the "ban."

But Trump continued to lie about the "China ban" as the pandemic raged on,[17] and he never really stopped. He claimed that his order had saved "tens of thousands" or even "hundreds of thousands" of American lives, despite a complete lack of evidence that it saved any lives at all. No more than a few, in any case.

Trump's much-touted, bogus travel ban looks even more like a modified limited hangout — a partial measure meant to obscure a nefarious and all-encompassing program of sabotage — in light of his subsequent actions, moves that directly inflicted suffering and death, and were naked in their designs to do just that.

In the Obama administration "pandemic playbook," one of the key guidelines was to ensure an adequate supply of protective gear for health care workers.[18]

"Is there sufficient personal protective equipment for health care workers who are providing medical care?" the playbook advised the next administration to ask. "If YES: What are the triggers to signal exhaustion of supplies? Are additional supplies available? If NO: Should the Strategic National Stockpile release PPE to states?"

Without proper PPE, health care workers faced unimaginable risks.

They were certain to get sick and even die in significant numbers. Which is obviously a terrible thing in itself — but their deaths could also create a shortage of medical professionals.

That shortage, in turn, would lead to higher rates of death among victims of a pandemic.

But even as Trump received warning after warning about the coming pandemic throughout January and February, his administration — according to records inspected by the Associated Press — "largely waited until mid-March to begin placing bulk orders of N95 respirator masks, mechanical ventilators and other equipment needed by frontline health care workers."[19]

By March 20, New York state alone had confirmed 8,352 coronavirus cases, with 100 deaths.[20] One month later, that number was up to 209,278, and 18,929 of those patients were dead from the disease. Clearly, the PPE situation was critical.

If Trump had any intention of protecting the lives of health care workers — and coronavirus patients — he could have mobilized the federal government to distribute its own stockpile of PPE. He could have immediately invoked the Defense Production Act, which allows a president to direct private companies to manufacture supplies for the national defense.

Instead, Trump at one of the more than 40 coronavirus press briefings at which he appeared, and dominated, suggested that increased supplies of PPE were unnecessary because health care workers were stealing the stuff.[21]

"Something is going on, and you ought to look into it as reporters," Trump said in his March 29 appearance.[22] "Where are the masks going? Are they going out the back door?"

Just to make sure everyone got the point, Trump went on to state, "I don't think it's hoarding ... I think maybe it's worse than hoarding."

Trump didn't stop at simply fabulating about imaginary sticky-fingered nurses. Someone was indeed stealing PPE. Him.

Local governments in Colorado, Massachusetts, New Jersey, Kentucky, Texas, and Florida all purchased their own supplies of PPE, only to see federal agents intercept and seize them,[23] for reasons that have never been fully explained.

The Federal Emergency Management Agency denied that it was hijacking the PPE shipments, claiming instead that it was simply trying to forestall "the unintended consequence of disrupting the regular supply-chain deliveries to other areas of the country that are also preparing for the coronavirus."[24]

At an April 5 "briefing," if his self-gratifying jousting sessions with the White House press corps could be called that, Trump huffily defended FEMA.[25]

"What they've done is a miracle in getting all of this stuff. What they have done for states is incredible," he said, before turning on his heel and fleeing the podium.

Trump finally did sign an order activating the Defense Production Act on March 27,[26] requiring General Motors and other big companies to start manufacturing ventilators — a crucial piece of medical equipment for keeping COVID-19 patients alive. Then Trump sent hundreds of the ventilators produced at taxpayer expense to foreign countries — including at least 200 to Russia.[27]

Overseas ventilator shipments were not a new occurrence under the Trump administration. As the Obama administration geared up preparation for a possible pandemic in 2015, it contracted with a Pennsylvania company to produce an inexpensive ventilator called the Trilogy Evo Universal. The machine was finally approved by the Food and Drug Administration in 2019, and Trump's Department of Health and Human Services ordered 10,000, to be added to the federal stockpile.

But according to *ProPublica* reporting, by the end of March 2020, not a single Trilogy Evo Universal had been delivered to HHS[28] — and the Trump administration never even tried to obtain the machines it had ordered — again, at taxpayer expense. Instead, the company sold them abroad.

A month after finally flipping the switch on the Defense Production Act, after weeks of foot-dragging, to produce needed ventilator machines, Trump was much quicker to use the DPA — but this time, he wasn't even pretending to use the law to save lives. He used it to kill people — or at least, to put them in grave danger.

Meat processing plants dotted across the country were slammed by coronavirus outbreaks through March and April, and into May. A CDC report released on May 1, 2020, counted close to 5,000 meat plant workers who had tested positive for the virus, spread over 115 plants in 19 states.[29] As of April 27, 20 meat packers were dead from COVID-19, according to the CDC.

The CDC surmised that meat processing facilities were especially conducive to spread of the coronavirus — the same phenomenon was taking place at meat plants in Australia, Canada, Spain, Brazil and other countries around the globe — because crowded assembly lines where workers gut, strip and otherwise mutilate animal carcasses to package them as human food are not especially amenable to six-foot-apart social distancing requirements.

"The pace and physical demands of processing work made adherence to face covering recommendations difficult," the CDC wrote, "with some workers observed covering only their mouths and frequently readjusting their face coverings while working."

Not only that, but meat plants, the CDC said, "have difficulty adhering to the heightened cleaning and disinfection guidance," which sounds bad not only for preventing the spread of coronavirus, but for meat in general.

"A thousand people might work a single eight-hour shift, standing shoulder to shoulder as carcasses whiz by on hooks or conveyor belts," wrote *Wired Magazine* reporter Megan Molteni.[30] "Often, workers get only a second or two to complete their task before the next hunk of meat arrives."

It all sounds appetizing, indeed. But quality of the meat aside, workers' lives were clearly at great risk from the meat-packing outbreaks.

In fact, to control the outbreaks, 13 U.S. meat processing plants closed down during March and April.

The outbreaks appeared not to trouble Trump — but the closed meat plants certainly did. On April 28, he signed an executive order activating the Defense Production Act to force endangered workers back into the infected facilities.[31]

The order classified meat packing plants as "critical infrastructure," and not only ordered them to open up and get their slaughterhouses grinding again, but also shielded the companies that own the plants from legal liability, if workers did indeed catch the virus.

By May 28, according to an *Associated Press* report, 24 more workers had died out of another 3,000 who came down with the virus,[32] following Trump's order sending them back into the meat plants.

The actual number of infections among the meat workers was almost certainly higher, a United Food and Commercial Workers International official told the *AP*. Many states were simply withholding data, on the numbers of infections and deaths in the plants, if they were collecting that data at all. The union compiled the heartbreaking figures on its own, by surveying workers and the records at the plants themselves.

His Defense Production Act order to herd workers into the virus's line of fire was just one example of Trump taking deliberate actions to kill people in the midst of the pandemic.

But like the virus itself, which hit African-Americans and other minorities disproportionately hard,[33] Trump's death sentence for meat packing workers also targeted the working poor — meat packing workers earn $28,450 per year, according to the average compiled by the Bureau of Labor Statistics[34] — and minorities.

According to figures by the Center for Economic and Policy Research, 44 percent of meat packing workers are Hispanic, while another 25 percent are African-American.[35] More than half of all "frontline" meat packing workers are immigrants, according to the CEPR demographic data.

The first data showing that African-Americans were taking the brunt of the pandemic began to emerge in early April. *ProPublica* reported on April 3 that in Michigan, with a 14 percent Black population, African-Americans accounted for 35 percent of coronavirus cases — and 40 percent of those who died from the disease.[36]

Less than two weeks after that revelation, a series of protests broke out in several cities.[37] Composed mainly of white demonstrators who appeared largely middle class, these protests demanded that state governments immediately end the stay-at-home measures and business closures that had been imposed in mid-March to control spread of the novel coronavirus.

In Florida, North Carolina, Virginia, Michigan, Minnesota, Maryland, New Hampshire, Idaho, Texas, California and elsewhere, these protests were supposed to be a "grass-roots" uprising of concerned citizens who claimed to be suffering economic hardship that posed a greater risk than the pandemic.

In reality, the "reopening" protests were part of "a wide-ranging and well-financed conservative campaign to undermine restrictions that medical experts say are necessary to contain the coronavirus," according to reporting by *The Washington Post*.[38]

Though the *Post* reporting gave the protesters a hearing, allowing that "the activism is often organic and the frustration deeply felt," it also identified the deeper motive behind the "network of right-leaning individuals and groups, aided by nimble online outfits," who put the "reopening" protests together. Namely, the fear that economic disaster resulting from health-related shutdowns "could damage President Trump's political prospects."[39]

It all made a bizarre kind of sense. Trump took every step possible to cause mayhem and death with the out-of-control virus. And then his surrogates and allies provided him political cover with a ginned-up "protest" movement supposedly aimed at minimizing the politically destructive economic damage wrought by the pandemic.

Even if the protests failed to produce "reopenings," they at least shifted the burden of economic destruction onto governors, placing Trump on the side of success. It was those damn governors, mostly Democrats, who refused to "open" their states, causing economic collapse. Trump stood above them, heroically fighting for "liberation."

If there was any doubt, Trump — who, himself, had begun calling for "reopening" in late March, demanding the economy be "opened up" by the Easter holiday[40] — hopped onto his Twitter account to announce his approval.

"LIBERATE MICHIGAN!" he tweeted on April 17,[41] in his oft-employed all-caps idiom. He added "LIBERATE" tweets for Virginia[42] and Minnesota[43] as well, moments apart.

On April 17, the United States had already lost approximately 34,000 lives to the coronavirus pandemic,[44] out of more than 705,000 total cases. But that was but an inkling of what was to come.

As could have been easily predicted, "reopenings" led to more death and destruction. States that had begun allowing businesses to open up in mid-May saw surges in coronavirus infections that by late June threatened to overwhelm their health care systems. Arizona, Florida, and Texas were among the most egregious examples,[45] each hitting new highs in daily infection totals almost every day for weeks.

Did Trump intervene, or do anything to help the states slow the now-rampant virus? On the contrary — he did his own version of "opening up," holding an in-person rally June 20 in Tulsa, Oklahoma — his first since March. He went ahead with the rally, insisting on a ban against safety measures such as mask-wearing and social distancing inside the Bank of Oklahoma Center Arena despite the fact that Tulsa was in the middle of its own record-setting surge in coronavirus cases.[46]

Before the rally, workers at the BOK Center placed "Do Not Sit Here" stickers on seats, in order to cause Trump's fans to stay a safe distance away from each other. But Trump campaign officials, following their boss's wishes, forced them to remove the stickers.[47]

What was the point? Trump's insistence on a laissez-faire approach to health and safety at his rally seemed certain to lead to more infections, and as a result more death. Within four days of the rally, Tulsa had indeed suffered a new record spike in cases — though health officials claimed that it was "too soon to attribute any increase in infections to President Donald Trump's campaign rally."[48]

Attributable or not, there was no question that Trump knowingly brought his viralpalooza smack into the middle of a hot zone. And on June 30, 10 days after the precaution-free Trump rally, the state of Oklahoma recorded 585 new coronavirus infections in one day.[49] That was a state record.

The one-day high could not be attributed solely to an increase in testing.[50] Though the 15,404 diagnostic tests performed on that day were also a high for Oklahoma, the previous daily high in testing was 14,886, only three days earlier. That day produced 299 new cases.

By that date, cases were hitting new highs nationwide. The United States was initially believed to have hit the "peak" of the pandemic on April 24 when, according to Worldometers data, the country recorded 39,116 new cases.[51] And indeed, daily cases generally declined after that, dropping as low as 18,700 on May 11.

Feeling confident, or perhaps smug, most states began the "reopening" throughout May, with Trump as their "biggest cheerleader," as *The Washington Post* put it.[52]

By mid-June, predictably, case counts began rising again.[53] On June 25, the number topped 40,000, exceeding April's supposed "peak." Two days later, more than 47,000 Americans were logged in with the coronavirus.

Trump, as well as Vice President Mike Pence, took the line that the spike in infections was nothing more than a reflection of more testing. The seemingly unstoppable plague was actually a sign that they were doing a great job! But back in the real world, that wasn't the case.

"We're doing so much testing, so much more than any other country," Trump gloated to a Christian Broadcasting Network interviewer on June 24.[54] "And to be honest with you, when you do more testing, you find more cases. And then they report our cases are through the roof."

Cases really were through the roof, testing or not.[55] As data published by *ProPublica* showed, in many states, the rate of increase in new cases significantly outsripped the increased testing rate. At the same time, hospitalization rates were back up, and death rates (though lower than in April) held steady.

If the pandemic were genuinely subsiding, and the higher caseload was a mere illusion conjured up by Trump's imagined lush outlay of testing, hospitalizations and deaths would show noticeable declines. As the *ProPublica* report made clear, that wasn't happening.

Diagnostic testing for the SARS-CoV-2 coronavirus is perhaps the most important factor for controlling the pandemic. In countries like South Korea — where the professional baseball league was able to start its season on May 5,[56] less than six weeks after the scheduled opener — Iceland, and Germany, governments were able to bring the pandemic under control with a program of testing, which detects people who carry and can spread the bug without getting sick themselves.

"To truly end the crisis, keep deaths low, and allow the economy to recover," according to *Vox.com* science writer Umair Irfan, "testing has to happen on an enormous scale."[57]

And yet despite his repeated and false claims that the U.S. had conducted testing "far more than any other country," Trump was especially hostile to the very idea of testing.[58] Absurdly, on June 15, he called testing a "double edged sword" because it "makes us look bad."

"Without testing, or weak testing, we would be showing almost no cases," he wrote, perhaps wishfully.

On that same day, he told reporters, "If we stop testing right now, we'd have very few cases, if any,"[59] as if somehow failing to detect coronavirus cases would erase them from existence.

In June, in a *Wall Street Journal* interview, Trump dismissed coronavirus testing as "overrated."[60] He also said, in that June 19 *Journal* confab, that if cases spiked again, he would not push to increase testing.

Case numbers were already on a rapid rise[61] when Trump spoke to the *Journal*. Topping more than 33,000 on that very day, the country hit its highest one-day case-total since May 1 according to Worldometers data.

The very next day, Trump held his quickly infamous Tulsa rally at which he made a rather startling admission — but one that should not have been unexpected after his previous, cavalier statements on the need for testing.

"Here's the bad part. When you do testing to that extent, you're going to find more people, you're going to find more cases," Trump told his adoring fans in Oklahoma. "So I said to my people, 'Slow the testing down, please.'"[62]

Slow the testing down?

That seeming confession set off a wave of concern and outrage from health experts, congressional Democrats, and even some members of Trump's own administration.[63] But Trump's defenders in the White House claimed that he was "joking" when he made the "slow the testing" remark.

Trump himself contradicted the spin when he told a reporter three days after the rally, "I don't kid," when asked if he was, in fact, kidding about slowing testing.[64]

His hostility, or at best indifference, toward testing was evident as early as January, when Trump despite receiving reports and briefings on the looming pandemic (as we discussed in the previous chapter) took exactly zero steps to put a nationwide testing program in place.

Researchers in Germany created the first test for the novel coronavirus on January 20,[65] a week before that White House huddle when aides brainstormed how to get Trump to do something about the imminent biological invasion.

With Trump refusing to take the wheel, the CDC put the first U.S.

tests into circulation on February 5.[66] The results left something to be desired. The tests simply didn't work, a calamity that *MIT Technology Review* called "baffling."

As a result, according to the MIT report, by early March when other countries had tested "millions" of their citizens, the U.S. managed barely more than 1,600.

Why did this disaster happen? The CDC couldn't say. The health agency, which typically takes the lead in distributing information to the public in health crises, was muzzled. Trump appointed himself lead public health spokesperson,[67] appearing at the White House podium daily to spout nonsense, and often outright propaganda.

CDC experts were mostly barred from Trump's daily briefings, despite their own multiple requests.

"We continued to ask for approval," a CDC spokesperson told *Yahoo! News*.[68] "We were not given approval. Finally, we just stopped asking."

With his daily press "briefings" at his disposal, rather than do anything about the massive testing failure, Trump sought to cover his ass. He played his usual card. He blamed Obama.[69]

On at least four occasions in late March and early April, Trump nonsensically claimed that his administration "inherited" tests that were "broken" and "horrible."

On March 13, in what quickly became one of the signature moments of his presidency, Trump declared, "I don't take responsibility at all."[70]

Of course, in reality, Trump "inherited" no tests at all, because the novel coronavirus was not discovered until late 2019, and the "broken" test was created by the CDC in 2020. There was no such thing as SARS-CoV-2 when Obama was president, and therefore, no such thing as a test for SARS-CoV-2.

The Trump administration, in perhaps its single most malignant act — or non-act — never put together a national program for coronavirus testing at all.[71] Coordinated with a program of tracing the contacts of infected persons, and isolating coronavirus patients, the consensus of health experts was that an aggressive testing program was the best and perhaps only way to beat the pandemic.

Well, let's take a moment here to acknowledge something: it's not quite true that the Trump administration did *nothing* to create a testing program. In fact, what they did was even worse and more homicidal than nothing.

Not everyone in Trump's inner circle was in on his game of testing denial, at least not at first. A blockbuster piece of reporting for *Vanity Fair* by Katherine Eban on July 30 revealed that Trump's son-in-law Jared Kushner had been working behind the scenes in the early months of the pandemic to create a national testing program — the exact type of program essential to containing any pandemic, "a secret project to devise a comprehensive plan that would have massively ramped up and coordinated testing for COVID-19 at the federal level," Eban reported.[72]

And then — Kushner's program, developed in secret, simply disappeared. Kushner decided "for reasons that remain murky, to scrap its proposal," according to Eban. But as she reported later in the same article, maybe those reasons weren't so murky after all.

"The political folks believed that because it [i.e., the coronavirus] was going to be relegated to Democratic states, that they could blame those governors, and that would be an effective political strategy," one source told the *Vanity Fair* scribe.

The Trump "political folks" (likely, as it often is, a reference to Trump himself) made a clear decision to attack states led by Trump's political opponents, with a deadly virus. The spirit of Jani Beg's catapults lived on. Or perhaps, the spirit of Shoko Asahara, aimed squarely at more than half the population of the United States. Pick your (biological) poison.

In any event, the result was that Trump casually shunted testing programs on to individual states, whose efficacy in creating and carrying them out varied widely. According to a Harvard Global Health Institute study, the United States would require 4.3 million tests every day to achieve "suppression" of the pandemic.[73] That is, to crush the viral spread to the point where daily new cases reach, to use the Trumpian phrase, "close to zero."

Under "close to zero" conditions, something resembling normal daily life could resume, more or less safely. But by July 1, without a national testing program, the U.S. was conducting only 500,000 or 600,000 tests per day, approximately.[74]

A long way to go to reach 4.3 million. It should also be noted that the Harvard study came out on the low end of the spectrum. Other studies have put the minimum anywhere between 5 million and 20 million tests per day,[75] to squelch or at least constrain the pandemic.

For that matter, according to the Harvard Global Health study, a cool million tests per day would be needed to reach mere "mitigation" of the pandemic.[76] "Mitigation" means slowing the spread of the virus enough to stop it from overwhelming the country, as long as strict social distancing requirements and other restrictions remain in place.

"There is a challenge with this approach," wrote the study's authors.[77] "As states open up, mitigation level testing is often not sufficient to prevent new outbreaks."

With numbers at only about 50 to 60 percent of mitigation-level testing requirements (at best), and states "reopening" at Trump's urging throughout May and June, it was hardly a surprise that after a brief lull during which the pandemic appeared to plateau, the virus really found its footing, and suddenly spread like, well — a virus!

On June 15, the United States recorded 20,901 new coronavirus cases.[78] That number was more than any other country in the world.[79] On July 1, the U.S. had 51,097 cases. In a little more than half a month, the daily case load shot up by 240 percent.

The frightening case inflation was not attributable, as Trump and Pence repeatedly claimed, to an increase in testing. On June 15, there were 447,739 tests performed in the U.S., according to COVID Tracking Project data.[80] On July 1, there were 621,114 — an increase of roughly 38 percent.

By July 1, 131,389 Americans were dead from coronavirus infection.[81] But of course, without adequate testing, the death toll was seriously undercounted, as the CDC itself would acknowledge.[82] The agency recorded only deaths of patients who had a confirmed novel coronavirus infection. No test, no death. At least, not an official COVID-19 death, anyway.

Nonetheless, Trump continued to gaslight the country, claiming that U.S. testing was "by far the most, and best, in the World,"[83] and that "the United States leads the world in coronavirus testing!"[84] He made the claims dozens of times, on Twitter and in statements to the press.

But as of July, among countries with populations of at least one million people, the U.S. ranked 14th in per capita testing, according to the Worldometers data on July 2.[85] The U.S. ranked third among those countries in cases per capita.

Indications of Trump's aversion to doing the one thing most essential for stopping the pandemic surfaced early. On March 12, *Politico* reporter Dan Diamond told *NPR* that Trump "made clear" inside his administration that he did not want aggressive testing for coronavirus, and that Trump's stated priority pulled up the reins on any national testing program.[86]

"The lower the numbers on coronavirus, the better for the president, the better for his potential reelection this fall," Diamond told *NPR* host Terry Gross.

Why Trump believed that failing to test for the coronavirus — the only way to bring it under control — would help his reelection remains a mystery. By Election Day, November 3, the U.S. was averaging nearly 90,000 cases per day[87] — a simply inconceivable number just a few months earlier — and almost 240,000 Americans were dead.

Did Trump genuinely believe that the pandemic would "just disappear,"[88] as he said over and over, and on July 1 when the country was in the midst of a catastrophic spike in infections? Or October 15, when he said the pandemic was "going to peter out and it's going to end" even without a vaccine?

Was he truly that delusional?

Trump hardly kept his distaste for widespread testing a secret, even early on. Asked about passengers who in early March were stuck on a cruise ship that was being ravaged by the virus, off the West Coast, Trump said he wanted to keep them on board.

"I would rather have them stay on, personally," Trump said, during his lone visit to the CDC.[89] "I don't need to have the numbers double because of one ship that wasn't our fault."

In late June, Trump made good on his claim that he had told "my people" to "slow the testing down." Just five days after Trump made that admission — albeit framed as a boast — to his fans, his administration announced that it would cut off federal cash for 13 drive-through testing sites as of June 30.[90]

Seven of those sites, more than half, were in Texas, where Republican Governor and Trump loyalist[91] Greg Abbott's overeager reopening[92] — including allowing bars to open back up as early as May 22 — had set off a tidal wave of new infections, throwing the state into a crisis.

Two days before the administration announced that the Texas testing sites would close by the end of June (a deadline later extended by two weeks), Texas hit its all-time high in both new cases and COVID-19 hospital admissions.[93]

The two Texas senators, Ted Cruz and John Cornyn, were both hardcore Trump allies. Yet even *they* protested the defunding of the testing sites.

The reality is that, beyond cutting funds for some testing sites, there wasn't much Trump could do to slow testing down because he never created a national testing strategy, much less a functioning program.

"If you look at every country on Earth that has got a handle on the virus, it's because they had a national testing program in place early, aggressively," said New York congressional rep Patrick Maloney, in a June interview.[94] "We have never gotten our act together on that at the federal level. And we are paying a terrible price for it."

There was one other thing Trump could do to "slow the testing down," however.[95] And the day after his Tulsa rally, two Senate Democrats reported that he was doing it.

Two months earlier, Congress allocated $25 billion toward nationwide diagnostic testing and contact tracing programs — as well as collecting data on racial and ethnic inequalities in the impact of the pandemic. But by the time Trump declared his desire to "slow down the testing," only over half of those dollars, give or take, were spent.

When cutting funds for testing did not appear to be working to his satisfaction, Trump took another, even more clearly malicious action to slow testing. In late August, with cases topping 40,000 per day[96] (down from about 60,000 a month earlier), and deaths over 1,100 daily, the CDC announced a puzzling change to its testing guidelines.[97]

Under the new guidelines, which *CNN* gingerly described as having "perplexed some doctors," the CDC said that people who showed symptoms of possible COVID-19 no longer needed to be tested. In fact, they didn't need to be tested even if they had been in contact with someone who was definitely carrying the virus.

"This is key to contact tracing, especially given that up to 50 percent of all transmission is due to people who do not have symptoms," former Baltimore Health Commissioner Leana Wen told *CNN*. "One wonders why these guidelines were changed — is it to justify continued deficit of testing?"

Wen was onto something. Of course Trump wanted a "deficit of testing." Within a day, a CDC official told *CNN* that the health agency was pressured to make the change "from the top down."[98] The "top" was clearly a reference to the White House — that is, to Trump.

The CDC's Trump-appointed director, Robert Redfield, quickly took steps to soften the revelation[99] that the once-independent public health agency was now essentially acting as an arm of the White House. In what was described as "walking back" the new guidelines, he allowed that "all close contacts of confirmed or probable COVID-19 patients" could, in fact, be tested. But on the CDC's public web site itself, the newly altered guidelines remained the same.

At about the same time, the Trump administration announced what, on its surface, looked like a major concession to the need for testing that it had ignored and derided for months. On August 26, the Food and Drug Administration announced that it had granted rush approval to a new type of test,[100] produced by an outfit called Abbott Laboratories.

The spiffy new test, according to *The New York Times*, cost just $5 and took a mere 15 minutes to run.[101] Just 24 hours later, the Trump administration declared that the government would shell out $750 million to buy 150 million of the Abbott test kits.

Sounded great! Except the test, known by the brand name BinaxNOW, had back in May been the target of a rare FDA warning. The tests were too likely to produce results that were wrong.[102] Also, the test is primarily used to sift out confirmed cases of coronavirus infection from the larger pool of "probable" cases. BinaxNOW wasn't generally used to screen the general population. It was primarily used on people already showing symptoms.

Any other type of use could produce a large number of false results and, according to a *Daily Beast* report,[103] "dilute" the total number of COVID-19 cases in the country — exactly what Trump in numerous public statements said that he wanted to happen.

The cuts to testing were alarming, but they weren't the first cuts Trump made in the midst of the pandemic. In late April, the National Institutes of Health suddenly and inexplicably eliminated funds for a joint U.S.-Chinese research program that was looking to determine how coronaviruses leap from bats to human beings,[104] as the 2019 novel coronavirus was believed to have done.

The NIH gave no explanation for the sudden end to the research, which was conducted at a lab in Wuhan, China, where the outbreak originated. A statement by one agency official proffered, "At this time, NIH does not believe that the current project outcomes align with the program goals and agency priorities."

But just about 10 days earlier, Trump told a writer for the right-wing site *Newsmax*, "we will end that grant very quickly."[105]

He also claimed, "the Obama administration gave them a grant of $3.7 million."

In fact, the five-year grant from the NIH to the group EcoHealth Alliance ran from 2014 to 2019 — when it was reapproved by the Trump administration.[106]

At the time Trump eliminated the grant, two months into the 2020 pandemic, the Wuhan lab was the subject of various unfounded conspiracy theories pushed most prominently by Trump loyalist Tom Cotton, the Republican senator from Arkansas, and echoed by Trump as well.

In congressional testimony on June 24, Dr. Anthony Fauci confirmed that orders to cut the NIH coronavirus research funding came from the White House.[107] But a White House official passed the buck, claiming that the cuts were entirely the responsibility of the Department of Health and Human Services. HHS, however, said only that the program "was not in compliance with NIH's grant policy," whatever that means.

Trump's evident efforts to avoid widespread testing, then "slow down the testing" when it started to ramp up, may have been his deadliest actions of the pandemic. To a large extent, Trump got his wish to "let this wash over the country,"[108] as he expressed repeatedly to top administration officials, including Fauci, in early April — a time when more than 10,000 people were already dead from coronavirus.[109]

Fauci, according to *Washington Post* reporting, explained to Trump that "many people would die" if the virus was allowed to "wash over" the United States.[110]

After that, Trump apparently stopped telling people that he wanted the virus to "wash over" the country. He just did it.

Holding back testing and steadfastly refusing to even think about, much less implement, a nationwide testing program accomplished that goal pretty well.

Fauci's repeated insistence that the pandemic was, in fact, as bad as it looked clearly irritated Trump. The anti-shutdown "protesters" were chanting "Fire Fauci" as an integral part of their coordinated campaign in April.[111] Trump himself retweeted a post with the hashtag "#FireFauci" on April 12.[112]

Never mind that, because he holds a civil service position, Fauci cannot be arbitrarily fired by Trump or anyone else.[113] By mid-July, as the virus surged to frightening, new record numbers, Trump effectively benched the preeminent infectious disease expert.

According to a *Washington Post* report, Trump ignored Fauci, refusing to meet with him at all, much less listen to his expert advice.[114] In one interview, Trump said that Fauci was "a nice man but he's made a lot of mistakes." And in another, asked about Fauci's assessment that the country was "not in a good place" with the coronavirus, Trump shrugged him off, saying, "I disagree with him."

Behind the scenes, according to the *Post*, Trump and his aides took their cold shoulder toward Fauci to another level, leaking a "lengthy list of the scientist's comments from early in the outbreak" to the media,[115] in an attempt to publicly discredit him.

Another method Trump employed for allowing the viral "wash" effect under which "many people would die" was his active discouragement of masking. On April 3, the CDC (finally!) issued a recommendation that Americans wear a facial covering while in public.[116]

Why? Because as the medical journal *Lancet* reported, use of such masks "was associated with a much lower risk of infection."[117] Subsequent studies confirmed the conclusion.

In June, a study at Cambridge and Greenwich Universities in the United Kingdom showed that "population-wide" facemask use would keep the coronavirus "reproduction rate" under 1.0.[118] In other words, each infected person would infect no more than one other person, on average, and may not infect anyone at all. An "R" number of 1.0 or lower means that the pandemic will not increase, and is on its way toward going away.

Other studies showed that widespread mask-wearing would cut down the transmission of the virus by 75 percent. The simple, facial mask was almost as good as a vaccine, except much cheaper and easier to make and buy.

And yet, Trump was hardly enthusiastic about this development which, had he championed it, could put the country on a path out of the crisis.

"With the masks, it's going to be really a voluntary thing," he mused at an April 3 press conference.[119] "You can do it, you don't have to do it. I'm choosing not to do it, but some people may want to do it and that's OK."

In mid-May, he softened somewhat, saying that he would wear a mask privately, but not when he was seen by TV cameras.

"I didn't want to give the press the pleasure of seeing it," Trump said,[120] after refusing to wear a mask while visiting a Ford manufacturing plant in Michigan — where mask-wearing was required for all visitors and employees.

Trump's refusal to publicly don a facial mask had an effect. According to social scientist Peter Glick, writing in *Scientific American*, Trump was signalling that "appearing to play it safe contradicts a core principle of masculinity: show no weakness. In short, wearing a mask emasculates."[121]

While a poll taken in early April showed that 72 percent of Americans said they planned to regularly wear masks,[122] it quickly became clear that plenty of Americans had no such plans.

"It's submission, it's muzzling yourself, it looks weak - especially for men," said one anti-mask protester,[123] quoted by Arizona Republic reporter BrieAnna J. Frank.

At "reopening" protests around the country, few of the angry demonstrators were seen wearing masks — even though widespread masking would make a quickler reopening safer and easier.

Finally, on July 11, Trump was photographed wearing a mask in public, when he paid a visit to Walter Reed military hospital.[124] But according to a CNN report, it took "pleading" from his top aides to persuade him to slip one on.[125]

Trump's capitulation to mask-wearing came months too late. As the country saw an alarming surge in coronavirus cases in June and July, health officials said that the widespread resistance to wearing masks, as well as the failure to maintain adequate person-to-person social distancing, had directly resulted in the increases.

The virus was indeed washing over the country.

Masks may have been similar to a vaccine, but only a vaccine would actually *be* a vaccine. The Trump administration had a program to oversee the national effort to find a COVID-19 vaccine, BARDA, or the Biomedical Advanced Research and Development Authority.

BARDA was led by immunologist Rick Bright. So of course, as seemed somehow inevitable, Trump fired him.[126]

In congressional testimony after his April dismissal, Bright contended that he was canned for objecting to Trump's repeated and enthusiastic endorsements of the anti-malaria drug hydroxychloroquine, as a treatment for COVID-19.

Bright said that he wanted the government to invest taxpayer dollars in "safe and scientifically vetted solutions, and not in drugs, vaccines and other technologies that lack scientific merit."

Taking a cue from Trump, perhaps, Americans obtained hydroxychloroquine prescriptions in February and March at a rate more than 86 percent higher than usual.[127] But studies soon showed that the drug had no real effect on coronavirus infections, and could even cause heart trouble and other health problems.

But Trump wasn't finished. As the summer of 2020 heated up, he turned his deadly sights on America's children. On July 7, as case numbers ballooned, topping 50,000 per day on a regular basis,[128] and the U.S. hit its highest one-day death toll in 27 days (993),[129] Trump announced that he was "very much going to put pressure on governors and everybody else to open the schools, to get them open."[130]

The day before, Trump had unleashed one of his signature, all-caps tweets (with a triple exclamation point added for emphasis): "SCHOOLS MUST OPEN IN THE FALL!!!"[131]

At a White House event, Trump accused local and state school officials of keeping schools shut down "for political reasons."

Trump nonchalantly shrugged off the potential dangers of cramming kids into classrooms, saying, "young people do extraordinarily well" when infected by the virus.[132]

While it was true that children, in particular very young children, appeared to be less susceptible to contracting the coronavirus,[133] for reasons that remain poorly understood, they are far from invulnerable.

Schools in Israel reopened in May, but many were shut down again two short weeks later when more than 200 kids and school staff tested positive for the virus.[134] A similar spike in China's capital of Beijing forced school re-closures there in mid-June.[135]

While some public health experts also advocated sending kids back to school in the fall,[136] they did so knowing the risks. They thought the damage caused by keeping children at home was worse, however.

Research showed that even young people, widely believed to be at low risk from the virus, could suffer long-term lung damage even if they were asymptomatic.[137] Put another way, young people who didn't even know they had the disease were still damaged by it. They may not get sick now, but they would develop a preexisting condition that may stay with them for the rest of their lives.

They would never be able to receive treatment for that condition, however, if Trump got his way. Even as the early summer surge accelerated to unsustainable levels, the Trump administration appealed to the Supreme Court to repeal the Affordable Care Act, better known as "Obamacare."[138]

If Trump succeeded, the Obamacare requirement for health insurance companies to cover patients with preexisting conditions would also be deep-sixed. Many of those young people handling their coronavirus infections "extremely well" would eventually become older people, who would need health insurance to handle their weakened lungs.

Of course, Trump handled his assault on Americans who had pre-existing conditions, and those who would soon develop them thanks to him, in his usual way. He lied about it.[139]

"I will ALWAYS PROTECT PEOPLE WITH PRE-EXISTING CONDITIONS, ALWAYS, ALWAYS,ALWAYS!!!" Trump rather brazenly lied, in a June 29 tweet[140] — after previously telling the same lie approximately 100 times, by a *Washington Post* count.

- Blowing off early warnings of the incipient pandemic threat.
- Refusing to set up a national testing plan, and telling his "people" to "slow down the testing."
- Repeatedly and incessantly lying about the dangers of the coronavirus.
- Pushing for early "reopening" — as early as Easter!
- Stealing supplies of PPE bound for state health care systems.
- Stalling on activating the Defense Production Act to make more PPE.
- Publicly cheering bogus "protests" against health-mandated economic shutdowns.
- Forcing workers back into coronavirus-infested meat processing plants.
- Discouraging the wearing of masks by the American public.
- Cutting or eliminating research into understanding the coronavirus.
- Firing his own vaccine research chief.
- Pushing questionable, even quack "treatments" for COVID-19.

The bullet points could go on and on. Each and every one of those actions by Donald J. Trump, President of the United States, demonstrably killed Americans.

Or at a minimum, they endangered American lives.

All in all, Trump's pandemic "response" precisely mirrored the effects of a massive biological warfare attack by a hostile foreign power, or terrorist organization. Was that just a coincidence? A result of Trump's "failures" and incompetence?

I don't think so — not given his own extreme measures to shield himself from the coronavirus, his lying to the public about its dangers, the repeated early warnings both before and after the virus landed stateside. All are clear evidence that he knew what he was doing. He knew he was causing harm. He knew he was killing people.

But the mass slaughter, a body count that topped 325,000 by Christmas, was not the only destruction Trump caused, and knew he caused. The United States economy caught its own disease, and the Trump solution was about what you'd expect.

CHAPTER FIVE
. . . .

WORDS THAT NOBODY EVER HEARD OF BEFORE

"We're going to have just a tremendous surge. I think it's gonna be like a rocket ship. I really believe that. We'll have to see what happens. But there's a lot of things happening but with all of that, we still have to remember all of the people that perished."

— *Donald Trump, April 11, 2020*[1]

In the state of Washington, where the United States' first case of coronavirus infection was detected on January 20,[2] Governor Jay Inslee took a dramatic step, before any other state government had done much of anything.

Certainly, the federal government had not been willing to directly interfere with the daily routines of Americans by March 11, when Inslee ordered public gatherings of more than 250 people banned.[3] It would be another five days before Trump would announce a set of non-binding guidelines to "slow the spread."[4]

Those were, initially, supposed to stay in place for only 15 days.[5] The "slow the spread" suggestions emphasized working from home, avoiding "discretionary travel," and of course encouraged hand-washing and stifling sneezes into one's elbow.

Even though the guidelines noted that "bars, restaurants, food courts, gyms, and other indoor and outdoor venues where groups of people congregate, should be closed,"[6] that was just a suggestion, Trump noted, not a federal order.

One month after issuing those guidelines, Trump was already posting new guidelines for "Opening America Up Again."[7]

But on March 11, before any of that, Inslee tried to drive home the deadly seriousness of the coronavirus pandemic. Asked if he would be imposing legal penalties for those who flout the public gathering order, Inslee drew the situation in stark terms.

"The penalties are you might be killing your granddad if you don't do it," Inslee said.[8]

The order effectively cancelled the Seattle Mariners' home opener, which at that point was just 15 days away. But of course, the very next day, Major League Baseball ditched Opening Day, and as it turned out, its regularly scheduled season anyway.[9]

The National Basketball Association also shut down on March 12, a move prompted by a player, Rudy Gobert of the Utah Jazz, who tested positive for the virus.[10] Oddly enough, just three days earlier, Gobert had "jokingly" made a show of rubbing his hands all over a bank of microphones after a press conference.

The National Hockey League also decided to "pause" its season on March 12,[11] while MLS, the American pro soccer league, did the same.[12] Even the XFL, a brand-new pro football league in only its first season, closed down operations on that day.[13] Less than a month later, the XFL declared bankruptcy and said it had "no plans" to play another season in 2021.[14]

The sudden evaporation of all major sports in the country was stunning,[15] and in addition to costing the sports industry billions, left Americans facing the reality of what was about to hit them — not merely a health disaster, but an economic collapse like most people alive in 2020 had never seen or even imagined. Not only would basketball and other sports need to shut down, so would pretty much everything.

How bad was it?

The International Monetary Fund predicted that the lockdown —

not only in the U.S., but worldwide — would set off "the worst recession since the Great Depression, and far worse than the Global Financial Crisis."[16] That is, the crisis of 2008, which cratered the American and global economies in the final year of the previous Republican administration of George W. Bush.

But the coronavirus collapse made the Bush meltdown look like prosperity.

The World Bank served up an even more dire diagnosis. The economy would contract by 5.2 percent,[17] worse than at any time since the Great Depression of 1929 to 1939.[18] But the sheer, planet-wide scale of the pandemic, and economic shutdown, would actually make this collapse, the World Bank predicted, the worst in 150 years.

That was a reference to the "Long Depression," which extended from 1873 to 1896.[19] That crisis, as the sobriquet implied, was a long, drawn-out period of deflation and economic panic that caused businesses to go under, world powers to realign — *out with the U.K., in with the U.S.* — and militaristic authoritarianism to tighten its grip, paving the way for the Great War (aka World War I) from 1914 to 1918.

The economic disaster was something even Trump could not lie his way out of, though he certainly tried. The first indications that the coronavirus pandemic would set off an economic disaster came courtesy of the stock market, which began plunging in late February. After a startling 3.5 percent drop on February 24, Trump took to Twitter, absurdly declaring "Stock Market starting to look very good to me!"[20]

The market (that is, the Standard & Poor's 500) plunged another three points the following day. Within a week, the index had dropped eight points. On February 26, back on Twitter, Trump blamed the fall on cable news, saying "Low Ratings Fake News MSDNC (Comcast) & CNN are doing everything possible to make the Caronavirus (sic) look as bad as possible, including panicking markets, if possible."[21]

Trump concluded his tweet with the sunny pronouncement, "USA in great shape!"

By March 18, the Dow Jones Industrial average had plunged to a figure just under 19,000, literally wiping out all of the gains it had made since Trump took office.[22]

The stock market crash had to be especially galling for Trump. Since he assumed office, the rising stock market had been perhaps his favorite thing, other than himself, to brag about. He clearly viewed the easily understandable number — *up = good! down = bad!* — as his failsafe to reelection.

According to a count by *Politico,* in the first year of his administration Trump publicly bragged about high stock market numbers "once every 35 hours," including 25 times in the 29 days from January 3 to February 1 of 2018.[23]

So when the market went into a dizzying tailspin in early 2020, one might think it would have spurred Trump to action. As he watched the coming coronavirus crisis sap the market of its strength, of course he would quickly take control of the crisis, leaping into action to take the necessary steps to slow it down and hold off a coming recession, or depression.

One might think. But that's not what happened.

Trump continued to do nothing with regard to coordinating a national strategy or plan of action to face the virus. Instead, he continued to lie, exaggerate and cast blame anywhere but himself as the pandemic, with ever accelerating velocity, began to "wash over" the United States.[24]

In an impressive analysis of 260,000 words publicly uttered by Trump between March 9 and April 17,[25] *The New York Times* found 600 instances of self-congratulation by Trump, and 110 times he blamed others. He mentioned the already-staggering death toll, then at about 33,000,[26] "only fleetingly," the *Times* reported.

Some of the "self-congratulation" cited by the *Times* study was, in fact, whining and self pity. Such as on April 13 when, with the U.S. death toll topping 29,000, he kvetched that he had been "brutalized for the last four years," adding, "I used to do well before I decided to run for politics."

And yet, in all of that time, when Trump was making public appearances as part of a coronavirus "briefing" on a daily basis, no reporter asked him the most obvious question: "Why are you lying?"

Indeed, why *was* he lying?

Not that any reporter would expect an honest answer from Trump to that (or any) question. A *Washington Post* tabulation put Trump at 19,127 "false or misleading claims" (i.e. lies) by June 1, 2020, the first 1,226 days of his term.[27]

No need to whip out the calculator. I'll do the math for you. That's 15.6 lies per day. Even though no honest answer may have been forthcoming, the question "Why are you lying?" sure seems worth an ask.

Was he simply an inveterate liar, a mentally disturbed person who couldn't help himself? A degenerate who lies in any situation even when the truth would suffice?

He spat forth a notably blatant lie in an interview with Chris Wallace of Fox News (of all places) on July 19, when Wallace asked him why his administration — at the height of the pandemic — was battling in the Supreme Court to overturn the Affordable Care Act (aka Obamacare), stripping an estimated 23 million Americans of their health insurance.[28]

Wallace asked him why he wanted to destroy Obamacare without any replacement plan?

"We're signing a health care plan within two weeks," Trump shot back, indignantly.[29] "A full and complete health care plan, that the Supreme Court decision on DACA gave me the right to do."

There was no such plan.[30] Trump and the Republicans in Congress had never presented a credible alternative to the ACA in the decade since the law was passed. Trump was simply making shit up, to cover for yet another decision designed to result in mass suffering and death.

Maybe he believes his own lies, so in some epistemological sense, they're not really lies? Mary Trump hinted at that possibility, when she authored her psychobiography of her uncle.[31]

"The lies may become true in his mind as soon as he utters them, but they're still lies," she wrote. "It's just another way for him to see what he can get away with. And so far, he's gotten away with everything."

Maybe Trump's glaring pathology could indeed explain his callous lies in the face of mass death. But lying about obvious economic conditions would not even serve his need for emotional fulfillment. The economy should have been something he actually cared about — if only insofar as a strong economy was traditionally seen as any incumbent president's best shot at reelection.[32]

The stock market would somehow eventually rebound to something resembling health. The reasons why it bounced back are better left to professional economists and market analysts. I will venture a guess, however, that the congressional bill — the CARES Act — blasting $2.3 trillion back into businesses and individual households was a significant factor.[33]

More than anything else, the stock market bounce-back showed just how disconnected from the everyday reality of life in America the investor casino really was.

Even as the market gained back some of its losses, the official national unemployment rate launched skyward, from a reasonable 4.4 percent in March, to a disastrous 14.7 percent a month later, according to the Bureau of Labor Statistics.[34] By June the rate had come down a bit, to 11.1 percent — still higher than in any month in any year since 1940, but enough for Trump to declare the day the June jobs report hit the streets "a very big day for our country."[35]

He also took the opportunity to announce that the U.S. had, at that point, come "largely through" the "horrible pandemic" due to "the greatest economy in the history of the world."

It was another lie. Despite the seemingly encouraging ease in unemployment percentage, an average of 1.5 million Americans filed new jobless claims each week in June.[36] That number was more than twice the previous one-week record of 695,000 set in 1982.[37]

"It's still more than twice the worst week of the Great Recession," economist Heidi Shierholz told *The New York Times*.[38] "It's a sustained hemorrhaging of jobs unlike anything we've seen before."

Why was Trump lying? Did he honestly believe that, by putting a public happy face on the economic devastation, he could magically wish it away? Or was he simply attempting to "give people hope," as he claimed. That's how he explained away his early denialism about the virus, including his repeated dismissals of the virus as "the flu," among other disastrous bullshit.

"This is really easy to be negative about, but I want to give people hope, too," he said at a March 31 White House appearance, during a coronavirus "task force" purported briefing.[39] "You know, I'm a cheerleader for the country."

He was still at it in the July 18 Wallace interview. Pressed by the Fox News anchor about his claims that the virus was "going to sort of disappear," Trump stuck to his fantasy.

"I will be right eventually," Trump replied.[40] "You know I said, It's going to disappear.' I'll say it again."

That was the same interview when Trump, confronted by Wallace about the massive U.S. coronavirus death toll — quickly approaching 145,000 at the time — replied, "It is what it is."[41]

The March 31 "briefing" was the one that sparked some of the more credulous elements of the political press to praise Trump for his new "somber" tone regarding the deadly pandemic.

In comments compiled by rather gobsmacked *Vanity Fair* reporter Caleb Ecarma,[42] media outlets declared that after Trump's weeks of denial and fancifully incanting that the virus would simply vanish, the briefing marked "an absolutely new message and new tone from Trump" (*Politico*), that he was "sounding different today. Scale of death appears to have changed his tone, at least" (*New York Times* reporter Eric Lipton). And that Trump now appeared, "grave, sober, grim, realistic" (Karen Travers of ABC News).

Trump's own later comments rendered the charitable media interpretations of his "tone" nonsense. But the March 31 event was also where Trump made what should have been an admission that caused the assembled press to leap from their socially distanced chairs.

Asked by *CNN* correspondent Jim Acosta whether he "knew (the pandemic) was going to be this severe when you were saying this was under control", Trump blithely admitted that his earlier statements had been willful lies.

"I thought it could be. I knew everything," he replied.[43] "I knew it could be horrible, and I knew it could be maybe good."

"I knew everything."

This blunt confession after weeks of denial, obfuscation and non-action would, one might surmise, have been taken as a bombshell by the assembled media, and the public. But it wasn't. Like many of Trump's utterances, it just slipped by. As yet another in an endless torrent of dubious and often ludicrous statements, it just didn't register.

It should have. The admission was demonstrably true.

Trump's seemingly ignorant statements generally get a pass because he is, in matter of actual fact, ignorant[44] — as if that's a legitimate excuse for a United States president. But on March 31, Trump exploded his own "ignorance" excuse.

As we've outlined in our previous two chapters, Trump did indeed know everything. He was warned about the coming pandemic *ad nauseam* going back to November of 2019. But more telling, and more important, than his lies about what he knew, were his actions.

He took none. Or almost none. Despite the fact that he "knew everything" he did basically nothing. He "knew it could be horrible" and yet he elected to let it "wash over the country."

Trump explained away his lies by claiming, "I want to keep the country calm, I don't want panic in the country."[45] But as *CNN.com* columnist Chris Cillizza astutely noted, "Trump's attempts to undersell the virus to the public had real-world consequences — including a very slow start to testing for the virus in this country and our current shortages on masks and ventilators."

He was lying about the economic devastation as well. Though he never boasted that "he knew everything" about how painful life had become for millions of Americans, he obviously did. He saw the monthly jobs report and, as we have noted, could barely shut up about the stock market.

Instead, he portrayed the economic devastation as the easily reversible result of sensible health policies that he misleadingly attributed to himself.

"We did it the right way," he said in an April 11 Fox News interview with "Judge" Jeanine Pirro.[46] "We took care of social distancing and all of the things, words that nobody ever heard of before, frankly, and phrases."

In reality, by July, Trump was taking active measures to sabotage not only any pandemic mitigation measures, but the economy as well. As Democrats and Republicans opened up negotiations for a new round of badly needed economic relief funding, Trump threw a new wrench in the works by insisting that the relief bill must "block billions of dollars for states to conduct testing and contact tracing," according to a *Washington Post* report.[47]

To repeat, because it cannot be repeated enough, testing and tracing are the DNA of any program with a prayer of slowing a pandemic. Any move to "zero out" funds for test-trace programs would be, effectively, a death sentence for thousands of Americans.

But Trump was so determined to end the funds for those programs that his insistence put him at odds not only with the Democrats he despised, but with the very Republicans in the Senate who made the concept of "President Donald Trump" a reality.

Clearly, when Trump said he wanted his "people" to "slow the testing down," he wasn't screwing around.[48]

At the same time, as Trump and his administration threw down the testing-tracing gauntlet, the already-cratered U.S. economy was speeding toward a new cliff. A package of increased unemployment benefits, including a $600 per week add-on, that had been a lifesaver for millions who lost jobs or freelance gigs thanks to the out-of-control coronavirus, was set to go out with a whimper at the end of July.

The emergency relief package, known as the CARES Act, was passed by Congress and signed by Trump on March 27.[49] Totaling $2 trillion, the package authorized the $600 payments, but also provided checks of $1,200 to every American with $75,000 or less in annual income.[50]

But as badly as those relatively minuscule "stimulus" checks were needed, Trump risked delaying their disbursement[51] — at least for people who received the paper checks, rather than direct bank deposits — by insisting that his own signature appear on them.

"The president is not an authorized signer for legal disbursements by the U.S. Treasury," *The Washington Post* observed, dryly.[52]

The package also included an initial $350 billion in funds to be loaned, largely on a forgivable basis, making them grants rather than loans, to "small" businesses.[53] Congress insisted on establishing an independent watchdog group,[54] to make sure that the money was not misused by the Trump administration, or given to Trump's pals.

But Trump immediately fired the chief watchdog, Glenn Fine, who had previously served the same oversight role at the Pentagon.[55] Sure enough, according to an investigation by *ProPublica*, "businesses tied to President Donald Trump's family and associates stand to receive as much as $21 million" in cash from the PPP loan fund.

In addition, businesses that rented space from Trump or Jared Kushner took in $3.65 million in those loans, and funnelled it straight to Trump or Kushner businesses as rent.[56]

Trump-related businesses that got loans included a hydroponic lettuce farm in which Donald Trump Jr. was an investor, which took about $150,000. The same amount of cash also went to a Florida dentist who was one of the elder Trump's golfing buddies.

The petty graft was typical of Trump, of course. But allowing the additional $600 unemployment payments to expire was a more aggressive act of eco nomic sabotage.

The $600 bonus benefits were not only essential for the Americans who needed them, they propped up an economy that was otherwise on its knees, and tumbling chin-first toward the canvas. A J.P. Morgan Chase study showed that rather than fall seven percent — the typical amount of decreased spending by people on unemployment — spending by those receiving the new aid actually jumped by 10 percent.[57]

But people who kept working during the pandemic lockdowns, and did not receive the benefits, reined in their spending by 10 percent, according to the J.P. Morgan Chase research.

Trump and many Republicans claimed that the $600 per week payments actually hurt the economy, by discouraging low-wage workers to get back on the job, where they make less money than they would on the expanded unemployment.

"It gave you a disincentive to work last time," Trump said in an interview.[58] "We want to create a very great incentive to work."

But was Trump really talking about an "incentive," or was he actually trying to force workers back into spaces where they were more likely to contract the virus? As we recounted in the previous chapter, this was the same Donald Trump who invoked the Defense Production Act to shove workers back into meat processing plants,[59] where some of the country's worst outbreaks were underway — after dragging his feet on using the law to compel manufacturing companies to produce badly needed medical supplies.

Not working was "precisely the point," as Duke University's Gabriel Rosenberg wrote in *The Washington Post*. The original $600 payments were designed, he wrote, to "reinforce the public health measures needed to stop the spread of COVID-19 by providing positive incentives for people to cooperate."[60]

Rosenberg summed up the idea behind the payments, saying, "we should pay people to stay home — and pay handsomely. Why? Because such a strategy works to stop an epidemic."

On the other hand, cutting back or cutting off the payments would likely have the opposite effect, making the pandemic worse.

"Because many workplaces can be crowded settings, and many jobs involve a high level of interaction with the public, these settings could allow virus to be spread easily among workers," the CDC cautioned, stating the obvious in a July 10 posting.[61] In Oregon alone, 48 workplaces recorded concentrated outbreaks by early July,[62] three weeks before the $600 "top-off" payments were set to expire, and workers would be compelled to find jobs — if they could.

University of Chicago economists claimed that two of three workers receiving the benefits made more on the expanded unemployment than at their jobs[63] — a sad statement considering that even with an average state unemployment payment of $370 factored in, the "topped off" benefits gave a worker laid off during the pandemic an income equivalent to just over $50,000 per year.

By comparison, the annual cost of living in San Antonio, Texas in 2019 was $58,504.[64] In San Jose, California, a person would run up a tab of more than $99,000 simply by being alive.

Keeping the $600 payments in place as the pandemic raged on through 2020 seemed like an obvious move. But as we've said before and will surely say again — that's not what happened.

Instead, at the urging of Trump administration officials, Senate Majority Leader Mitch McConnell — the day after the $600 benefit ran out for about 30 million Americans,[65] or almost 20 percent of the country's working population[66] — announced his intention to offer only a $200 per week unemployment benefit.[67] And even that pittance did not end up happening.

It's almost as if Trump and the Republicans didn't care about what happened to the country, and were deliberately making everything worse. But that couldn't be true! Could it?

Trump claimed *ad nauseam* prior to the pandemic that under his leadership, the U.S. economy was "the greatest in the history of the country." In reality, measured by growth rate, the economy was stronger in the latter years of Obama's term,[68] as well as at numerous other points in history.

Not surprisingly, actual reality did not stop Trump from bragging about what existed only in his imagination. Even in mid-July, he boasted, "I created the greatest economy we've ever had. And now, we're creating it again."

The opposite was true. Trump was actively sabotaging the economy, and he appeared to be doing so on purpose. Former Hillary Clinton campaign adviser Jennifer Palimieri, from her experience helping to run Clinton's campaign against Trump, saw first hand that he was not the out-of-control windbag that he was often taken for. He did, in fact, know what he was doing.

"What we do know about this guy is that he is able to be disciplined. He is able to stick to a plan," Palmieri said on an MSNBC *Meet the Press Daily* broadcast July 16. "Why he would not do that now in the face of so much death, so much economic distress and his political standing continuing to fall? Maybe it will force him."

It didn't force him to do anything. If Trump was disciplined and sticking to a plan, the plan was to ruin the economy, not rebuild it. Perhaps his motive was economic. As we saw in Chapter 2, Trump holds deeply to a belief that chaos and destruction for society means profit and prestige for himself. As his niece, Mary Trump, quotes Donald Trump telling his brother Fred in 1981 (when New York City's unemployment rate hovered near nine percent[69]), "it's a fantastic time to take advantage of losers who bought at the height of the market."[70]

Describing the views of Trump's father, real estate tycoon Fred Trump Sr., the Trump niece wrote, "in life, there can be only one winner and everybody else is a loser."[71] There's no indication that the younger Trump ever deviated from his father's inculcated wisdom. For him to win, everyone else had to lose. And as president of the United States, for Trump "everyone" now meant *everyone*. He wins by making everyone in the country lose.

What I've called Trump's "apocalyptic vision" could also account for his puzzling behavior in his reelection year. As *Washington Post* columnist Paul Waldman asked in June, "why does it seem that Trump isn't even trying to win?"[72]

While it is impossible to say whether it would have guaranteed a Trump election victory, a steady hand on the pandemic response from the beginning would have boosted his chances, and his always-lacking prestige in the eyes of the public. Instead, his decisions were "substantively appalling, resulting in more death, misery and political instability," Waldman wrote. "But even from the standpoint of his own self-interest, they're almost incomprehensible."

On July 27, five months into Trump's stunning and deadly mishandling of the coronavirus crisis, the *Post* finally ran a news story attempting to answer the question, "Why not try harder to solve the coronavirus crisis?"[73]

Observing that "the best way for him to regain his political footing is to wrest control of the novel coronavirus," reporters Ashley Parker and Philip Rucker spoke to some of Trump's "loyal allies," who appeared "perplexed" by his determination to do exactly the wrong things.

"The president's inability to wholly address the crisis is due to his almost pathological unwillingness to admit error," the "allies" told the *Post* reporters, "a positive feedback loop of overly rosy assessments and data from advisers and Fox News; and a penchant for magical thinking that prevented him from fully engaging with the pandemic."

Trump aides and "outside advisers" tried to impress on him that he needed to "grapple with the reality of the virus" before the country could "reopen." But Trump was "largely unreceptive to that message," they said. Instead they found him "overly preoccupied with his own sense of grievance, beginning many conversations casting himself as the blameless victim of the crisis," according to Parker and Rucker's reporting.

There's no doubt that Trump's aberrant personality characteristics described in the *Post* report played an important role in shaping his destructive handling of the pandemic. But were there more specific motivations?

We know that from the time the virus was first discovered in China to the end of July when more than 150,000 Americans lay dead from the disease, Trump spoke on the phone to Vladimir Putin an extraordinary nine times, the latest call to that point on July 23. In that call, according to the Kremlin at least, Trump and Putin chatted about "arms control and Iran's nuclear program."[74]

Parker and Rucker's article was the first, at least in a major media outlet, to question why Trump acted the way he did, and to examine his reelection "strategy" in anything other than conventional terms. But even the two *Post* journalists did not take a step to the logical conclusion raised by their paper's own columnist, Paul Waldman: for some reason, Trump was not *trying* to win.

Throughout the entire campaign season, Trump acted as if he had it in the bag — as if he wasn't trying to win, but to seize power and hold it. He was unsuccessful in the end, but his post-election behavior was consistent with that of a wannabe dictator who believed he could cheat his way to a coup.[75]

Trump's apparent belief that he could stage a takeover in lieu of winning an election was also evident in his economic approach to the crisis, one that he shared with significant segments of the Republican Party in Congress. He called for cutting back relief funds for Americans,[76] a move guaranteed to leave millions desperate or destitute, and to accelerate the pandemic, with fewer than 100 days to go before the November 3 election. What sense did that make?

I'll close out this chapter with a brief digression. Because to me, the pandemic exposed the raw coercion that sits at the foundation of the U.S. economy, and arguably, the world economy. The GOP's pained refrain about how people will be "incentivized" to goof off rather than march into shitty-paying, shitty jobs where they are likely to contract a deadly virus, because the COVID-19 relief bill "pays you more not to work than if you were working,"[77] was about something even deeper and more insidious than their indifference to public health, and the death, suffering and sorrow of their fellow Americans.

They were admitting that the economy cannot function without those terrible things — without dangerous and soul-crushing forced labor that leaves its participants physically and mentally exhausted, and financially deprived. That system grinds down the health of those who work in it, even without a deadly virus floating around.

Maybe even more important, the system cuts people off from their ability to do what they believe is best, and what they are best at doing. The economy is fueled by thwarted dreams.

An economic system that needs propping up by coercion may not be worth preserving, but it appears to be what we've got. Thanks to the crisis of the pandemic, however, a slight crack in that system began to show. What frightens people like Trump more than anything, I suspect, is the possibility that for once, people other than himself may have experienced even a sliver of the agency that has sustained him for his whole life.

If he can't destroy the dreams and self-worth of others, what is he worth to himself?

CHAPTER SIX

RED DAWN

"Any way you cut it, this is going to be bad. ... The projected size
of the outbreak already seems hard to believe."

— *Dr. Carter Mecher,*
U.S. Dept. of Veterans Affairs,
January 28, 2020[1]

Just two days after Dr. Carter Mecher conveyed his anxiety about the pending coronavirus pandemic, on an email chain with dozens other U.S. government medical officials, Donald Trump confidently declared that the country had the viral outbreak "very well under control."

The group of medical experts and officials gave their protracted email correspondence the nickname "Red Dawn," a reference to the cheesy, 1984 movie melodrama about a Soviet invasion of the mainland United States. The joke, of course, was that the country was now facing a real invasion, not by a Cold War adversary, but by a deadly virus.

The first case of novel coronavirus infection in the U.S. was confirmed just four days before Mecher tapped out his gloomy email to the group.[2] But Trump remained publicly unconcerned, even as those medical officials were freaking out. A month later, on February 27, Trump declared that the coronavirus was "going to disappear. One day, it's like a miracle, it will disappear."[3]

He repeated that bizarre claim another 23 times by the end of July.[4] But the virus, obviously, did not disappear. The medical experts on the email chain possessed no information that was not accessible to Trump, the ostensible president of the United States.

"The president began to say [in March] that nobody could imagine that something like this could actually occur," biosecurity expert and Red Dawn emailer Dr. Dan Hanfling later told ABC News.[5] "The truth is that there was a group of us that had been trying to raise the alarm."

Trump repeated his surreal prediction, that the looming pandemic was "very much under control in the USA," less than a month later, on February 24.[6] In the interim, he had issued a series of statements shrugging off the crisis, saying that the country was in "very good shape," and that "it's going to be fine."

But during this period, the email chain continued. Every medical official and expert on the Red Dawn email chain knew that there was a massive crisis — apparently on the level of a Soviet invasion — on the horizon. Hanfling told ABC News that he wasn't sure whether the warnings in the emails ever made their way up to the higher echelons of the Trump administration. But that isn't really the point.

The point is that the info was out there, the predictions based on that info were widely discussed and shared. Trump could have known, should have known, and if he did not know, it is because he chose not to know.

Even a medical journalist who was not part of the email chain told ABC that she felt a sense of dread about the pandemic — then apparently confined to China — as early as January 2.

"It rapidly grabbed my attention and held it," she told the network.[7]

Yet Trump remained, at least outwardly, oblivious. While it seems plausible that he was unaware of the Red Dawn email chain itself, very similar warnings to the ones it contained were presented to him on January 29 in a memo by his top trade adviser, Peter Navarro.[8]

In the memo, as uncovered by *The New York Times*, Navarro directly warned Trump that (as *The Times* phrased it), "the coronavirus crisis could cost the United States trillions of dollars and put millions of Americans at risk of illness or death."

After the *Times* revealed the existence of Navarro's memo, Trump denied that he had seen it — or a subsequent memo by Navarro, which included his dire imprecation of an "increasing probability of a full-blown COVID-19 pandemic that could infect as many as 100 million Americans, with a loss of life of as many as 1-2 million souls."[9]

"I didn't see them, but I heard he wrote some memos talking about pandemic," Trump claimed, at one of his White House coronavirus "briefings," so-called.[10] "I didn't see them. I didn't look for them either."

Why not?

Trump, as we've seen previously, was warned about the coming viral outbreak possibly as early as November.[11] CDC Director Robert Redfield[12] — appointed by Trump in 2018 and deemed an "abysmal choice" by veteran medical reporter Laurie Garrett — was told by medical authorities in China about the outbreak on January 3.[13]

At the time, however, Trump was involved in formulating what he appeared to see as his signature accomplishment — a new trade agreement with China. As the pandemic wreaked devastation into the summer, Trump did a 180 on China, repeatedly calling the pandemic "the China virus" or even the more blatantly racist "kung flu."[14] But in the early months of the crisis, he not only praised the Chinese response, but participated in the Chinese cover-up.

Trump repeatedly assured the public that the coronavirus would "miraculously" go away, when the weather "gets a little warmer."[15] He made that claim on February 10. But just two days earlier he had spoken by phone with Chinese Communist Party leader Xi Jinping, who fed Trump the "warm weather" idea.

How do we know about this bizarre phone call? Trump himself told us about it.

"I had a long talk with President Xi," Trump said at a White House meeting of business leaders on February 10.[16] "He feels very confident. And he feels that, again, as I mentioned, by April or during the month of April, the heat, generally speaking, kills this kind of virus."

Along with his questionable characterization of COVID-19 as "the China virus," Trump concocted a story that a nefarious Chinese government had sandbagged him with the pandemic, ruining his (fictional) "greatest economy in history."[17]

But that story — like so many of Trump's stories — was just that: a story. And not a very good one.

"Trump collaborated with Xi, concealed the threat, impeded the U.S. government's response, silenced those who sought to warn the public, and pushed states to take risks that escalated the tragedy," wrote *Slate* columnist William Saletan.[18] "He's personally responsible for tens of thousands of deaths."

Trump, then, to recap…

- Knew about the coming pandemic as early as January, probably much earlier.

- Lied about it to cover up China's role so he could get his trade deal in the bag.

- Used the virus as a deadly weapon — a deadly *biological* weapon — against his political opponents.

The accusation that Trump essentially collaborated with China in minimizing the virus in order to nail down a trade deal is not exactly an original one.[19] Democratic presidential candidate Joe Biden said the same thing, in a June 17 publication for the blogging site *Medium.com*.

"Why didn't he act when the warning signs were so clear? Why did he ignore his briefings from the intelligence community, the warnings from his own team, and from me?" Biden wondered aloud. "Why did he repeatedly praise the Chinese government and President Xi as the coronavirus spread? Because he wanted to have a trade deal with China as a talking point for his re-election campaign."

It was quite a remarkable accusation for a presidential candidate to make against a sitting president — that Trump allowed a deadly pandemic to kill thousands of Americans so he could score a political point.

At the same time, Biden's allegation was so unsurprising that it passed with barely any notice from the major media, perhaps because that sort of cynically transactional behavior was tediously predictable from Trump.

As a January *Atlantic Monthly* article noted — at which time Trump was facing impeachment over an attempted "quid pro quo" with the Ukrainian government — "Trump has embraced this style of quid pro quo politics throughout his business career, and from his perch in the White House, he now encourages it in others."[20]

The only problem with the Biden theory is that nothing Trump did during the entire coronavirus crisis (or before) showed that he was actually concerned about winning the election. Where was the evidence that he was trying to win?

"The three most significant threats to Trump's reelection are the pandemic, the country's terrible economic situation, and the eagerness of Democrats to turn him out of office," wrote *Washington Post* columnist Paul Waldman in late June.[21] "In every case, the president has chosen not just to avoid taking actions that might help him win, but to actively worsen his situation."

Commentator and author Sarah Kendzior made the same point in an interview a month later.

"Trump is not trying to win the election," she said.[22] "He's trying to *steal* the election. A person who wants to win an election tries to win people over and expand their base."

Even MSNBC host Chuck Todd, that most middle-of-the-road of political commentators, appeared to realize what Trump was doing, noting Trump's unusual approach to trailing his opponent, Joe Biden, by a substantial polling margin.

"He's seemingly been looking for ways to disrupt the vote and sow doubts about its result," Todd said in a broadcast during the opening day of the Republican National Convention in August, "rather than trying to catch up the clean way."[23]

Trump did nothing to "expand his base." While "expanding the base," otherwise known as "getting more people to vote for you," is always a fundamental of political campaigning, for Trump, it seemed especially important. He was the loser of the 2016 popular vote by a significant margin of nearly 3 million votes, or 2.1 percentage points.[24] The grand total of votes across the three "swing" states — Michigan, Wisconsin, and Pennsylvania — that gave him his Electoral College victory was fewer than 80,000,[25] out of nearly 137 million votes cast.[26]

If anyone needed to persuade voters to turn his way, it was Donald Trump. Going all-out to crush the pandemic would've been one pretty effective way to sway voters. So would rescuing the drowning economy. Trump did neither. On August 19 he tweeted out a call for his followers to boycott Goodyear Tires because the company supposedly would not allow its employees to wear Trump's red "MAGA" caps at work.[27] (Goodyear said Trump's claim was a "misconception."[28])

But Goodyear is one of the top 100 employers in the crucial "swing state" of Ohio. How was Trump trying to win the election?

In *The Atlantic*, commentator Franklin Foer noted that Trump was going "through the motions of pursuing an outright victory," his true objective was "discrediting the political process itself."[29]

"He disparages the rules that govern politics and the institutions that facilitate it," Foer wrote. "He seems to want his supporters to believe that their electoral participation will be rendered meaningless."

Suffice to say, all of Trump's seemingly insane actions start to make sense when we realize that he was never trying to "win the election," but instead to seize power, and hold it.

In that regard, as 2020 rolled on into the late summer, with the election less than three months away and Trump trailing in the polls by more than eight points[30] (by comparison, Barack Obama beat John McCain in 2008 by seven[31]), he continued to take no steps to do anything about the COVID-19 pandemic.

He just kept right on doing things to make the crisis worse. He continued to plug the non-existent virtues of malaria drug hydroxychloroquine as a supposed treatment for coronavirus infection,[32] despite no evidence that it worked and significant evidence that the drug could harm patients.

In late July, on his Twitter account, he promoted a video featuring quack physician Stella Immanuel,[33] who in addition to touting hydroxychloroquine as a "cure for COVID," also claims that DNA from "space aliens" is used in pharmaceutical medicines, and that gynecological ailments are the result of women having sex with witches.

Asked why he was publicizing Immanuel by White House reporters, Trump called her "very impressive," and "an important voice." He then added, "I know nothing about her."

He went back on Twitter to spread more disinformation, retweeting one tweet that was removed by Twitter itself for containing misinformation about COVID-19. The tweet seemingly approved by Trump accused Anthony Fauci,[34] the government's top infectious disease expert, of "suppression" of hydroxychloroquine to cause more COVID deaths and "hurt Trump."

In an interview with, of all people, *Barstool Sports* founder Dave Portnoy, Trump again rebuked Fauci, lying that the longtime public servant wanted the U.S. economy "closed up for a couple of years."[35] Trump then went on to boast about ignoring Fauci.

Moving into mid-August, the U.S. coronavirus death toll crept up on 170,000,[36] and Trump appeared to sideline not only Fauci, but his other top scientific adviser on the pandemic, Dr. Deborah Birx. At an August 12 White House "press conference," he introduced his new adviser. Dr. Scott Atlas, whom *CNN* described as "a fellow at Stanford University's Hoover Institution who frequently appears on Fox News."[37]

Though he had a medical degree, Atlas was not — unlike Fauci and Birx — expert (or even trained) in the field of infectious diseases.[38] Atlas was instead a radiologist, meaning that his speciality was reading X-rays and other forms of medical imaging.

Nonetheless, Trump fell for him because he "adopted a public stance on the virus much closer to Trump's," according to *CNN*. In particular, Atlas had his back on what had become Trump's latest issue as of late summer, 2020 — sending kids back to school.

On July 6, Trump blasted out one of his signature all-caps, multi-exclamation-point tweets, declaring, "SCHOOLS MUST REOPEN IN THE FALL!!!"[39]

As we recounted in Chapter Four, earlier in the year Trump issued an order forcing workers in meat-packing plants around the country back to work, even as the plants were the sites of rampant coronavirus outbreaks. A few months later, he had something similar in mind for the country's children.

He ignored the cautionary example set by Israel, which, after doing a successful job suppressing the virus through March and April, reopened its schools in May. Within days, as *The New York Times* reported, one Jerusalem high school saw a series of new cases which "quickly mushroomed into the largest outbreak in a single school in Israel, possibly the world."[40]

Students brought the virus home, infecting their families. Within weeks, hundreds of schools across the small country closed down again. Israel soon experienced an outbreak far worse than the one it had seen in the early days of the pandemic. On May 31, the country's seven-day average of daily cases was 50 in the country of 9.1 million. By July 30, it peaked at 1,732. Adjusting for population, that would equal about 62,500 cases per day in the United States. The actual U.S. was averaging about 70,500 cases per day at that time.

Nonetheless, Trump pushed on, threatening to "cut off funding" for schools that resisted his command to reopen[41] — a threat that had no legal basis, but nonetheless reflected his drive to compel children and teenagers back into schools with no plan to keep them safe from the virus.

Atlas backed him up, claiming in his numerous Fox News appearances that children "have no risk for serious illness" and are "not significant spreaders."

Trump's appointed Health and Human Services Science Adviser Paul Alexander put it more bluntly, writing — incorrectly — in an internal HHS email that "infants, kids, teens, young people, young adults," have no "or little" risk.

"We want them infected," he wrote.[42]

Alexander got his wish. In the final two weeks of July, 97,000 children tested positive for the virus,[43] and at least 25 died from the viral infection in that month alone. Overall, 20 kids under the age of five died from the disease in the United States, by the end of July.[44]

A study published in *JAMA Pediatrics* found that while young kids generally exhibited milder symptoms of COVID-19 than adults, children under age five who contracted the virus carried much larger amounts of it in their nasopharynx (that's the top of your throat, behind your nose) compared to older kids and adults.[45] The finding would appear to suggest that a sneeze from a little kid could be more deadly to a grownup than one from another grownup.

A large-scale study in South Korea, covering 65,000 children, found that teenagers spread the coronavirus with effectiveness equal to adults.[46] At the same time, despite their seeming resistance to becoming symptomatic from SARS-CoV-2, some children — a small number, but more than zero — developed a horrifying condition known as MIS-C, aka Multisystem Inflammatory Syndrome in Children.[47]

According to the CDC, under this particular condition, "different body parts can become inflamed, including the heart, lungs, kidneys, brain, skin, eyes, or gastrointestinal organs."

Yet in August, Trump went on (for some reason) a sports talk radio show to insist that "young kids, almost none have a serious problem" from COVID-19.[48] On August 5, he told the country that children were "almost immune" to the virus. The next day, the American Academy of Pediatrics released a study showing that over the previous four weeks, cases among children exploded, zooming upward by 90 percent.

"Immune means that if they were exposed to the virus, their bodies would fight it off without any chance of them getting infected," Dr. Dara Kass, a medical contributor to *Yahoo! News,* explained.[49] "We know a hundred percent that is definitively false."

Facts never deterred Trump, and they didn't this time either. In the August 12 edition of his daily White House "press conference," events which tended to function more as a forum for Trump to air his various grievances and insult his perceived enemies, he once again implored, "We've got to open up our schools and open up our businesses," while conspicuously continuing to offer no actual plan to do so without setting off new and uncontrollable coronavirus outbreaks.[50]

On that same day, according to a *Washington Post* report, the United States recorded more coronavirus deaths than on any single day since the middle of May.[51] The country's rolling, seven-day average of COVID-19 deaths topped 1,000 for the 17th straight day.

Trump's indifference to the potential for killing children was, sadly, no surprise. Given a chance to express some feeling or emotion or any reaction at all to the mounting national death toll, Trump told reporter Jonathan Swan, "They are dying. That's true. And you — it is what it is."[52]

Shocking as his callous disregard for the lives of thousands of Americans may have seemed, it was no surprise. Trump used the same phrase in an interview just two weeks earlier. Asked by Chris Wallace of *Fox News* about the 1,000 per day death tally, Trump replied, "It came from China, they should have never let it escape, they should have never let it out but it is what it is."[53]

One high school in Georgia opened its doors to students in early August, and promptly suspended one student who posted a photo on social media showing a packed school corridor with none of the kids wearing a mask. Days later, six students and three staffers tested positive for the virus, and the school shut down, switching to online classes.[54]

That school was part of Georgia's Cherokee County School District, where 1,100 students and staff ended up in two-week quarantines after 59 positive cases just 10 days after schools reopened on August 3.[55]

Trump's White House in July issued a press release calling for school reopenings, partly on the basis of data supposedly showing that "99.96 percent of all [COVID-19] fatalities are adults."[56]

While it was true that the vast majority of those who perished were older, it was also true that, as vice-chair of the American Academy of Pediatrics Committee on Infectious Diseases Dr. Sean O'Leary told *CNN*, "We've had 90 deaths in children in the U.S. already, in just a few months. Every year we worry about influenza in children, and there are roughly around 100 deaths in children from influenza every year."[57]

The United States passed 170,000 COVID-19 deaths on August 13, 2020.[58] Obviously, 90 was, as Trump himself shrugged, "a tiny fraction" of that formidable total.[59] But it was still 90 dead kids.

Just as a point of comparison, for all of the country's very justified outrage over school shootings, those horrific incidents claimed a total of 114 children's lives over a 10-year period from 2009 to 2018, and no more than 37 in a single year (2018).[60]

Those 90 child-deaths occurred primarily during a period of school closures, social distancing, and other contagion mitigation measures in most states. Jamming children into school buildings appeared a sure thing to make the death toll go up. Especially because the preponderance of data showed that the risk of contagion was at its highest in crowded, indoor spaces.[61]

So as we have asked so many times already — and we're only a little more than halfway through this book — why? Why was Trump obsessively focused on sending children back to school with no mandated safety protocols, knowing that kids could die?

According to a *CNN* analysis, Trump and his campaign advisers believed that forcing schools to reopen would prove "widely popular," particularly with one group of voters Trump would, at least in a conventional election, absolutely need to win in November: white suburban women.[62]

But how did that even make sense? Why would suburban women,

white or otherwise, be enthusiastic about sending their kids into a coronavirus breeding colony? The prospect was so risky that even "abysmal choice" CDC Director Redfield contradicted Trump, stating that even "the White House" should not be allowed to "pressure" school districts to open their doors to students.

Trump's answer was to say that the government would provide 125 million reusable masks to schools across the country.

"Of all the mind-bending coronavirus decisions that Trump has made, the political risks of his back-to-school gamble are perhaps the greatest," wrote CNN.com columnist Maeve Reston.[63] "At a time when he is struggling with shrinking support among women, moderates and seniors, he is urging parents to send their children back into the classroom even though much is still unknown about the long-term risks to their health and how rapidly they could spread it to vulnerable adults, including grandparents and teachers."

Reston said that Trump's school fixation was "clearly" driven by "his desire to get the economy moving again — which he thinks is the lynchpin of his reelection chances."

But as we discussed in the previous chapter, given ample opportunities to pour stimulus into the economy, Trump demurred. And continued to do so, allowing the Senate to go on vacation from August 13 to September 8 without anything close to an economic program of relief package in place. The day before the Republican-led Senate split for the links, Trump himself declared that a new relief package was "not going to happen."[64]

It is certainly possible that Trump was just blundering and stumbling, not sure what could help him win the election — if he was even trying to win — but it is also possible that he had some other motivation for his school opening compulsion, the same motivation that compelled him to let the coronavirus "wash over" the country in the first place.

By the middle of August, at least 2,000 students and teachers across the United States were in quarantine due to COVID-19 exposure.[65] At the higher education level, the University of Notre Dame, and University of North Carolina both shut down, shifting to online classes only, within days of bringing students back to campus.[66]

The fast-expanding school crisis was utterly, even tediously predictable. The CDC in a confidential 96-page report obtained by *The New York Times* warned that school openings carried the "highest risk" for creating new outbreaks of infection.[67]

Outside of the government, doctors belonging to the Infectious Disease Society of America warned in July against reopening schools.[68]

"The simple answer is no," Northwestern University med school prof Dr. Tina Tan told *CNBC*, in a comment typical of the medical pros' reaction to Trump's school push. "When you have such surges of disease in the community, you're basically asking for trouble if you open schools, because you're bringing in individuals from all across the community that potentially may be exposed to it."

But way back in January, the various authors of the sadly prophetic Red Dawn emails were saying the same thing.[69]

"Any way you cut it, this is going to be bad," Mecher wrote in his January 28 entry on the email chain.[70] "You guys made fun of me screaming to close the schools. Now I'm screaming, close the colleges and universities."

By late February, the participants in the email chain had learned of a study showing that otherwise seemingly healthy people — "asymptomatic" became the popular term — could spread COVID-19 infection with the same potency as those who were sneezing, wheezing, and coughing from the virus. At that point, they decided to put together a plan, "Four Steps to Mitigation,"[71] and bring it to Trump.

"Mitigation," of course, referred to the drastic steps needed to block the virus from spreading — closing businesses, imposing stay-at-home orders, banning group gatherings, and so on. But Trump and his advisers weren't interested.

"A presidential blowup and internal turf fights would sidetrack such a move," *The New York Times* reported. "The focus would shift to messaging and confident predictions of success rather than publicly calling for a shift to mitigation."

So, to sum up…

- Even as dozens of experts were fervently warning of the coming pandemic in a January-February email chain, Trump supposedly remained oblivious.

- One of Trump's top advisers, Peter Navarro, handed Trump a memo outlining the potential for millions of lost lives and trillions in economic destruction. Trump claimed he never saw the memo.

- Trump shunned calls by experts to impose measures that would mitigate the viral spread, choosing instead to focus on "messaging."

- That messaging included Trump's incessantly repeated proclamation that the pandemic would simply "disappear," and it would be "like a miracle."

Early in the pandemic, on February 28, Trump gave a test-run to one of his favorite "messaging" tropes — dismissing the virus as a "hoax."[72] Trump had already deployed the word "hoax" to dismiss the investigation into his ties to Russia, and his pressure campaign against Ukraine that led to his impeachment.[73]

At his February 28 campaign rally in North Carolina, Trump again dropped a "hoax," this time on the coronavirus.

"Now the Democrats are politicizing the coronavirus They have no clue, they can't even count their votes in Iowa," he said, referring to the then-recent debacle in the Iowa Democratic primary.[74] "This is their new hoax."

Despite a brief outbreak of hand-wringing over whether Trump had *really*, technically called the coronavirus pandemic a "hoax," exemplified by a vaguely ridiculous *FactCheck.org* "fact check" decrying how a Democratic political ad "twists" Trump's words,[75] his intent was clear

— to pollute public discussion of the coronavirus crisis with yet another unfounded "hoax" accusation. And why not? It worked for him pretty well before.

Perhaps understanding that calling the pandemic a "hoax" just wouldn't catch on, as more than 1,000 Americans died every day, Trump pulled back on that terminology rather quickly. But he never gave up the idea, claiming in a July interview that on November 4, the day after the 2020 election, "everything will open up."[76] As if the entire pandemic were the doing of Democrats attempting to damage him.

Trump may have been saying more than he realized during that February 28 rally, when he cited the "new hoax" as one in a series, starting with the "Russia hoax."

"One of my people came up to me and said, 'Mr. President, they tried to beat you on Russia, Russia, Russia.' That did not work out too well. They could not do it. They tried the impeachment hoax," Trump rambled, before adding that the coronavirus was "their new hoax."[77]

Why would he link the Russia scandal, the Ukraine scandal, and the coronavirus pandemic all in a single stream of his consciousness? Which one of these things is not like the others?

Maybe they were all alike after all. Not because they were all hoaxes, but because they were all part of a pattern in Trump's mind. We've earlier documented how the pandemic also marked Trump's busiest period of communication with Vladimir Putin. In August, Trump floated the idea of holding a face-to-face meeting with Putin sometime before the election.[78] He also said that he wanted to hold a meeting of the G7 group of economic world leaders in the United States, and that he planned to invite Putin — even though Russia was kicked out of the group in 2014 as a penalty for its annexation of Crimea.

Why was Trump communicating with Putin at such a frantic rate during the pandemic crisis — to the point where he felt the need to converse with the Russian strongman in person?

The possible answer goes back years, into the depths of Trump's outwardly strange and subservient relationship to the former KGB man who has established himself as something like Russia's president for life.

CHAPTER SEVEN

. . . .

WILL HE BE MY NEW BEST FRIEND?

"All of it was invented by people who oppose President Trump to undermine his legitimacy. I'm puzzled by that."

— *Vladimir Putin*
December 14, 2017[1]

Donald Trump wanted to be named *Time Magazine* "Person of the Year." Like, really badly.

He may have settled for any sort of accolade from the 97-year-old newsweekly. In October of 2012, he angrily tweeted, "I knew last year that TIME Magazine lost all credibility when they didn't include me in their Top 100..."[2] But in December of 2015, as his campaign for president was building unstoppable momentum, *Time* had the audacity to pick German Chancellor Angela Merkel as its "Person of the Year."

Trump responded by claiming that he had been the "big favorite" but that, "I told you TIME Magazine would never pick me."[3] He went on to add, gratuitously, that Merkel was "ruining Germany."

In 2019, three years after Trump finally, actually, had received the "Person of the Year" *Time* cover slot, Trump was enraged when he was passed over in favor of teenage Swedish climate activist Greta Thunberg, deriding the pick as "so ridiculous."[4]

"Greta must work on her Anger Management problem, then go to a good old fashioned movie with a friend!" Trump wrote. "Chill Greta, Chill!"[5]

Even in 2016, when Trump actually collected the honor, such as it is, he griped that it somehow didn't meet his standards, claiming that the magazine called him in advance to tell him that he would "probably" be named "Person of the Year."[6]

"Probably is no good," he tweeted, claiming that he "took a pass" on granting *Time* an interview. A top content officer at the magazine scoffed at Trump's claim as "total BS." The magazine issued a statement noting that it does not announce the selection in advance of publication.

So covetous of the *Time* cover is Trump that he, according to a *Washington Post* report, mocked up a counterfeit cover with a picture of himself and the headlines "Donald Trump: The 'Apprentice' is a television smash!" and (in all caps), "TRUMP IS HITTING ON ALL FRONTS... EVEN TV!"[7] He hung the phony *Time* cover in five of the golf resorts that he owns.

Trump's undisguised envy and resentment toward anyone else who appears on *Time's* cover, then, makes a letter he penned to the 2007 "Person of the Year" recipient all the more curious. In that year, the honoree was Russia's president, Vladimir Putin.

"Dear President Putin," Trump gushed in the letter.[8] "Congratulations on being named *Time* magazine's 'Man of the Year' (sic) — you definitely deserve it. As you probably have heard, <u>I am a big fan of yours!</u> Take care of yourself. With best wishes, Sincerely, Donald J. Trump."

Signing with his favored thick, black Sharpie, he also used the pen to underscore the phrase, "<u>I am a big fan of yours!</u>"

The letter, which appeared publicly for the first time on page 432 of the 966-page fifth and final volume of the Senate Intelligence Committee's report on "Russia's Active Measures Campaigns and Interference in the 2016 U.S. Election,"[9] may be the earliest evidence of Trump's unfettered admiration for Putin.

The committee released the report on August 18, 2020. It also included a second letter from Trump to Putin, this one dated June 26, 2013. In that fawning missive, Trump — who at the time owned the

Miss Universe Beauty pageant — informed Putin that the pageant would take place in Moscow in November of that year. He invited Putin to attend as "my guest of honor," adding, "I know you will have a great time."[10]

At the bottom of that letter, again in his beloved black Sharpie, Trump jotted, "The world's most beautiful women!"

The letter was dated just eight days after a Trump tweet in which he wondered aloud if Putin would show up at the pageant, and "if so, will he become my new best friend?"[11]

When *The Washington Post* initially reported on the second Trump letter to Putin, on March 9 of 2018 — apparently without having seen it — the paper called it "the first known attempt at direct outreach by Trump to Putin."[12]

As the Senate Intel Committee report revealed, it wasn't.

In fact, before the pageant in 2013, Trump himself claimed that he had already met Putin personally, "once." He made that claim in an interview with late-night TV host David Letterman. He repeated his claim to have met Putin in May of the following year at a National Press Club speech, saying that he had spoken "indirectly and directly with President Putin, who could not have been nicer."[13]

And the year after that, he again claimed to have met Putin "once, a long time ago," in an interview with right-wing extremist talk show host Michael Savage.

Trump has also told Letterman that he had "done a lot of business with the Russians."

Trump's claims to have actually met Putin might have been his usual line of bullshit. He also claimed in 2015 that he and Putin had once been "stablemates" on the *CBS News* program *60 Minutes*, whatever that means, and as a result Trump said, "I got to know him very well."[14]

As it happened, Trump and Putin had indeed appeared on the same *60 Minutes* program, on September 27, 2015 — in separate, taped interviews. Putin's was recorded in Russia, Trump's in New York. How that let Trump get to "know him very well" remains a puzzle.

Less than a year later, Trump had changed his story entirely. Asked by *ABC News* interviewer George Stephanopolous about whether he knows Putin, Trump said, "I have no relationship with him. I don't — I've never met him."[15]

That was in late July of 2016, just over a month since three independent cybersecurity firms concluded that Russia was behind digital intrusions into Democratic National Committee email servers.[16] Then, during an October 19, 2016, presidential debate with Hillary Clinton, Trump again denied ever having met Putin.[17]

"I never met Putin. This is not my best friend," he said in response to a moderator's question. "But if the United States got along with Russia, it wouldn't be so bad. Let me tell you, Putin has outsmarted her [i.e. Clinton] and Obama at every single step of the way."

By that time, even the U.S. government itself was affirming that Russia was behind the DNC hacks.[18] Just 12 days earlier, the Department of Homeland Security and Director of National Intelligence issued a joint statement on behalf of 17 count 'em 17 U.S. intelligence agencies which had all arrived at the same conclusion.

Trump in the debates and at campaign rallies repeatedly stated that there was no way of knowing whether it was really Russia behind the hacking — famously stating in his September 26 debate with Clinton that the perpetrator may have been "somebody sitting on their bed that weighs 400 pounds."[19]

In reality, Trump knew exactly what had happened.[20] As an official presidential nominee, he received regular intelligence briefings — which as far back as August 17, 2016, included the details about the Russian hacks.

Coupled with Trump's baffling and disconcerting affinity for Putin and all things Russia, it was only natural to wonder if there was some connection between the Russian cyberattack on Trump's political opposition, and Trump's denials and inexplicable (at the time) affection for Putin.

Trump's lawyer-turned-nemesis Michael Cohen believes that Trump's guy-crush on Putin is easy to explain.[21] Trump worships the almighty buck, and he perhaps mistakenly pegged Putin as the world's richest man.

It should be noted that anti-Putin crusader Bill Browder says that from his personal observations, he puts Putin's fortune at more than $200 billion.[22] If true, that would, indeed make Putin the world's richest person. Though Trump bete noir Jeff Bezos in August of 2020 also reportedly edged past the $200 billion mark.[23]

Trump was also smitten with Putin's ability "to take over an entire nation and run it like it was his personal company — like the Trump Organization, in fact," according to Cohen in his tell-all memoir.

And yet, Trump's idolatry of Putin appears to run deeper than that, back into his early affinity for Russia in general, which dates back to 1987.

When the Senate Intelligence Committee released the fifth volume of its report on the Russian operation, it shed a little more light on why Trump may have gushed so effusively about Putin.

Trump was engaged in a deal to build a "Trump Tower Moscow," a deal that would have been worth "hundreds of millions of dollars" to Trump, the report said, were the Tower to actually go up.

"While these negotiations were ongoing, Trump made positive public comments about Putin in connection with his presidential campaign," the report said.[24]

Trump lawyer Cohen and Felix Sater — a Soviet-born, mob-linked business associate of Trump's and longtime pal of Cohen's — "sought to leverage Trump's comments, as well as subsequent comments about Trump by Putin, to advance the deal."[25]

Whatever the reason, Trump's awestruck praise of Putin, and utter refusal to criticize him, continued throughout his term in office. But our purpose here is not to detail every strangely jovial interaction between Trump and Putin. What's important is that Trump either had or, as is sorely obvious, craved a close friendship with the Russian strongman, who came up through the ranks of the Soviet KGB.[26]

If Trump's claims to have met Putin "once, a long time ago" were true, then their relationship extends back further than anyone has been able to document. If they're just more of Trump's bluster, well, we at least know that forming a relationship with Putin had always been a high priority for Trump — going back to at least 2007, as his "I'm a big fan" letter released by the Senate Intel Committee revealed.

So what does all of this have to do with the 2020 pandemic? Glad you asked.

While we're not going to rehash the whole Trump-Russia scandal in this book it is worth noting as we did toward the end of the previous chapter that Trump himself connected the Russia "hoax" with the coronavirus "hoax," in his own mind.

What we will focus on here is not merely that Trump had, and maintained, a relationship with Putin, but that he maintained a strangely subservient relationship. He appeared to rely on Putin — for advice and a weird kind of mentorship. While there's no "smoking gun" (yet), all of the circumstantial evidence tells us that Trump did *whatever Putin wanted him to do.*

In the introduction to this book, we described an incident in which it appears that Putin himself fed Trump a cover story that was initially used to explain the infamous Trump Tower meeting between Trump Jr., Kushner, Manafort and a group of Kremlin-linked Russians.

Later in 2016, after he became president-elect, Trump oddly took Putin's side against the U.S. government.[27] The outgoing Obama administration hit Russia with sanctions, expelling 35 diplomats whom it identified as "intelligence operatives."

The sanctions were a punitive measure for Russia's sabotage of the 2016 election, which as U.S. intel agencies concluded was intended to damage Clinton and help Trump get elected. In a highly out-of-character move, Putin declined to reciprocate, demurring on smacking back at the U.S. with sanctions of his own.

Though the Obama sanctions were backed even by many Republicans in Congress, Trump had little to say about them. But he did have something to say about Putin.

"Great move on delay (by V. Putin)," Trump tweeted on December 30.[28] "I always knew he was very smart!"

It should be noted, however, that — his supposed smartness aside — in restraining himself from lashing back at the sanctions, Putin was following the advice of his ambassador, Sergey Kislyak, who had spoken to Trump's incoming national security adviser, Michael Flynn.[29]

In their phone calls, Flynn asked Kislayk to be "even-keeled" in response to the Obama sanctions, and that they would have "a better conversation" once Trump assumed office. Why Flynn was conducting what amounted to diplomacy with Russia before he assumed office and after Russia had tampered with the 2016 presidential election, well, that's another question for another time.

The sanctions issue did not go away once Trump was inaugurated. That Trump would lift sanctions on Russia as a kind of quid pro quo for the election sabotage operation was a central theme of the Steele Dossier,[30] and plenty of mainstream speculation in the months and years after he took office. And Trump did little to dispel the theory.[31]

Within days of taking office, Trump attempted to remove sanctions against Russia over its invasion of Ukraine and annexation of Crimea, without getting anything in return from Putin, according to a report by Michael Isikoff of *Yahoo! News*.[32] Of course, Trump had already received something from Russia — his election victory. Or illegal aid in achieving it, at least.

The attempt to unilaterally lift the sanctions was stopped by State Department officials who waged an ultimately successful bureaucratic battle to stymie Trump's effort at sending the gift to Putin.

But when Congress in 2018 passed new sanctions on Russia over the election interference operation and nonstop incursion into Ukraine,

Trump simply refused to put them into place.[33] His administration's excuse was that the mere "threat" of new sanctions would "deter" Russia — though the actions for which the Russians were being sanctioned had already taken place and therefore could not be deterred.

Trump's anti-American praise of "V. Putin" as "very smart" echoed his assertions as far back as 2013 that the Russian leader was "outsmarting our country."[34] Rather than attack or criticize Putin, Trump declared his alleged "outsmarting" of "our country" to be "a great job" by the Russian strongman.

Trump returned to his theme of Obama's allegedly being "outsmarted" by Putin.[35] At the 2019 G7 summit in France, with the world watching, he gleefully announced that Putin "outsmarted" Obama by annexing Crimea from Ukraine in 2014 — the very violation of international law that got Russia booted from the G7 (then the G8) shortly thereafter.

Obama was behind the expulsion of Russia from the group because he found the annexation of Crimea personally "embarrassing," Trump postulated. He followed up by declaring that he wanted Russia back in the G7, though the country still claimed the Crimean territory as its own and had done nothing to atone for its international aggression.

"President Putin totally outsmarted President Obama on Crimea and other things including the 'red line' in the sand," Trump said on the White House lawn that same week, before departing for France.

The most striking public example of Trump's submissiveness to Putin came at a July, 2018, one-on-one summit meeting between the pair in Helsinki, Finland.[36] They spent more than two hours behind closed doors, with no one else in the room besides their respective translators.

Trump snatched away his own translator's notes after the meeting, and swore the interpreter to silence.[37] No record exists of the conversation outside of the Kremlin — as by all accounts, Putin allowed his interpreter to retain the notes.

But it was what followed the meeting that immediately gained notoriety as perhaps the most mortifying moment of the Trump era. With Putin standing alongside him at their twin podiums, Trump — as *CNN* reporter Jeremy Diamond put it, delivered "a stunning rebuke of the U.S. intelligence community," essentially taking Putin's side over his own country on the election-hacking issue.[38]

"President Putin was extremely strong and powerful in his denial today," Trump babbled, adding, "President Putin says it's not Russia. I don't see any reason why it would be."[39]

Trump didn't stop there. Putin apparently told Trump that he would allow Russian investigators to interrogate the Russian intelligence agents accused by Special Counsel Robert Mueller of carrying out the election-hacking attack.

It was a rather crude and probably halfhearted attempt to control the cover-up himself. Nonetheless, Trump enthusiastically hailed Putin's "offer" as "incredible."

Perhaps most laughably, Trump resurrected his supposed discussion with Putin — which had started the previous year — about the prospective U.S.-Russia collaboration on what Trump called "an impenetrable Cyber Security unit."[40] In other words, Putin was suggesting that he, himself, investigate the cyberattacks that he ordered — and Trump thought that idea was just terrific.[41]

The "joint working group" would also give Putin direct insight into how U.S. intelligence, and Mueller, figured out that he personally ordered the election attack, and identified the specific intel agents who carried it out.

Trump never pushed to make the collaboration happen. Even his own supporters in Congress decried the idea as risible. But that Putin even thought there was a chance Trump would go for it says quite something about how he sees the handler-asset relationship.

Any why not? On May 10, 2017, when Trump had been in office for less than four months, he held an impromptu Oval Office meeting with Kislyak and Putin's longtime foreign minister, Sergei Lavrov. In that meeting, Trump blurted out the classified details of an intelligence operation involving Israel in Syria.[42]

If Trump was willing to give up such highly sensitive information to Russians once, why wouldn't he do it again? You can't blame Putin for trying.

A couple of years later, Trump's administration again expressed enthusiasm for allowing Putin to investigate his own crimes. When top Putin critic and political adversary Alexei Navalny was poisoned on August 20, 2020, Trump himself offered no comment saying that he was looking into it, and his administration waited five days to make a statement.[43]

When U.S. Ambassador to Russia John Sullivan finally spoke out, he called on Russia to undertake an "immediate, comprehensive, and transparent investigation" into Navalny's poisoning.[44] Later that day, a "deeply concerned" Secretary of State Mike Pompeo said that "If these reports (that Navalny was poisoned) are proven accurate," the U.S. would be "ready to assist" a "comprehensive investigation."[45]

The administration's reticence about Navalny's poisoning came about two months after a *New York Times* report revealing that, as early as February, Trump has been told by U.S. intelligence agencies that the Russian government was paying "bounties" to Taliban extremists to kill American soldiers in Afghanistan.[46]

Not only did Trump say little publicly about the bounty reports, and certainly never issued any words of rebuke to Russia over the reported atrocities, in his repeated calls with Putin he — by his own admission — never mentioned the bounties at all, and continued to dismiss the reports as false.

"That was a phone call to discuss other things, and frankly that's an issue that many people said was fake news," Trump told *Axios* reporter Jonathan Swan, in an interview televised on HBO.[47]

What were those "other things," and why did Trump and Putin speak by phone a remarkable nine times during the pandemic, starting with that December 29 golf course chat? The orgy of chat included five Trump-Putin calls in three weeks starting on March 30,[48] a crucial period for the virus as daily case totals topped 30,000,[49] the country went into an economic deep-freeze, and Trump continued taking no meaningful action beyond his daily press "briefings."

Whatever was spoken between the pair in those calls, the American — and global — public may never know because Trump and his Praetorian Guard sealed any records of the conversations on a highly classified, top-secret computer server.[50] The server's existence came to light during the flurry of revelations about Trump's illegal pressure campaign against the Ukrainian government, in which Trump attempted to force Ukraine to help him smear Joe Biden by holding back a crucial package of military aid.

The record of Trump's July 25, 2019, phone call with the Ukrainian president, Volodymyr Zelensky, was secreted away on that server. And as it turned out when reporters from *CNN* did some digging, so were "phone calls with Saudi Crown Prince Mohammed bin Salman and Russian leader Vladimir Putin."[51]

The network reported that a transcript of "at least one" of the Trump-Putin calls was hidden on the server. But with no information made public about any of the calls during the pandemic, beyond cursory "readouts," it seems safe to conclude that either no records of the calls were kept, or they are under lock and key on that server, or a similar one.

In the Kremlin, Putin and Co. were also less than eager to see the contents of the calls exposed.

"We would like to hope that we would not see such situations in our bilateral relations, which already have plenty of quite serious problems," Putin's longtime press flak, Dymitri Peskov, delicately told reporters.[52]

So we don't have the hard evidence. But we do know a few important facts that can help us understand what was *probably* discussed in those calls. First we know…

- All of Trump's relationships are transactional.

Even his wife, Melania, appears to understand that her husband always has an angle. Asked in 2005 (the year they were married) whether she would be in a relationship with Donald Trump if he weren't rich, she answered, frankly, "If I weren't beautiful, do you think he'd be with me?"[53]

His former "fixer," lawyer and all-around right-hand man Michael Cohen, in his book, described Trump's total lack of genuine emotional relationships.

"He has a million acquaintances, pals and hangers on, but no real friends," Cohen wrote.[54] "I urge you to really consider that fact: Trump has no true friends."

Cohen goes on to describe how for a decade he believed he was Trump's true friend, even "family," as Trump himself assured him. But the moment Cohen was no longer useful, he was cut adrift, ending up in federal prison for helping Trump pay "hush money" to adult film star Stormy Daniels.[55] Because the cover-up of Trump's brief sexual tryst with Daniels was clearly designed to protect his chances in the 2016 election, the unreported payoff was a clear violation of campaign finance laws.

In court documents, Trump himself (under the nomenclature "Individual 1") was named as having orchestrated the crime, but because he was a sitting president, he slithered away from any indictment while allowing Cohen — a man who once boasted that he was ready to "take a bullet" for Trump — to take the fall.

Maybe the most blunt illustration of Trump's transactional, "what's in it for me" view of life came in an *Atlantic* magazine report by Jeffrey Goldberg, which revealed Trump's contempt for American soldiers killed in action.[56] To Trump, they're all "losers" and "suckers."

Standing with his Chief of Staff John Kelly, over the grave of Kelly's 29-year-old son, a Marine killed in Afghanistan, Trump actually said to Kelly, "I don't get it. What was in it for them?"

"He can't fathom the idea of doing something for someone other than himself," one retired general told Goldberg. "He just thinks that anyone who does anything when there's no direct personal gain to be had is a sucker. There's no money in serving the nation."

- Trump is always, *always* ready to talk to Putin

We've already detailed the December 29 call from Putin that Trump took even though it interrupted one of his sacrosanct golf outings. Trump's eagerness to put himself at Putin's disposal, however, was evident in the earliest weeks of his term.

In January 2017 when Britain's then-Prime Minister Theresa May became the first foreign leader to visit Trump in Washington, D.C.,[57] he went on a tirade right in front of her when he learned that a top adviser told Putin that he'd take a message and Trump would call him back.

"Somebody just mentioned in passing that Vladimir Putin had asked for a call with him, and right in front us he absolutely shouted down Mike Flynn," May's ex-chief of staff, Nick Timothy, recounted in a 2020 interview.

Adding that Trump "like really shouted" at Flynn, he quoted the new president, who had been in office for only a week, bellowing at Flynn, "If Putin wants a call with me you just put him through."

This outburst at Flynn would have occurred on January 27[58] — just one day after Acting Attorney General Sally Yates personally warned White House Counsel Don McGhan that Flynn "essentially could be blackmailed by the Russians" because he had lied to the FBI about his sanctions talks with Kislyak, and "the Russians knew this, (and) that they likely had proof of this information."[59]

Even presumably knowing that Flynn was compromised by the Russians, Trump could not tolerate the national security adviser exercising discretion when it came to piping calls from Putin straight through. He forced Flynn to resign 17 days later, later citing Flynn's lies to the FBI as the reason for his firing.[60]

Trump already spoke by phone to Putin at least 16 times prior to the golf course call in late December, 2019. That made a total of 24 calls, plus two face-to-face meetings, for a total of 26 discussions between Trump and Putin — that were publicly known — in the 46 months between Trump's inauguration and the end of August, 2020.

That appears to be more contact than the previous three U.S. presidents, whose terms in office covered 24 years, had with a Russian leader, put together.[61]

- Trump would do anything for Putin.

Anything? Maybe that's an exaggeration, but the list of actions and policies Trump took as President of the United States that served Russian interests more than his own country is an impressive one.

One example: during the 2020 Republican National Convention Trump featured a video showing him in the White House with six U.S. citizens who were held hostage in countries such as Turkey and Iran.[62]

At the same time, Russia had imprisoned two former U.S. Marines[63] — one for 16 years the other for nine — on charges that their families insisted were phony, and which drew protests from Trump's own ambassador to Moscow. But Trump said and did nothing.

Trump also became entranced by the "theory" that Ukraine — not Russia — tampered with the 2016 presidential election, and on the side of Hillary Clinton, not himself. He was so invested in plugging the phony claim that it was a key part of the July 25, 2019, phone call to Ukraine President Zelensky that ended up getting Trump impeached.

But according to a Senate Intelligence Committee report released in August 2020,[64] the "Ukraine interfered" canard was concocted by a Russian intelligence agent who worked closely with Trump's 2016 campaign chief Paul Manafort. That the Ukraine "theory" was Russian propaganda had been widely known.[65] Putin himself peddled the tale as far back as 2017. But Trump grabbed onto it and made it his own, giving the Russian disinformation the imprimatur of the U.S. presidential seal.

Trump in the 2020 campaign attempted to make a major issue out of his opponent's supposed mental decline, even releasing a series of online ads alleging that Joe Biden "has suffered cognitive decline over the past four to five years," as *Fox News* put it.[66]

Now, the "cognitive decline" smear had also been used in the primary campaign by supporters of Biden's rival candidate Bernie Sanders. So maybe Trump just latched on to that. However, according to an *ABC News* investigation, the Russian propaganda-meisters also pushed a "scheme to promote 'allegations about the poor mental health'" of Biden.[67] And we know this confluence of narratives was not a coincidence, because U.S intelligence agencies circulated a warning bulletin throughout the government, sounding the alarm about Russia's attempt to tar Biden as a mental invalid.

The Trump administration Department of Homeland Security killed that bulletin. The memo, "Russia Likely to Denigrate Health of U.S. Candidates to Influence 2020 Election," was turned in to the DHS for review on July 7, according to *ABC*,[68] after a top DHS official demanded a "hold on sending this one out."

The bulletin was never seen again.

Even as the Senate Intelligence Committee[69] warned in August that Russia was sabotaging the 2020 presidential election just as it had the 2016 one, Trump administration Director of National Intelligence James Ratcliffe declared that the administration would no longer offer briefings to Congress about election interference, clearing the path even more cleanly for Russian to help Trump all over again.

Trump's longtime confidant Roger Stone was, according to multiple investigations including the August Senate Intelligence Committee report, Trump's go-between with Wikileaks, giving the supposed "transparency" site cues for when to dump Russian-hacked Democratic emails online.[70]

When Stone was convicted on seven counts of lying to Congress and witness tampering, Trump granted him a reprieve, commuting his 40-month prison term down to zero.[71]

By his lying, Stone slowed and obstructed an investigation into

Trump-Russia collusion in the 2016 election.

The list of Trump's giveaways to Putin goes on and on. In October of 2019, his sudden pullout of U.S. troops from the Syrian/Turkish border was a "gift to Russia," according to Trump's own former U.S. special envoy to the region, Brent McGurk.[72]

Though he never went through with it, Trump seriously considered pulling the United States out of the 75-year-old, post-World War II NATO alliance[73] — the West's most powerful bulwark against Russian aggression.

Shortly before the Republican National Convention in 2020, Trump announced that he would withdraw about one-third of United States troops in Germany. *CNN.com* columnist Nic Robertson called the inexplicable move "his last gift to Putin before the election."[74]

Whether it was actually his "last" is debatable. But point taken. As Robertson himself wrote, "Trump is the gift that keeps on giving for the Kremlin."

In the waning days of his lone term, as Trump flailed in defeat, refusing to concede defeat to Joe Biden and claiming that the election was "rigged" against him[75] — and even privately threatening that he would refuse to vacate the White House[76] — news broke that the Russians had pulled off a massive cyberattack against the U.S. government,[77] including the Pentagon and intelligence agencies, and a number of private corporations.[78]

But even as the stunning scope of the online espionage assault became clear, Trump said not a word about it in public.

We still don't know what Trump and Putin discussed on those nine phone calls,[79] from the December 29 golf course chat to the July 23 call in which the two supposedly discussed "arms control issues." But as we've established in this little chapter, we *do* know that Trump eagerly anticipated each and every call with Putin, and continually acted in ways that may as well have been dictated by the Russian leader himself.

Did Putin also dictate to Trump when it came to handling the coronavirus pandemic? They sure talked a lot during the crisis. Was Putin advising Trump on how to handle, or not handle, the devastating coronavirus attack?

As I said, we don't know. I don't pose those questions as a sneaky way of pushing a conspiracy theory without actually taking responsibility for it — though the "just asking the question" technique is a favorite of conspiracy mongers, including Trump himself.

No, I'm putting those questions out there as a plea for someone with greater resources than I have to investigate them. A congressional committee. A special prosecutor. A major news organization. We need to know exactly what Putin and Trump discussed in those calls, that very likely sit inside a top-secret computer server, if records exist at all.

As we'll see in the subsequent chapters, Trump's response was not altogether different from how Putin himself handled the coronavirus pandemic in Russia — by largely ignoring it, then pushing for a bogus "vaccine" months ahead of any safe or reasonable schedule.

Was Trump's biological warfare attack on the United States, in the form of "let it wash over the country," his real "last gift to Putin?"

Or perhaps more precisely, was unleashing the virus to wreak havoc and death across the U.S. his payback to Putin, not so much his "last gift," but his end of the bargain in a quid pro quo?

The surprise would be if it weren't. We know that for Trump, everything is a transaction. He places no value on anything, not even human life, except what he thinks he can get out of it. Why would he suddenly change, due to the pandemic or for any reason?

We also know that, for what we can assume are largely transactional reasons, Trump is besotted with Vladimir Putin. Now, admittedly, it seems like his transactionality with Putin goes beyond a mere material or cash exchange. Trump appears to crave Putin's approval and attention, like no one else.

In her book about her uncle, Mary Trump — a clinical psychologist — gives a clear portrait of Trump's craving for his father's approval.[80] But she notes that as he built his own empire (albeit with the elder Trump's financial backing) he became "unmoored" from the need to please his own father. Perhaps Putin played the role in Donald Trump's life that was once played by Fred Trump.

Why, exactly, Trump served as Putin's poodle remains a mystery. All that is clear is that he was — and he was getting something out of the relationship. But what? And does it have a connection to Trump's "wash over the country" approach to the pandemic? The definitive answer will take a congressional investigation, or a prosecutor — or a special "truth commission" whose only job is to get to the bottom of what really happened to the United States when it fell into the clutches of Donald J. Trump.

CHAPTER EIGHT

....

THIS IS THEIR NEW HOAX

"I watched Fox Business. I watched Lou Dobbs last night. I watched Sean Hannity last night. Tucker last night. Laura. I watched <u>Fox & Friends</u> in the morning."

— *Donald Trump*
Describing his diet of television. September 10, 2020.[1]

Donald Trump A/B tested a wide array of excuses and cover stories for his refusal to do anything to stop the coronavirus pandemic. But the silliest — though he didn't seem to think it was silly — may have been his claim that he was distracted by "hoaxes."

ABC News anchor David Muir flat-out asked Trump, in a May 5 interview, what he did to "restock those cupboards that you say were bare?" Muir was referring to Trump's bogus assertion that his predecessor, Obama, had somehow depleted the federal government's supply of personal protective equipment,[2] badly needed by health care providers as they treat coronavirus patients.

Of course, the cupboards weren't bare.[3] And of course, though PPE supplies were short relative to the requirements of a major pandemic, Trump did absolutely nothing to restock them in his then-three years in office — despite repeated warnings from experts that the stockpile needed rebuilding.

Why not?

"Well, I'll be honest. I have a lot of things going on. We had a lot of people that refused to allow the country to be successful. They wasted a lot of time on Russia, Russia, Russia. That turned out to be a total hoax," Trump told Muir in the ABC interview.[4]

But "Russia, Russia, Russia" wasn't the only "hoax" supposedly distracting Trump from the looming pandemic. Next up was "Ukraine, Ukraine."

"Then they did Ukraine, Ukraine and that was a total hoax, then they impeached the president of the United States for absolutely no reason, and we even had 197-to-nothing vote by the Republicans," he rambled.

The impeachment proceedings against Trump were supposedly another distraction.[5] Not only did Trump himself claim this to be the case, so did other Republicans, including Senate Majority Leader Mitch McConnell.

In an April 2 letter to Senate Democratic Leader Chuck Schumer, Trump nonsensically blamed the impeachment proceedings for New York's then-rampaging coronavirus outbreak.[6]

"If you spent less time on your ridiculous impeachment hoax, which went haplessly on forever and ended up going nowhere (except increasing my poll numbers), and instead focused on helping the people of New York, then New York would not have been so completely unprepared for the 'invisible enemy,'" wrote the President of the United States, on official White House letterhead.

Trump dismissed, or appeared to dismiss, the pandemic itself as a "hoax" in a campaign rally speech on February 28, a date which, it should be noted, fell exactly three weeks after he told Bob Woodward that he knew the coronavirus to be "deadly stuff."[7]

Speaking to his usual crowd of adoring, fanatical supporters in North Charleston, South Carolina, Trump ran down the inventory of "hoaxes" that, in his mind at least, Democrats had perpetrated against him.

"They tried the impeachment hoax. That was on a perfect conversation. They tried anything. They tried it over and over," Trump extemporized. "They'd been doing it since you got in. It's all turning. They lost. It's all turning. Think of it. Think of it. And this is their new hoax."

As Democrats, including Biden, quickly pounced on Trump for referring to the virus itself as a "hoax," fact-checking orgs such as *Factcheck.org* were just as quick to split that hair, noting that Trump was saying that the Democratic response to his response to the coronavirus was the "new hoax," not the coronavirus itself.[8]

As his interviews with Woodward later revealed, rather unsurprisingly, Trump was well aware that the coronavirus was no "hoax," but in fact was a "killer" and "the plague."[9] Whether he meant to say that the disease was a "hoax" in that February 28 rally or not is somewhat debatable. But it is not debatable that Trump continued to *act as if* the pandemic was a hoax, throughout the spring, summer, and into the fall. On September 21, the final day of 2020's long, traumatic summer, Trump told an Ohio rally crowd that the coronavirus "affects virtually nobody."[10]

Throughout the late summer and into the fall — prime campaign season for the 2020 presidential election — Trump held a series of rallies at which his supporters rarely wore masks, and packed tightly into indoor arenas, as if the pandemic simply did not exist. These "superspreader" events actually killed one of Trump's most prominent supporters.

Herman Cain, the former Republican presidential candidate who had been CEO of the restaurant chain Godfather Pizza, showed up maskless at Trump's June 20 rally in Tulsa, Oklahoma.[11] Less than two months later, he was dead of COVID-19.

As for Trump, he said he was "not at all concerned" about the indoor, no-mask rallies, because "I'm on a stage, and it's very far away."[12]

On the same day that Trump told his fans that the virus "affects virtually nobody," more than 204,500 Americans were already dead from the disease,[13] with a total upwards of 7 million cases — 2.55 million of them active at that moment.

A couple of days later, when a reporter asked Trump why he had said nothing publicly to acknowledge the massive loss of American life — the fifth-worst mass-casualty disaster in U.S. history[14] — Trump's only response was, "Go ahead. Uhhhh. Anybody else?"[15]

Clearly, and perhaps understandably, Trump did not want to talk about the staggering, soul-shattering death toll. Not only did he claim that various "hoaxes" had distracted him from paying proper attention to the pandemic, but he attempted to create a series of distractions of his own, to shift the media and public zeitgeist away from the mass tragedy that continued at a rate of approximately 1,000 deaths per day as summer turned to fall.

In May, as the body count blew past the 100,000 mark,[16] Trump went to his go-to for whenever he was feeling particularly aggrieved: his imagined permanent persecutor, Barack Obama.

Trump announced the existence of something called "Obamagate" — more than three years after Obama left office — declaring this nebulous event "the biggest political crime in American history."[17] He demanded prison sentences for members of the previous administration who had, in his feverish imagination, conspired against him. He accused Obama himself of leading a "coup."

Never mind that Obama, not Trump, was president when the hazy events of "Obamagate" took place, so what he meant by a "coup" was not altogether clear. So what the hell was he talking about?

"For years, Trump has claimed without proof that Democratic partisans within the Justice Department and the FBI abused their powers to investigate members of his campaign and undermine his presidency," wrote *CNN.com* reporters Marshall Cohen and Jeremy Herb.[18] "'Obamagate' appears to be an extension of this underlying theory."

The reporter noted that the "theory" also, perhaps primarily, "served as a diversion from the coronavirus pandemic, as the nationwide death toll passed 80,000 and the unemployment rate tripled to a staggering 14.7 percent."

"Obamagate" was far from the only "diversion" Trump served up in May. He threatened to cut off federal funds to states that planned to allow universal voting-by-mail in the November election.[19] In fact, Trump's obsession with mail-in ballots, which he falsely claimed were susceptible to widespread fraud, ran from spring through summer into the autumn months.[20]

In the September 23 installment of his unending series of press conferences, with the COVID-19 death total topping 206,000, Trump amped up his inane claims about "the ballots" to 11, essentially promising to hold power by a coup,[21] unless somehow "the ballots" were no longer used.

"I've been complaining very strongly about the ballots and the ballots are a disaster," Trump said, responding to a question about whether he would allow peaceful transition of power if he were to lose the election. "Get rid of the ballots and you'll have a very peaceful — there won't be a transfer, frankly. There'll be a continuation."

Trump made good on his threat, or tried to, refusing to acknowledge his decisive election loss, and whining about the "rigged election" for weeks on end.[22] Behind the scenes, weeks after his defeat, he told his advisers that he would refuse to physically vacate the White House even once election victor Joe Biden was inaugurated.[23]

The prospect of a president refusing to give up power even after an electoral defeat was certainly a distraction, one difficult to ignore. In a six-week period in April and May — and following the end of his impeachment trial, when Trump beat the rap — he created yet more chaos by firing or forcing out five federal inspectors general, including the State Department's IG.[24]

Those were the very people whose job it was to investigate Trump and his cronies. The firings included Michael Atkinson, the intelligence agencies' IG. It was Atkinson who handled the whistleblower complaint that originally fingered Trump in the Ukraine "quid pro quo" caper, and set off Trump's first impeachment.

At one point in May, Trump declared that he, himself, was taking a cycle of hydroxychloroquine,[25] the anti-malaria drug that he repeatedly and wrongly pushed from the bully pulpit as some sort of treatment or cure for coronavirus infection. That came just a few weeks after Trump bizarrely suggested the possibility of injecting industrial disinfectants to stop the disease.

Whether he was doing so consciously, or just because it's what he does, Trump was carrying out the advice of his former adviser and campaign chief Steve Bannon, who famously counseled that the way to deal with the media was to "flood the zone with shit."[26]

Neither Bannon nor Trump invented this "flood the zone" method of propaganda. According to a 2014 RAND Corporation report,[27] Russia pioneered the technique, which RAND dubbed the "Firehose of Falsehood," at least as far back as 2008 when Putin sent troops into the Republic of Georgia, to prevent the country from aligning with the West.[28]

RAND described the "Firehose" as consisting of two main elements: "high numbers of channels and messages and a shameless willingness to disseminate partial truths or outright fictions." But even more importantly, the propaganda is "also rapid, continuous, and repetitive, and it lacks commitment to consistency."

Trump adopted the Russian propaganda technique pretty much right away in his presidency, but dialed it up to a new level when the pandemic hit. As we know from Bob Woodward's reporting, on January 28, 2020, Trump's national security adviser, Robert O'Brien — who would later contract the coronavirus himself[29] — warned him that the pandemic "will be the biggest national security threat you face in your presidency."[30]

The general view is that Trump shrugged off that dire imprecation. But he didn't. He took it to heart in his own way. *The Washington Post* maintains a database of Trump's public lies,[31] showing that Trump's own firehose of falsehood rapidly accelerated once the virus came to America.

From his earliest mention of the coronavirus in January through the middle of July, Trump spewed more than 1,000 "false or misleading claims," also known as lies, about the viral invasion. That impressive total was second only to the 1,200 lies he told about his impeachment.

Trump also fulfilled the "rapid, continuous, and repetitive" requirements of the Putinesque propaganda method, coughing up lies at a personal record pace. In Trump's first 100 days, according to *The Post*, he pumped out lies at a rate of about five per day. During the pandemic crisis, he easily topped 20 false public statements every day, on average.

He has always been a repetitive propagandist. The *Post* database records 500 examples of Trump repeating a single fabulation at least three times.[32]

Following the Russian "firehose" model outlined by RAND, Trump's propaganda was repeated and amplified by multiple sources[33] — including Fox News, One America News (a minor cable channel that gained national notoriety with its unwavering pro-Trump stance), and on social media, primarily Twitter and Facebook.[34]

"Receiving the same or similar message from multiple sources is more persuasive," even if those sources tell differing versions of the same message, the RAND report concluded.

The social media outlets were not only part of Trump's Russian-style propaganda efforts, they were actually Russian. At least to a significant degree. Russian "bots" and trolls disseminated pro-Trump messaging, repeating and restating many of his favorite lies. Ultimately, by 2020, the Russian online trolls often simply retweeted Trump's own tweets, or quoted his glaringly phony claims.[35]

Trump by that point was not merely benefiting from Russian internet propaganda, as he had in 2016. He was driving it.[36]

His to-the-letter adherence to Russian propaganda techniques may have been just a coincidence. Or, more accurately, a confluence of like minds. As his former lawyer Michael Cohen recounted, Trump was a longtime practitioner of the "Big Lie."[37] He launched his political career as de facto leader of the "Birther" movement, peddling the racist lie that

Barack Obama was born not in the United States, but in Kenya.

But the "Big Lie," most often associated with Hitler,[38] was a different technique than the "Firehose of Falsehoods." The Russian version was more like a torrent of lies, some big, some small, none genuinely intended to fool or persuade — but instead to short circuit the target's ability to respond rationally, or make any sense at all out of a given situation.

The Russian propaganda method, RAND wrote, "makes no commitment to objective reality." Sometimes what the propagandist says is actually true. Other times, it is simply invented out of thin air. Again, there's no real effort to win over new converts to the cause, whatever that cause may be. The point, instead, is to overload the infospace with "shit," as Bannon would say, taking advantage of the natural human tendency to intellectual laziness, and the difficulties in distinguishing between true and false information.

The nonstop "firehose of falsehoods" from Trump was just one way in which he emulated, or at least drew inspiration from, Putin's own approach to the coronavirus in his own country. While we don't know exactly what was said between Trump and Putin in the December 29 impromptu golf course call, we know that on a July 23 call the two discussed "efforts to defeat the coronavirus pandemic while continuing to reopen global economies," according to a White House flak.[39]

That White House statement was deja vu all over again, because we also know that the pandemic came up in a June 1 phone call between the Russian strongman and his U.S. would-be counterpart. After the Kremlin revealed that call, a White House statement confirmed that Trump and Putin chatted about "the latest efforts to defeat the coronavirus pandemic and reopen global economies."[40]

Sliding backwards in time a few weeks, Trump and Putin chatted about the pandemic on May 7. The administration statement about that call was somewhat more specific, saying that Trump informed Putin that "the United States is working hard to care for Americans at home" but "is also ready to provide assistance to any country in need, including Russia."[41]

Trump made good on the pledge, sending $5.6 million worth of medical aid to Russia just two weeks later.[42] That aid package included 200 ventilator machines — after Trump had told governors of U.S. states in March that when it came to the desperately needed ventilators, "try getting it yourselves."[43]

The U.S. medical aid to Russia also followed a shipment of medical supplies going the other way, from Russia to the U.S. on April 2.[44] The 45 ventilators in that delivery were not only manufactured by a company under U.S. sanctions, they were not usable, due to what was described as "voltage issues."

The rest of the shipment was basically useless as well, including such items as household cleaning gloves and chemical warfare gas masks. Russia sent the U.S. treasury a bill for $660,000 to cover what was essentially a planeload of garbage.[45]

But when Trump was asked whether the shipment served as P.R. for Russia, rather than actual help for Americans, Trump waved off the suggestion.

"I'm not concerned about Russian propaganda. Not even a little bit," Trump told reporters, clearly telling the truth, at least that one time.

After a March 30 phone call, the Kremlin announced that Trump and Putin had talked coronavirus in that call as well. That was the first of a blizzard of calls between the two at the height of the pandemic — five calls in three weeks.[46]

Adding those to the July 23, June 1 and May 7 calls, plus the December 29 golf course chat, Trump and Putin spoke on the phone an astonishing nine times during the pandemic. In the introductory chapter to this book, I quoted former U.S. Ambassador to Russia Michael McFaul, who was stunned that the U.S. president called any world leader — much less Vladimir Putin — that frequently. Just to make the point, McFaul's quote merits an encore.

"That would be a crazy number of calls to any foreign leader," he wrote on his Twitter account "But to Putin? What on earth were they discussing? So strange."[47]

Strange indeed!

McFaul posted his tweet two weeks prior to the July 23 call. He did not even reference the December 29 call.

With either the White House or Kremlin confirming that Trump and Putin discussed coronavirus in four of those nine calls, are we to believe that the topic never came up in the other five? If they spoke about what was then just a localized epidemic in China on December 29, what did they say?

Without the transcript, we obviously cannot know. But we can look at the behavior of the two leaders following that call. If we see similarities in how Trump and Putin responded to the nascent pandemic (spoiler alert: we do), then it would seem reasonable to conclude that they talked about it on December 29.

Of course, any such similarities could be a coincidence, or the result of Trump's slavish emulation of Putin and Putinism. Plus, there was one major difference between the two: while a bored Trump eventually gave up on safety, paying little attention to health protocols[48] — and ended up contracting COVID-19 himself as a result — Putin did the opposite. The Russian strongman protected himself scrupulously. More on that one rather large difference later in this chapter.

Like Trump in the U.S., Putin's earliest response to the coronavirus outbreak in Russia was to deny it was real. He went even further than Trump, in fact. In January, Moscow hospitals began reporting an unusually high number of pneumonia cases[49] — a number up 37 percent from the previous year, according to a *Reuters* report which cited Rosstat, the country's official stat-keeper.

Yet the Russian capital's health department publicly claimed that pneumonia cases were down from 2019 by eight percent. Putin, according to the *Reuters* reporting, dismissed the claims that excess pneumonia cases were actually coronavirus, being deliberately misreported.

"Putin has complained that Russia is being targeted by fake news to sow panic," Reuters reported.

That *Reuters* report was dated March 19. On March 26, the Kremlin, via the Russian state media "watchdog" organization Roskomnadzor, ordered Facebook and Twitter to delete posts with supposed "fake news" about the coronavirus outbreak.[50] Facebook actually went along with it, censoring what Roskomnadzor called "socially significant false information" on the number of Russian COVID cases.

At that point, Russia had reported just 840 cases, a low figure that understandably aroused widespread public suspicion. A "fake" story posted on Twitter claimed that the city of Moscow planned to impose a curfew on its citizens as a public health measure. The city's mayor vehemently denied the story — only to impose a curfew after all, along with other strict lockdown measures, just three days later.[51]

About a month later, Moscow's mayor admitted that the actual number of coronavirus cases in his city was probably three times higher than the official figures.[52]

The Reuters report of Putin's "fake news" complaint came 10 days after Trump tweeted, "The Fake News Media and their partner, the Democrat Party, is doing everything within its semi-considerable power (it used to be greater!) to inflame the CoronaVirus situation, far beyond what the facts would warrant. Surgeon General, 'The risk is low to the average American.'"[53]

Trump tweeted using the phrase "fake news" 58 times between January 1 and March 31 alone. Of course, not all of those tweets dealt with the pandemic. Though, on March 18, he attacked the topic again.

"I always treated the Chinese Virus very seriously, and have done a very good job from the beginning, including my very early decision to close the 'borders' from China - against the wishes of almost all. Many lives were saved. The Fake News new narrative is disgraceful & false!"[54]

As we've covered earlier, Trump's much-touted (at least by himself) closing of the "borders" with China was itself fake news, at least to an extent. Trump's order allowed 12 exceptions to the China travel ban, and thousands of travelers arrived from China after the January 28 "ban" took effect.[55]

The China "ban" was the only step Trump, to that point, had taken to cut off the virus. Putin took the same step, slamming shut Russia's 2,700-mile land border with China — the sixth-longest in the world — on January 30,[56] two days after Trump announced his "China ban." Putin also grounded all international passenger flights in and out of Russia.

On March 12, Trump also extended the flight restrictions, this time suspending travel — for a 30-day period only — from 26 European countries, those in the "Schengen zone" where cross border travel is allowed without restrictions.[57] But at the time, the U.S. already had 1,635 known coronavirus cases,[58] and 41 people had died.

The leaky "ban" did not apply to U.S. citizens, or permanent residents, or families of either. And by the time Trump got around to imposing it, at least 1.8 million travelers from Europe, where the virus was then more prevalent than in any other region in the world, had already flown into the United States.[59] Despite Trump's repeated, racist references to COVID-19 as "the China virus," epidemiologists, according to a *Washington Post* report, believed that "the U.S. outbreak was driven overwhelmingly by viral strains from Europe rather than China."[60]

But the most devastating flaw in Trump's European "ban" was the timing. There was a two-day lag between Trump's announcement and when the restrictions actually went into effect. Nor did Trump make clear that Americans were exempted from the ban. The result — a massive crush of passengers at European airports, scrambling to get home.[61]

Dr. Anthony Fauci, who at that point was still a mainstay at the White House coronavirus task force before being effectively sidelined by Trump, warned that the crowding was the exact opposite of the social distancing required to stem the spread of the virus.[62]

And indeed, as *The Post* reported two months later, rather than seal off the U.S. from the virus, Trump's European travel clampdown "delivered one final viral infusion." Travelers from Europe who were already infected, or picked up the virus in airport crowds, "became part of an influx from Europe that went unchecked for weeks and helped to seal the country's coronavirus fate."[63]

So, while Putin's early response to the coronavirus pandemic bore strong similarities to Trump's, it was more sinister, with an outright cover-up attempt, and at the same time, more effective.

There was an even more nefarious aspect to Putin's cover-up, crossing a line that not even Trump approached. As doctors charged with treating coronavirus patients began to make public rumblings about the Putin government's shortcomings in handling the outbreak, they also began to plunge out of windows.[64]

In one instance, Russian doctor Alexander Shulepov recorded a video in which he blew the whistle on the insane work conditions for medical personnel there. Shulepov tested positive for coronavirus, but was not allowed to miss even a single shift, he complained.

That was in late April. But days later, Shupelov recorded a video mysteriously recanting his allegations, claiming he was "just being emotional" when he made them. On May 2, as he was being treated for the disease in a Russian hospital, he fell out of a second story window, and fractured his skull.[65]

Shupelov survived. Authorities said he must have slipped when he was smoking at the window, and Shupelov's wife, Maria, was barred from speaking publicly about what happened to her husband. Two doctors who had also complained about their conditions and the government's response weren't so lucky.

Dr. Yelena Nepomnyashchaya, who spoke out about the lack of personal protective equipment for health care workers, somehow fell 50 feet to her death from a hospital window in Krasnoyarsk, a city in Siberia, eventually dying of her injuries on May 1.[66] Nepomnyashchaya was not known to have contracted the virus — unlike another female doctor, Natalya Lebedeva, who plunged 60 feet on April 24. Lebedeva was reportedly blamed for somehow causing a viral outbreak in Star City, a military area outside of Moscow that has long been the home base for Russia's cosmonauts.

On December 19, it happened again. Alexander Kagansky, 45, a leading Russian geneticist and molecular biologist, was found on a street in St. Petersburg, apparently having fallen from a high window,[67] and stabbed in the stomach to boot.[68]

Kagansky was reportedly working on a coronavirus vaccine with researchers in Scotland. Russia had approved its own "Sputnik V" vaccine in August, but even the Russian public responded to the domestic vaccine with skepticism, leaving medical centers where the vaccination was offered mostly empty.

The remarkably similar deaths of the four doctors could, of course, be a coincidence, a tragic series of accidents. Doctors in other countries, including the U.S., certainly did their share of complaining about inadequate government measures. Yet somehow, none plummeted to terrible fates from high windows.

Trump certainly took measures of his own designed to silence and sideline voices critical of his pandemic agenda — which was essentially to pretend that the pandemic did not exist and just get on with "normal" life.

Fauci said that he was prevented from appearing on Sunday news talk shows for a period of time in March. Eventually Fauci was replaced on the coronavirus task force by Scott Atlas, a radiologist and Fox News talking head who advocated a dangerous "herd immunity" approach[69] — that is, pretending that the pandemic did not exist and getting on with "normal" life even as the virus was left unchecked to infect and kill millions.

Another example of Trump and Putin taking similar tactics in their dealings with the pandemic, with Putin taking the more extreme approach, came in their claims about a vaccine. As the 2020 election drew closer, Trump appeared increasingly desperate in his insistence that there would be a COVID-19 vaccine available for widespread use by November 3, Election Day.[70]

Obviously, that didn't happen, and was never going to happen.[71] Despite Trump's own objections, the Food and Drug Administration determined that it required at least two months of data on the safety of any vaccine, before issuing even an expedited, emergency authorization for its use.

Trump absurdly condemned the FDA's requirements as a "political hit job," making clear (for anyone who didn't get it already) what his own motives for demanding a quick vaccine actually were.[72]

Despite not facing an election, because he never really does, Putin went even further than Trump. On August 11, he announced that Russian scientists had, in fact, developed a vaccine — and it was ready to inject into actual Russians.[73]

To say Putin rushed the vaccine into public distribution would be quite an understatement. According to the medical journal *The Lancet*, "at the time of approval, the vaccine had not even started phase 3 trials, nor had any results on the earlier stage trials been published."[74]

Putin claimed that his own daughter had taken the vaccine, and later said that "dozens" of his "close relatives" and working associates had been vaccinated.[75] He did not, however, say that he had received the shot himself.

Nonetheless, vaccine or no vaccine, on October 9 Russia reported its highest single-day spike in cases,[76] with 12,126 new ones bringing the country's total to 1.3 million, 22,000 of whom had perished.

After that December 29 phone call, Trump and Putin both:

- Called reports of the virus's dangers "fake news."
- Stifled critics of their respective responses.
- Shut down international flights.
- Pushed for an untested, rushed vaccine.

One Russian citizen who was not infected, however, was Vladimir Putin. And this was another major difference — perhaps the most significant difference — between him and Trump.

After months of, by his own admission to Bob Woodward, "playing it down"[77] — the dangers of the coronavirus, that is — and worse, openly disdaining the most basic health precautions, on October 2 Trump revealed the inevitable.[78] He had the coronavirus.

His pal and mentor, Putin, took the exact opposite approach. Since visiting a hospital in March and shaking ungloved hands with a doctor who specialized in treating coronavirus patients, and who subsequently tested positive himself,[79] Putin quickly went into virtual isolation and stayed there.

"The contrast with Russian President Vladimir Putin could not be more stark," *CNN* reported.[80] "The authoritarian leader Trump admires so much is living in a bubble."

While Trump was golfing, holding daily press conferences and, starting in July, campaign rallies with few if any precautions, Putin was remaining in his residence, conducting business by phone and video conference as the Kremlin took what *CNN* called "extreme measures" to protect the country's leader-for-life.[81]

Any visitors hoping to see Putin were first required to quarantine for two weeks, then pass through a "disinfection tunnel" installed in his home,[82] among other drastic but, frankly, sensible steps.

As a result, Putin and Trump communicated yet again. Shortly after Trump announced his positive test, which sent him to Walter Reed hospital the next day, Putin sent him a telegram saying "get well soon."

CHAPTER NINE

. . . .

OCTOBER SURPRISE

"I feel so powerful. I'll walk into that audience. I'll walk in there,
I'll kiss everyone in that audience. I'll kiss the guys and the
beautiful women. Everybody. I'll just give ya a big fat kiss."

— Donald Trump, October 12, 2020[1]

In the early morning hours of October 2, 2020, as the American coronavirus crisis was rolling into its ninth full month and more than 212,000 Americans were dead, @realDonaldTrump posted to his Twitter account. That in itself was hardly unusual. Long before he occupied the Oval Office, Trump was fond of tweeting late at night, and into the early morning.[2]

This tweet, however, was one of a kind, and not merely for its relatively (for Trump) subdued tone. After more than eight months of downplaying the pandemic, lying about it, pretending it was no big deal, and taking every possible step to make it worse and cause more Americans to get sick and die, Trump himself had now contracted the virus.[3]

"Tonight, @FLOTUS and I tested positive for COVID-19," he announced in the Twitter post.[4] "We will begin our quarantine and recovery process immediately. We will get through this TOGETHER!"

What Trump did not reveal in the tweet, or in a lengthy, phone-in to Sean Hannity of *Fox News* earlier in the evening of October 1, was that he already knew he was COVID-positive. He had tested positive earlier that day using a "rapid" test, according to a *Wall Street Journal* report.[5]

Positive results from rapid tests are "usually highly accurate," according to the Food and Drug Administration.[6] It's the negative results that can be iffy and need confirmation with a more sophisticated test. Trump received a positive result from the rapid test, but didn't reveal that fact even to Hannity — the Fox News host with whom he is so close Trump reportedly phoned him each night before bedtime.[7]

His cover-up of the initial positive test was not only a harbinger of how Trump would handle his entire bout with the virus, but an extension of the deadly disinformation campaign he had waged from the beginning.

We've covered some of that disinformation earlier, and we'll go into it a little deeper in the next chapter. But suffice to say, an extensive study of 38 million English-language media articles by Cornell University found that none other than Donald Trump was "the single largest driver of misinformation around COVID."[8]

He continued to drive COVID misinformation, or disinformation, as a COVID victim. His personal White House doctor Sean Conley — an osteopath — "served as Trump's publicist in a white coat," wrote *Atlantic* reporter James Hamblin, "reassuring Americans at every turn that Trump is doing well, while leaving out conspicuous details."[9]

One such conspicuous detail was that Trump's illness was so severe, he required oxygen on October 2.[10] Conley and the White House left that one out, though he soon reversed course and admitted that not only did Trump need extra oxygen, his blood-oxygen levels dropped below normal at least twice, on October 3 and again on October 4.

Trump's three-day hospital stay at Walter Reed National Military Medical Center was clouded with fuzzy or false information about his health, but culminated not in a show of humility by the suddenly vulnerable Trump, or a display of newfound empathy for the 215,000-plus Americans who had died[11] and millions more who had been sickened or otherwise affected by the virus — but instead in what was widely described as a Mussolini-like moment, Trump returned to the White House on October 6 after pressuring doctors to release him from the hospital early.[12] There, he climbed a set of steep stairs leading to a balcony overlooking the White House South Lawn. Turning to face outward toward no one in particular, he made a show of stripping away his protective face mask and saluting, for some reason, in the general direction of the Marine One helicopter that flew him back from Walter Reed.

"Most frequently, Mussolini had himself photographed on balconies," another *Atlantic* writer, Anne Applebaum, noted of the Italian facist dictator she compared to Trump.[13] "The Italian cameramen who made his newsreels often filmed him from just below these structures, so that the perspective was always that of the crowd, looking up adoringly at the Leader."

Trump's callback to the founder of fascism was likely deliberate. On an even more risible note, prior to leaving the hospital, Trump had the bright idea to exit for the cameras while appearing "frail at first when people saw him," according to a *New York Times* account. But after a few moments he would stand up straight, and rip open his shirt revealing a bright red Superman "S" across his chest.

"He ultimately did not go ahead with the stunt," *The Times* dryly noted.[14]

The aborted Superman gimmick could be charitably called silly, but the facsist display he did finally stage was unsettling, to say the least. Perhaps even more serious, and dangerous, was the lesson he took from his bout with the deadly disease which he personally had inflicted on the country.

"Don't be afraid of Covid. Don't let it dominate your life," Trump tweeted shortly before leaving the hospital,[15] a message he reiterated in a video posted online the following day.[16]

Even after Trump himself was temporarily felled by the virus, he continued his campaign to push Americans — 215,852 of whom had died by that point[17] — back into the teeth of the pandemic. As erratic as he had been for most of the summer, and as erratic as he would become over the following days, he remained on-message about that one imperative: the coronavirus must continue to spread. Or, one might say, to "wash over" the country.

Not that there was ever any possibility that Trump would soften his posture. As we've argued throughout this book, Trump's mission from the beginning was to attack America with the disease, wreaking mayhem and death, at least in part because — as has been his stated belief — he expected to profit from picking up the pieces.

Trump also claimed that far from being slowed down by his illness, after his treatment he felt "better than I did 20 years ago!"[18]

He may well have. He was being administered dexamethasone, a powerful steroid that lowers the body's immune response.[19] In many serious cases of COVID-19, much of the damage is caused by the patient's own immune system going berserk, in what's called a "cytokine storm," killing not only the virus but the patient's own, healthy cells as well.

While the steroid is effective in controlling the worst effects of coronavirus infection, it has a few side effects as well. Those include, according to medical professionals cited by *The New York Times*, "euphoria, bursts of energy and even a sense of invulnerability."[20]

Though Trump claimed on October 10 that he was off the drug, he continued to be photographed with bandages on the back of his right hand, suggesting ongoing intravenous injections.[21] Dexamethasone can be given by IV.[22]

On October 12, even though he likely remained contagious and had not fully recovered from the disease, he held a campaign rally in Sanford, Florida. At the rally, he declared to his supporters that he was now immune to coronavirus (probably not true[23]) and was so sure he was not contagious that he wanted to wade into the crowd planting big kisses on "the guys and the beautiful women."

In the weeks following his "recovery" from COVID-19, in the final month before the 2020 election, Trump's messaging, if you could call it that, was all over the place. He blasted out 477 tweets and retweets in 10 days, on such topics as the "rigged election," California's imaginary program to dump "millions of gallons" of water into the Pacific Ocean, and in one particularly memorable retweet, a bizarre internet conspiracy "theory" claiming that Osama bin Laden was still alive and that Barack Obama and Joe Biden had the Navy SEAL team that killed bin Laden murdered in a "blood sacrifice."[24]

All perfectly normal!

But as crazy as Trump got, he remained consistently "on message" about one thing — the need for the American people to return to normal life as the virus swept across the country unimpeded.

During that same 10-day period, Trump's administration quietly adopted the policy of "herd immunity" advocated in an online statement calling itself "The Great Barrington Declaration."[25] The statement was much like any other internet "petition," allowing pretty much anyone to digitally "sign."

Many of the signatories to this new policy statement were obviously gags.[26] The names included "Dr. Johnny Bananas," "Dr. Person Fakename," and another whose "name" was simply the opening lyrics to "Hey Macarena."[27]

"Herd immunity" was a sham, pseudoscientific gift wrap for exactly the same Trump non-policy that governed his entire, deadly approach to the pandemic. In theory, "herd immunity" happens when enough members of a population are infected with the contagion of the moment that the disease burns itself out.

In reality, "herd immunity" was "a fringe component of epidemiology. This is not mainstream science. It's dangerous," National Institutes of Health Director Francis Collins told *The Washington Post*.[28] "It fits into the political views of certain parts of our confused political establishment."

"Herd immunity" would also kill 1,385,800 Americans,[29] if in fact it could actually be achieved, with another 2.3 million hospitalized, according to one estimate. Other estimates, such as the one cited in the introduction to this book, put the death toll at nearly twice that.

In September, Scott Atlas, the radiologist and Fox News talking head brought on to the White House coronavirus task force by Trump specifically to advocate for "herd immunity," vigorously denied that he advocated such a plan, calling reports that he did an "overt lie."[30]

But a month later, a White House aide told the *Post* that the Great Barrington Declaration "is endorsing what the president's policy has been for months. The president's policy — protect the vulnerable, prevent hospital overcrowding, and open schools and businesses — and he's been very clear on that."[31]

In other words, "herd immunity," albeit with the additional wrinkle of "protecting the vulnerable," referring primarily to senior citizens — something Trump was doing only half-heartedly.

In July, he announced a program that would distribute $5 billion to nursing homes across the country,[32] and require that they test their staff on a more regular basis.[33] Perhaps not surprisingly, however, *The New York Times* reported that nursing home chains with "long histories of safety violations and misusing public funds" had deployed an army of Washington lobbyists, "many with close ties to the Trump administration."[34]

Was Trump "protecting the vulnerable" or funneling cash to his pals? The $5 billion package was just one part of the billions dumped into the nursing home industry by the Trump administration, according to the *Times* investigation.

The unnamed White House official who spoke to *The Post* wasn't doing much more than stating the obvious. As far back as late March when daily deaths had already climbed well over the 1,000 mark on their way to the 2,000-plus level they would hit in April, Trump was already pushing to relax guidelines restricting group gatherings and social distancing, so that by the Easter holiday, "You'll have packed churches all over our country. I think it would be a beautiful time."[35]

Despite Atlas's public indignation at the suggestion that he was a booster of "herd immunity," reporting by *The Washington Post* in October confirmed that not only did he favor "allowing infections to spread naturally among most of the population while protecting the most vulnerable and those in nursing homes until the United States reaches herd immunity, which experts say would cause excess deaths,"[36] but he actively opposed common sense measures agreed by an overwhelming consensus of scientists to slow contagion.

Atlas on his own Twitter account made the phony claim that mask-wearing does nothing to prevent transmission.[37] (Twitter blocked Atlas's tweet at potentially harmful "false or misleading content.") He also opposed increased testing — the core of any anti-pandemic program — shooting down attempts by Fauci to allocate $9 billion in unspent money that had been earmarked for that purpose, according to the *Post* report.

At the same time that Atlas was muscling his way to the top of Trump's coronavirus task force, becoming the only "scientist" who could hold Trump's attention — by telling him exactly what he wanted to hear — Trump hit the campaign trail to publicly disparage the very idea of concern about the deadly pandemic at all.

"They are getting tired of the pandemic, aren't they?," he grumped at a campaign rally in Prescott, Arizona, on October 19 — 15 days out from an election he was trailing by nearly 11 points.[38] "You turn on *CNN*, that's all they cover. 'COVID, COVID, Pandemic, COVID, COVID.' You know why? They're trying to talk everybody out of voting. People aren't buying it, *CNN*, you dumb bastards."

So Trump was just plain sick of the whole thing, ready to move on, if only *CNN* hadn't annoyingly kept reminding him that the virus was still out there. Earlier in the day on October 19, on a campaign conference call with reporters listening, Trump also asserted that Americans were simply bored of the pandemic and no longer wanted to engage in the burdensome process of protecting themselves from it.

"People are tired of COVID. I have these huge rallies. People are saying whatever. Just leave us alone," Trump claimed on the call. "They're tired of it."

He also claimed that people were "tired of hearing Fauci and all these idiots," referring to other scientists and public health experts.

At the same time, Trump repeatedly made glaringly false promises of a "cure," and that a vaccine would somehow emerge prior to the November 3 election. At one point in early October, he reportedly overruled the Food and Drug Administration on its rules for verifying the safety and efficacy of a potential vaccine.[39]

Shortly after he got out of the hospital following his own bout with COVID, he declared that "the vaccines are coming momentarily."[40]

"Momentarily."

The drug manufacturers themselves quickly shot down Trump's made-up campaign line. The major big pharma firm Johnson & Johnson had to shut down its own vaccine trial due to an "unexplained illness" suffered by one of its subjects.[41]

The Johnson & Johnson setback came a month after another drug-maker, AstraZeneca, shut down its own vaccine trial when not one but two test subjects came down with what were reported as serious neurological disorders shortly after being injected with the experimental COVID vaccine.[42]

Trump was unmoved by the stricter FDA safety protocols,[43] dismissing them as "a political move more than anything else," and in a tweet on October 6, "another political hit job!"[44]

When Trump went down with COVID, he was immediately administered a series of experimental drugs that would have been utterly inaccessible to anyone not the president, or at least a "VIP."[45] The drugs appeared to propel him to a speedy recovery, letting him get back out on the campaign trail within days.

On that same campaign trail, Trump shifted his rhetoric from promising a vaccine, to pledging a "cure" — just like the one he got. "We have — I call 'em cures. I don't call 'em therapeutics," he proclaimed, in his first interview after his release from the hospital, with Maria Bartiromo of *Fox Business News*.[46]

"Without a vaccine to tout, Trump was clearly in the market for another October surprise," wrote *Washington Post* columnist Philip

Bump.[47] "And with his coronavirus diagnosis last week, he stumbled onto one."

Despite Trump's own apparent quick comeback from COVID-19, no "cure" existed. Even the main therapeutic drug that Trump received — the experimental antibody "cocktail" known as Regeneron (which is actually the name of the company developing it) — was unavailable to the general public. The drugmaker said that it would have only 50,000 doses in the initial rollout, once it was approved for general use.[48] Hardly adequate at a time when the U.S. was slammed with an average of more than 60,000 new COVID cases detected every day.

In one of his post-hospital Twitter videos, Trump also claimed that "vaccines are coming momentarily."[49] It was a claim he had been making for some time.

Back on Labor Day, Trump claimed that a COVID-19 vaccine could be available "during the month of October," conveniently prior to the November 3 election.[50] Leaving no doubt about what his wishful thinking was aimed at, he also said that the non-existent vaccine could be distributed before "a very special date."[51]

"President Trump is getting this vaccine in record time," he said, disconcertingly referring to himself in the third person. "By the way, if this were the Obama administration, you wouldn't have that vaccine for three years, and you probably wouldn't have it at all."

Nor was the Labor Day press conference the first time Trump had made the phony claim about a vaccine arriving by November 3. One month earlier he told friendly interviewer Geraldo Rivera he was "optimistic" that the vaccine would be ready before election day[52] — but he claimed that while it "wouldn't hurt" his reelection chances, he was really just trying to "save lives."

Trump called the operation to produce a vaccine in record time, maybe even before his big day in November, "Operation Warp Speed." In October, however, one top pharmaceutical firm, Johnson & Johnson, had to put the brakes on the warp drive when one of its vaccine test subjects came down with an "unexplained illness."[53]

A few days later, the one company that had previously said it might actually have its version of a COVID vaccine finalized by November 3, Pfizer, announced that it would not ask the Food and Drug Administration for an "emergency use authorization,"[54] which would have been the only way to get the drug out to the public in time for voters to weigh in.

How would the hypothetical vaccine have reached millions of Americans quickly, maybe even before the election? As with so much in Trump's alternate reality, the answer was simple. The military would get the job done.

The U.S. military, Trump claimed, was "all mobilized" to distribute a vaccine to Americans.

"Logistically, we're using our military, our great military — a group of people, their whole life is around logistics and bringing things to and from locations — and they'll be able to take care of this locationally, and bringing it where it has to go very, very quickly," Trump said on July 28. "It's been fully set up. When we have that vaccine, it will be discharged and taken care of. It'll be a very rapid process."

But officials from the National Guard and U.S. Northern Command — which is responsible for defending the territorial United States[55] — told the McClatchy News Service in July that they had not even been "asked to plan or prepare for distribution."

From a president who early in the crisis stated his hope for the coronavirus to "wash over" the country, and who made good on his wish by embracing the dangerous quackery of "herd immunity," while claiming that his lies about the severity of the disease were well-intentioned efforts to prevent "panic," the torrent of lies about an incipient vaccine seemed particularly pathetic. Why would he make up such a transparently obvious tall tale?

The story may not have been complete fiction in Trump's brain. He made personal calls to drug company CEOs as the election approached, pushing them to step on the gas in their vaccine development.[56] Did Trump actually believe that millions of Americans would somehow be reassured by his empty "vaccine" claims, and reward him at the ballot box?

Maybe. There's no way to know precisely what was going on inside of his head. More likely, however, the blather about a vaccine, and a "cure," was part of Trump's own Russian-style "firehose of falsehoods."

"The confusion Trump's generating is on purpose — that's the strategy," wrote media critic Eric Boehlert.[57] "The goal is to create a nonstop loop of puzzlement to the point where it's not possible to understand what Trump's policy is for the defining public health crisis of our time."

Trump's propaganda "strategy" mirrored Vladimir Putin's almost exactly — a strategy "to confuse the public and to spread the idea that the truth is unknowable," journalist Luke Harden — a specialist in the Russia beat — said in describing the Putin plan. "It's a form of epistemological warfare."[58]

As we discussed in the previous chapters, Trump's nine phone calls with Putin during the pandemic were largely unexplained, and what the two discussed remained mysterious. But we do know that Trump, with the support of *Fox News* and other elements of the media, executed the Putin propaganda plan to perfection. If the goal was to short-circuit America's ability to respond rationally to the pandemic, and to Trump himself — mission accomplished.

CHAPTER TEN

. . . .

LYING IN STATE MEDIA

"Just stick with us, don't believe the crap you see from these people, the fake news. Just remember, what you're seeing and what you're reading is not what's happening."

— Donald Trump, July 24, 2018[1]

"To be effective, propaganda must constantly short-circuit all thought and decision. It must operate on the individual at the level of the unconscious. He must not know that he is being shaped by outside forces ... but some central core in him must be reached in order to release the mechanism in the unconscious which will provide the appropriate — and expected — action."

— Jacques Ellul
Propaganda: The Formation of Men's Attitudes (1962)

Election Day, November 3, 2020. The day that Donald Trump would finally square off against former Vice President Joe Biden in a battle to determine, among other rather important items, whether the United States would do anything to control the coronavirus pandemic. Anything at all.

As of that date, almost 240,000 Americans were dead from COVID-19.[2] That was approximately one of every 1,400 U.S. residents who were alive at the start of the pandemic, dead.

On Election Day itself, the country recorded 94,764 new coronavirus cases. At the time, that staggering number was a record, the single worst day of the pandemic in the U.S.A. The mark was broken the very next day, when the country topped 100,000 new cases for the first time — and climbed past the 120,000 level the day after that. In the first 10 days of November alone, the country recorded more than a million new cases — and another 1.76 million in the 10 days after that.

And yet, at least according to Election Day exit polls, only 17 percent of voters — fewer than one of every five — considered the pandemic the "issue that mattered most" in choosing whether to cast a ballot for Trump or Biden.[3]

If we date the start of the pandemic to the first reported case of SARS-Cov-2 infection in the United States,[4] January 20, not quite a full nine months had passed by the time voters went to the polls (even less for the 100 million or so who voted early, thanks to the pandemic). Economic misery went hand-in-hand with the mass death and suffering. Health measures that shut down businesses across the country caused an unprecedented, nearly Biblical economic calamity. More than 21 million Americans were receiving unemployment assistance.[5]

All of that, the direct result of the pandemic — and the near-total absence of any attempts to curtail it by the federal government, led by Donald Trump.

So how could a mere 17 percent say that the COVID-19 pandemic was not the most important issue facing voters — when by any objective standard, it was?

For that matter, how could thousands of people enthusiastically show up at Trump's campaign rallies? Many of these events were held in coronavirus hot zones, including 30 — 30! — in the nine days before the election. Trump's fans showed up mostly sans masks — the most effective and at the same time simplest tool against the virus.[6] They bunched together shoulder-to-shoulder, in direct contravention of the "social distancing" required to mitigate the viral contagion.

The results were predictable. One widely reported Stanford University study that focused on just 18 of Trump's late 2020 insane campaign rallies concluded that Trump alone was responsible for about 30,000 additional infections — and 700 deaths.[7]

As Trump toured his "superspreader" events around the country,[8] he repeatedly confirmed the thesis of this very book, stated way back in our introduction, all those words ago.

Namely — he was killing people on purpose.

The coronavirus pandemic was, quite literally, a biological warfare attack on the United States perpetrated by Donald Trump.

That Trump was somehow unaware of the destruction his campaign events were wreaking is simply not plausible. Why not? In state after state, Trump openly and brazenly defied local public health guidelines to hold the rallies,[9] guidelines of which he was well aware.[10] Prior to one indoor rally in Nevada, a reporter asked him directly about whether he believed his rallies were safe.

"I'm on a stage, and it's very far away," Trump replied.[11] But the question wasn't about him.

Nonetheless, he later proved he was fully cognizant of the fact that he was breaking safety rules. He promised his adoring fans, "If the governor comes after you, which he shouldn't be doing, I'll be with you all the way."[12]

His frenzied series of appearances were, at the time, the only mass gatherings taking place anywhere in the country. Rock concerts, Broadway shows, comic book conventions — every other type of event requiring large groups of hundreds or thousands all in one place were shut down.

Until he started inflicting his ego-assuaging rallies on the American people — starting with his own supporters — it was at least conceivably possible to dismiss Trump's horrific pandemic response as incompetence or mismanagement, a "failure." As if the millions of infections and hundreds of thousands of deaths were simply an accidental byproduct of Trump's stumbling, bumbling ineptitude.

But as he gleefully Air Force One-d from Pennsylvania to Michigan to Iowa to Florida and so on, it became more and more difficult to deny that Trump was deliberately spreading the virus. Or, as MSNBC host Chris Hayes put it, Trump proved himself to be "objectively pro-COVID."[13]

Beyond simply fulfilling Trump's mission to wipe out as many Americans as possible with the disease, his rallies were also part of a larger program, the program that made Trump's war against his own country possible in the first place — the propaganda campaign.

What were the aims of Trump's propaganda strategy? There were three main objectives, mostly successful.

- To "play down" the virus, convincing the population that the pandemic was either a hoax, or hugely exaggerated.

- To sideline safety measures, such as mask-wearing, in order to maximize deaths.

- To separate, in the public mind, the ideas of economic recovery and ending the pandemic.

Taken together, these objectives allowed Trump to get away with simply doing nothing as the virus devastated the country, causing mass casualties and economic calamity.

No less than the World Health Organization identified the "info-demic" as a significant cause of harm, a major factor in allowing the pandemic to spread.[14]

WHO defined the "infodemic" as "deliberate attempts to dissemi-nate wrong information to undermine the public health response and advance alternative agendas of groups or individuals."

The world's numero uno purveyor of that "wrong information" was none other than Donald Trump — according to a Cornell University study released in September.[15] In their survey of 38 million articles about the pandemic the researchers found that Trump's name came up 38 percent of the time.

"The biggest surprise was that the president of the United States was the single largest driver of misinformation around Covid," the study's lead author, Sarah Evanega, told *The New York Times*.[16] "That's concerning in that there are real-world dire health implications."

Dire indeed. By mid-November nine of the world's top 10 coronavirus "hotspots" were U.S. states[17] – and eight of them were "red" states, that is, states where a majority had voted for Trump.

Looking at Asian countries, where perhaps Trump's disinformation was not able to penetrate quite as comprehensively as in the West — as author Umair Haque did[18] — we see exactly how dire the consequences were. Adjusting for population, Taiwan would have suffered 18,000 deaths had it followed the Trumpian model. Instead, that country saw only seven deaths. Seven.

Vietnam suffered just 35 deaths, where it would have absorbed 73,000 under the American non-approach. South Korea saw 498 deaths from COVID-19. Taking the U.S. "strategy," it would have lost about 40,000. And so on.

Trump's propaganda campaign was a resounding success in its aim of persuading a dangerously large segment of the U.S. public that the pandemic was either not real, or no big deal. His goal was straightforward. If Americans could be gaslit into believing that the pandemic was either a hoax or at best, a wildly exaggerated threat, Trump wouldn't have to *do* anything. The American people themselves would beckon the deadly virus to "wash over" the country, causing thousands of deaths, untold suffering and economic deprivation.

That way, Trump could indeed fulfill his grandiose apocalyptic vision — in which he profiteers from the rubble of a ruined society — as well as pay his debt to Putin for aiding in his election, or whatever else he owes to the Russian strongman.

After all, even some of Trump's most ardent supporters agree that Putin intended to create chaos in the U.S. political system,[19] weakening it as much as possible — even as they fail to acknowledge that Putin's star agent of chaos was Trump himself.

The relentless propaganda assault had another purpose, one that might have worked if he hadn't telegraphed it so blatantly that even the media had plenty of time to prepare.

The purpose — win Trump the 2020 election.

The pandemic created, quite understandably, a general fear that standing in line at polling places, and entering voting booths, was quite dangerous. Hanging out in gathering places and prolonged proximity to other people were two of the easiest ways to spread the coronavirus.[20]

But if Trump could convince his own voters that COVID-19 was much ado about nonsense, they would be more likely to show up to vote on November 3, 2020 — while Democrats stayed home to avoid becoming deathly ill.

It worked, at least partly. In an election with a record 158 million (or more) votes cast,[21] about 101 million — almost two-thirds — cast ballots early.[22] Only 55 million, approximately, actually waited until November 3 to show up in person. The early votes were heavily Democratic, while Trump performed better on Election Day itself. The disparity created an illusion — or at least, Trump hoped that it did — in which he won the election but as the evening and week went on, millions of Biden ballots were mysteriously "found."

"We were getting ready for a big celebration, we were winning everything, and all of a sudden, it was just called off," Trump marveled in an election night appearance.[23] "We were getting ready to win this election. Frankly, we did win this election."

But he did not win the election. The propaganda campaign did not succeed in bringing home that prize for him. It did, however, succeed in accomplishing another goal important to Trump's chief patron.

"Putin is looking for innovative forms of disruption," wrote Russia expert Mark Galeotti.[24] "He encourages his agents and adhocrats to seize opportunities, fully aware that some, and maybe most, will fail. But that doesn't matter, because the very act of launching these attacks brings chaos and uncertainty, and when they do succeed, the judoka [i.e. Putin] can make his move."

Trump's biological warfare attack on the United States not only managed to kill hundreds of thousands of Americans, the information warfare element of the attack succeeded just as spectacularly. Through propaganda, Trump succeeded in exacerbating political and cultural division, grinding down public confidence in factual information, and sowing general anarchy among a large section of the U.S. population. The propaganda campaign followed the Russian "firehose of false-hoods" model identified by Rand Corporation researchers,[25] which we discussed in Chapter Eight.

"The primary objective is not to create a particular version of the truth but rather to cloud the truth and erode our ability to find it, cre-ating a sentiment that no narrative or news source can be trusted at all," another Russia expert, FBI official David Porter, said in late February, 2020, following a briefing to the House of Representatives.[26]

His remarks came a mere few weeks after the conclusion of Trump's first impeachment trial, and with the pandemic just beginning to en-croach into public consciousness.

Trump's propaganda program was perpetuated and amplified on an endless feedback loop by Fox News and other Trumpian media outlets.[27] Fox, beaming its own firehose of falsehoods to nearly 4 million people nightly,[28] was perhaps the most effective outlet for Trumpian propagan-da, all designed to drill home the theme that COVID-19 was nothing more than a vast conspiracy "to damage the Trump presidency."[29] An Annenberg Public Policy survey found that news consumers who re-lied mainly on Fox, Rush Limbaugh and other pro-Trump sources were likely to believe exactly that.

Another study, by Media Matters For America, watched Fox News for five straight days in early July, and found 253 cases of coronavirus falsehoods reported on the network, just in that short span.[30]

The largest slice of those reports, 115 of them, were flat-out lies about the scientific facts of the pandemic and how to prevent the disease, according to the MMFA study. Various Fox reports asserted that a rise in the coronavirus positivity rate (the percentage of people tested who return a positive result) was simply the result of more tests being conducted. Fox also repeatedly claimed that public health measures such as mask-wearing and social distancing were ineffective (they aren't), that the malaria drug hydroxychloroquine is an effective treatment for COVID-19 (no evidence for that), and that various public health experts were not to be trusted, for one reason or another.

Sometimes those attacks on qualified experts came from the network's favorite interview subject, Trump himself, who told host Sean Hannity on July 10 that Dr. Anthony Fauci had "made a lot of mistakes."

Even more often, they came from the network's own talking heads. Nighttime host Laura Ingraham was the worst offender in the MMFA study,[31] reeling off 63 falsehoods about the pandemic in that five-day period, or more than 12 per hour-long show.

Ingraham was not alone. Hannity also preached a cavalier approach to the pandemic on his own show. He repeatedly brushed off the deadly disease as a "common flu," and accused Democrats of "a shameful politicizing, weaponizing of, yes, the coronavirus."[32]

The idea that the pandemic was nothing but a "politicized" attempt to undermine Trump unified most of the Fox-perpetuated propaganda — though the network, at least early on, made a show of acting at least sort of responsibly. When Fox Business anchor Trish Regan in March characterized the pandemic as "yet another attempt to impeach the president," and an "impeachment scam," the network suspended her, and soon after that "parted ways" with the anchor.

Other Fox personalities, nonetheless, continued to press exactly the same claim, albeit in terms not quite as blunt.

The Fox propaganda did more than pollute the public debate, it appears to have actually killed people. A study published by the National Bureau of Economic Research showed that Fox viewers were statistically less likely to follow recommended public health procedures than people who get their information elsewhere — and that death rates tended to be higher in areas with higher Fox News viewership.[33]

But the "firehose of falsehoods" was only one element of this propaganda effort. As powerful as Fox News was, the ultimate megaphone was the behavior of Trump's own supporters and loyal chaos agents. By modeling the destructive behaviors described and urged by Trump, they created an environment where the taboo of flagrantly flouting sensible health measures was broken to the point of obliteration.

These Trump acolytes not only refused to wear masks to protect against the virus, they vociferously and sometimes violently railed against this simple, inexpensive yet highly effective safeguard against the disease.[34]

The weirdly resistant or, at best, nonchalant attitude toward mask-wearing flowed straight from Trump, who set a negative example by rarely donning a mask himself. When his own administration issued a national mask-wearing recommendation on April 3, Trump went out of his way to emphasize that he, personally, would not wear one.[35] At the same time, it's worth noting, most other major world leaders did don masks.[36]

He continued to dismiss or even ridicule mask-use, despite conclusive scientific findings that widespread use of facial coverings saved lives.[37] One study showed that universal masking in the United States could save about 130,000 lives between late October and February.[38]

But during an October 15 "town hall," Trump insanely claimed that "85 percent of the people who wear masks" actually contract the coronavirus.[39]

By mid-July, videos of unmasked people — presumably Trump supporters — putting on over-the-top public displays of petulance were regular features of social media. A woman at a Trader Joe's in Los Angeles was recorded shrieking at the grocery store's employees who asked her to either don a mask or leave.[40] In Brooklyn, New York, a woman in a bagel shop yelled and coughed on a fellow customer who reported her to an employee for not wearing a mask. A man at a Florida Walmart physically assaulted an employee there who asked him to put on a mask while inside the store. To cite just a few examples.

As childish as these viral video tantrums appeared to be, they did their part in creating an impression that there was some sort of debate taking place — an argument over whether mask-wearing was good and proper, and whether anti-maskers were suffering persecution of some sort.

The evidence that masks saved lives, for the wearer and others, was overwhelming.[41] But the sheer number of people visibly upset about them created the illusion that it was a two-sided question, that the "no mask" lunacy was somehow a legitimate point of view.

Mask-tantrum videos were just a small part of the propaganda campaign aimed at delegitimizing safety measures that could prevent COVID-19 deaths. The first visible signals of the carefully planned propaganda campaign came in April, just a single month into the pandemic, when a wave of "reopening protests" suddenly materialized in cities around the country.[42]

The "protesters" claimed to be ordinary middle-Americans, frustrated citizens desperate to resume their jobs, open their businesses or get much-desired haircuts, as they marched and agitated against state governors who had handed down business closure and "stay at home" orders. Those closures and other restrictions were tough. But as a CDC study showed, they were largely effective measures in stemming the contagion that threatened to kill citizens of their states, and overwhelm health care systems.[43]

Another study of "non-pharmaceutical interventions," led by researchers at Oxford University, showed that banning large gatherings (rock concerts, pro sports events with fans in attendance etc.) and closing "high-risk businesses" (restaurants, bars, and other indoor gathering establishments) was effective, and that closing schools and universities was "highly" effective is controlling the pandemic.[44]

In reality, the "reopening" protests were not grounded in reality. They were pure spectacle, organized and funded by pro-Trump right-wing political organizations.[45] And by outward appearances, they were coordinated with Trump himself, who was watching via Fox News.

On April 17, just two minutes after Fox News aired reports on "reopening" protests in Michigan, Virginia, and North Carolina, Trump jumped onto Twitter and called to "liberate" — or as he typed it, "LIBERATE" — those specific states.

As early as March 24,[46] just five days after the city of Los Angeles issued the continental United States' first "stay at home" order (the territory of Puerto Rico issued one on March 15),[47] Trump was already pushing to end the health-related restrictions by Easter, which was April 12.[48]

The earliest indication that Trump was executing a deliberate strategy of disinformation — though it wasn't revealed to the public until several months later — came in Trump's March 19 conversation with Bob Woodward. In that phone chat he flatly admitted, "I wanted to always play it down. I still like playing it down, because I don't want to create a panic."[49]

But Trump did more than just "play it down" to avoid creating a "panic." He deliberately passed dangerously incorrect information along to the American public, repeatedly likening the deadly disease caused by the novel coronavirus to a routine bout of the flu.[50]

In a February 7 interview with Woodward, Trump told the *All The President's Men* reporter that he knew the coronavirus to be "deadly stuff," and "more deadly than your, you know, your, even your strenuous flus."[51] He even told Woodward that the new disease was five times more deadly than the flu.

Less than three weeks later, Trump claimed from a White House podium that the disease was "a little bit like the flu. It's a little like the regular flu that we have flu shots for. And we'll essentially have a flu shot for this in a fairly quick manner."

Why? And why did he repeat this "flu" disinformation multiple times? Experts at Johns Hopkins University called that claim "not at all accurate."[52]

"Since December 2019," Johns Hopkins microbiologist Andrew

Pekosz wrote on October 20, 2020, "COVID-19 has killed more people in the U.S. than influenza has in the last five years."

Trump's estimate that COVID-19 was five times deadlier than the flu was pretty close to spot on. And yet, he relentlessly infected the media infospace with lethal propaganda. By October he was telling Americans to "learn to live with" the pandemic — just like we live with the flu.

"Flu season is coming up! Many people every year, sometimes over 100,000, and despite the Vaccine, die from the Flu," he tweeted on October 6.[53] "Are we going to close down our Country? No, we have learned to live with it, just like we are learning to live with Covid, in most populations far less lethal!!!"

(It should also be noted that the flu, at least since 2010, had not come close to killing 100,000 Americans in a single year.[54] And that by October 6, COVID-19 had already killed well over 200,000[55])

Not content merely to deceive the public, Trump also couldn't resist throwing in a little racism to spice things up, referring at one rally to the disease as "kung flu."[56]

The Trump/Fox News equating of COVID-19 with "the flu" ran into one particularly intransigent obstacle — the death count. If the coronavirus was basically harmless, why were hundreds of thousands of people dead? The number was significantly more than 325,000 by the time Christmas rolled around.[57] At its high point, on December 20, the U.S. seven-day rolling average topped 2,600 deaths per day.[58] That's one person dead every 33 seconds.

The propaganda campaign's answer to the thorny problem of mass casualties was as simple as it was obvious — deny the death totals. Denying reality had worked for everything else? Why not human mortality? As Trump told his fans, and as quoted in the epigraph to this chapter, "what you're seeing and what you're reading is not what's happening."

In August, Trump used his Twitter account to amplify yet another dark conspiracy fantasy.[59] (To call it a "theory" allows it too much dignity). He retweeted a post claiming that the CDC had "quietly" updated its website to "admit" that the actual number of coronavirus deaths was only six percent of the then-reported total, which was about 150,000 at the time.

This bizarre idea, that only about 9,000 had actually been killed by the pandemic, eight months into 2020, was widespread, with even Republican members of Congress publicly expressing "skepticism" over the official death counts.[60]

Needless to say, this grotesque fabrication originated with what *Scientific American* magazine charitably called a "gross misinterpretation" of how to read death certificates.[61] In a detailed debunking of the death-toll propaganda line, the venerable science mag noted that most death certificates list multiple conditions suffered by the deceased person that may have contributed to his or her demise. On six percent of certificates in a CDC survey, COVID-19 was the only listed condition. In the minds of the propagandists and conspiracy fantasists, that somehow meant that the other 94 percent did not die of COVID, but of some other cause.

"The idea that a death certificate with ailments listed in addition to COVID-19 means that the person did not really die from the virus is simply false," *Scientific American* wrote.[62]

Merely denying the true death totals was not enough for Trump, as it turned out. He wasn't happy until he had smeared the entire medical profession by imputing a sinister motive to the fictional under-counters.

In his October campaign rallies, he lied to his supporters, telling them that doctors were deliberately over-reporting COVID death figures — for cash.[63]

"If somebody's terminally ill with cancer, and they have COVID, we report them," he said in Waukesha, Wisconsin.[64] "And you know, doctors get more money and hospitals get more money. Think of this incentive. … If somebody has a really bad heart, and they're close to death, even if they're not, but they have a very bad heart and they get COVID, they put it down to COVID."

His new lie was a dark echo of a fiction he brewed up in March, at a time when his administration was rightly under fire for failing to prove adequate protective equipment, such as masks, for health care workers.

"That statement was made that they've been delivering for years, 10 to 20,000 masks," Trump said at a press conference.[65] "Okay, it's a New York hospital. Very — it's packed all the time. How do you go from 10 to 20, to 300,000? 10 to 20,000 masks to 300,000?"

The real answer was simple. Masks were in great demand and his government was doing nothing to produce more of them.

"Something's going on, and you oughta look into it," Trump said.[66] "Where are the masks going? Are they going out the back door?"

The mask itself became perhaps the leading avatar of Trumpian propaganda, both his own cavalier attitude toward wearing one, and perhaps more important, his frequent needling of those who did wear a mask. In private White House meetings Trump commanded underlings who dared to don the protective face covering, to "get that thing off!" And according to former coronavirus task force member Olivia Troye, inside the White House, "you were looked down upon when you would walk by with a mask."[67]

He mocked reporters at press briefings for wearing masks, and at one late-October rally in Michigan, he even took a potshot at Trump-loyalist Fox News host Laura Ingraham for taking this basic safety precaution.

"I can't recognize you. Is that a mask? No way, are you wearing a mask?" Trump jibed.[68] "I've never seen her in a mask. Look at you. Laura, she's being very politically correct. Whoa!"

Perhaps the crowning moment of Trump's propaganda campaign came when he, himself, contracted COVID-19. As we recounted in Chapter Nine, he made a relatively speedy recovery largely thanks to a battery of experimental drugs that would not be available to any ordinary American suffering from the disease.

Upon returning to the White House from Walter Reed hospital, Trump theatrically ascended the staircase to the South Portico entrance, stood on the balcony, dramatically turning to face outward toward exactly no one — except TV cameras — and stripped away his mask. He then turned and entered the White House maskless, with an active case of coronavirus infection.[69]

That was October 6. A week later he was back on the road holding his potentially deadly campaign rallies and using his own case of COVID as a propaganda talking point — claiming that he was now immune to the virus, a claim widely disputed by scientists and evidence.[70] He was so sure he was immune that he was willing to become physically intimate with members of his audience, he told them.

"I feel powerful," he exclaimed at a Florida rally.[71] "I'll kiss the guys and the beautiful women and everybody."

Trump's propaganda campaign, echoed and amplified by Fox News and other pro-Trump media, was designed to cause as many deaths as possible. The evidence of that outcome, as we've enumerated above, was too plain and well-documented for Trump (and the Fox personalities) to make the claim that they were simply oblivious. They had to know what they were doing, and they purposefully, deliberately kept it up to the very end.

The propaganda campaign was an important weapon in the biological warfare Trump waged on the U.S. throughout his final full year in office. Actually, "important" doesn't quite cover it. The propaganda was indistinguishable from the attack itself. The propaganda cleared the way for the virus to "wash over" the country, by causing too many Americans to ignore their own health, to be contemptuous of their own safety, and hostile toward the safety of others.

The propaganda needed its own push, however, and that came from the economic deprivation that was the immediate fallout from the pandemic.[72]

Americans out of work due to health-related shutdowns were understandably eager to return to their jobs, especially after the federal economic assistance package, known as CARES, expired at the end of July, months before the pandemic hit its peak. Trump's propaganda campaign succeeded in splitting the pandemic from the economy, creating the impression that workers could and should, simply ignore the virus and get back to their jobs.

Many would die as a result — something Trump openly acknowledged.

"It's possible there will be some [death] because you won't be locked into an apartment or a house or whatever it is," he said in May. "I'm viewing our great citizens of this country to a certain extent and to a large extent as warriors. They're warriors. We can't keep our country closed. We have to open our country."

Did Americans voluntarily enlist to be "warriors," inevitably succumbing to Trump's own attack? Maybe a few did. The Trumpian lieutenant governor of Texas, Dan Patrick, publicly announced that he was willing to die of the virus to get the economy humming again.

"There are more important things than living and that's saving this country," Patrick said.[73]

Meanwhile, back in the world of sanity, "saving the country" meant conquering the pandemic. As business journalist James Surowiecki demonstrated, the main problem with the economy wasn't business closures.[74] By the autumn months, most businesses had reopened at least partially anyway. The problem was "demand shock."

"What makes this demand shock exceptional is that the U.S. still has 40,000 to 50,000 new Covid-19 cases and 600 to 700 deaths every day," Surowiecki wrote.

"As a result lots of Americans are still leery of doing normal, not particularly indulgent things like eating out, going to the gym, or going to the movies."

That was in October. Less than two months later, cases were averaging more than 160,000 per day, with deaths easily exceeding 1,000 per day, even reaching above 2,000 on some days — and topping 3,000 for five separate days in December.[75]

As it turned out, even a powerful propaganda effort — which largely succeeded in allowing the deadly virus to sweep away American lives — was not enough. By the first of December, 10 states had lost one of every 1,000 residents to death by pandemic.

Despite the propaganda and seeming insanity of many Americans, most were not willing to sign up as "warriors," destined to die for the cause of Donald J. Trump.

Conclusion

"We're rounding the turn. You know, all they want to talk about is COVID. By the way, on November 4, you won't be hearing so much about it. 'COVID COVID COVID COVID.'"

— Donald Trump
October 26, 2020[1]

"The single biggest threat to man's continued dominance on the planet is the virus."

— Joshua Lederberg
1958 Nobel Laureate in Medicine[2]

In the 1995 Hollywood thriller *Outbreak,* which opens with that same Joshua Lederberg epigraph, a group of heroic scientists led by Dustin Hoffman race to contain a deadly epidemic afflicting a single California town — before the virus gets loose and sweeps through the country.

The theme of the movie, the question asked by the filmmakers, was this: How far is the United States government willing to go — what are our leaders willing to do — to stop a catastrophic pandemic?

In 2020, a quarter-century after that potboiler hit mall multiplexes, we found out exactly what the U.S. government is willing to do.

Nothing.

At least, that was the reality under the government led by one Donald J. Trump.

Given the urgent need to create a national diagnostic testing system, Trump did nothing.

A nationwide contact tracing system? None.

A national program of non-pharmaceutical mitigation measures to contain the viral spread? The best Trump could do was a postcard with his name on it, offering some general "guidelines" such as, maintaining "good hygiene" and staying home from work if you feel sick.[3]

(That postcard, incidentally, cost the U.S. Postal Service $28 million to print and deliver.[4])

While it was befuddling that Trump's policy of letting the Sars-COV-2 virus rake its scythe of death across the country somehow resulted in more than 74 million Americans voting in the 2020 election to let him keep going, seven million more than that voted for his opponent, Joe Biden.[5] So it seems reasonable to conclude that Trump's infliction of the havoc-wreaking disease on his own people played at least some role in his definitive rejection at the ballot box.

So we have to return to the question with which we began this book. Why?

Why did Trump seemingly make no effort to win the 2020 presidential election? Surely, taking — or even appearing to take — some sort of decisive action to protect Americans from the pandemic would have secured him some voters. Pushing for increased economic relief would certainly have been a help to his reelection effort also.

A study by the Peterson Institute for International Economics released in March, 2021, appeared to confirm just how badly Trump blew the election with his deadly COVID-19 "strategy.[6] If Trump had taken steps that made the pandemic a mere 30 percent less severe — taking into account both the health and economic impacts — he would have scored an Electoral College victory over Biden of 289-249. If only...

Why didn't he do it?

The answer goes back to my central premise. Trump inflicted this damage to the country, and the wave of mass death and suffering, deliberately. His assignment upon assuming the presidency was not to serve the country, but to destroy it from within.

As I detailed in our introduction, Trump committed too many plainly deliberate acts of destruction to get the benefit of the doubt on his pandemic response. As if those examples cited in my intro weren't enough, following his decisive electoral defeat to Biden, Trump embarked on yet another deliberate attempt to turn the country inside-out. He attempted to overturn the results of the election, refusing to concede despite the clarity of his loss. He tried to stage a coup — to overthrow the United States government and install himself as an unelected dictator.[7]

The great uncovered story of the Trump era — not only uncovered but adamantly resisted — was that America willingly, even gleefully, elevated a deranged psychopath to the presidency and kept him there for four interminable years. But just because Trump was a deeply and dangerously disturbed human being did not mean that his actions did not emanate from coherent, if darkly twisted motivations.[8]

I selected the phrases used in the subtitle of this book for a specific reason. Trump, as I believe the evidence in the preceding pages has demonstrated, does indeed harbor a deep-seated "apocalyptic vision." He embraces chaos and destruction because he believes they benefit him.

He also owes "a debt to Putin," first of all for helping him get elected in 2016, as has been extensively documented in several government reports — including the Mueller Report and the Senate Intelligence Committee Report on Russian interference in that year's election[9] — as well as numerous journalistic books and articles.

What are his other debts to Vladimir Putin? That remains a matter of speculation, better left for other works on the Trump era. But as we examined in Chapter Seven, Trump's infatuation with Putin goes back more than a decade, so perhaps his "debt" is as much as emotional one as it is political or financial. Putin bestowed upon him the approval from a powerful, autocratic figure — not dissimilar to Trump's own father — that Trump apparently craves.

Finally, the pandemic was an act of "biological warfare" committed by Trump against his own country, his own people — for all of the reasons explained in the previous chapters of this book.

I chose those rather blunt terms because I wanted to counter the incessant normalization of this pathologically destructive person in the press, and by other politicians, and to a large extent, the public. With terms like "biological warfare," I wanted to underscore — with a black Sharpie! — exactly how malignant and sadistic the Trump presidency has been.

Trump made very little attempt to hide his extraordinary callousness and indifference to the vast scale of human suffering he caused. The six-figure death toll "is what it is," he shrugged, telling Americans they needed to "learn to live with it."

A couple of months into his post-presidency, Trump again admitted his consciousness of the fact that his actions during the pandemic were the opposite of what they should have been. In a *Fox News* interview, he admitted — or perhaps boasted — that when to came to Anthony Fauci, the government's top infectious disease expert, "I didn't really listen to him too much because I was doing the opposite of what he was saying."[10]

His chief of staff, Mark Meadows, got in on the act, blithely revealing in October that "we are not going to control the pandemic."[11]

Meadows went on to claim that the Trump administration would "control the fact that we get vaccines, therapeutics and other mitigation areas." But predictably, once vaccines were approved and available in December, the Trump forces displayed yet more hostility to the American people.

Despite a stated goal of vaccinating 20 million by the end of 2020, only about 10 percent that many had actually received the shot by the time New Year's Eve rolled around.[12] Trump as usual sloughed off any responsibility.

"The Federal Government has distributed the vaccines to the states. Now it is up to the states to administer," he wrote on his Twitter account.[13] "Get moving!"

This was after promising the American people that "the full power and strength of the military" would be brought to bear in getting vaccines to the public.[14] "It's called logistics," Trump bragged in September.

The stated goal of "Operation Warp Speed," the Trump administration plan to spur private companies to develop COVID vaccines, was to have 300 million doses manufactured and distributed by the start of 2021.[15] But the administration in November turned down an offer to acquire 200 million doses, beyond the 100 million it initially agreed to buy.[16] And then, when time came to distribute the vaccines that it actually had purchased, Trump had no discernable plan to do so, beyond, "let the states handle it."[17]

And lest we again entertain the objection that this neglect was simple incompetence on Trump's part, "top Trump officials actively lobbied Congress to deny state governments any extra funding for the Covid-19 vaccine rollout last fall — despite frantic warnings from state officials that they didn't have the money they needed to ramp up a massive vaccination operation," according to a January, 2021, report by the health site *STAT News*.[18] Not only did Trump dump the responsibility for getting vaccines into arms onto underequipped state governments, he fought to deny them the resources to do it.

Okay — let's assume you've read the whole book up this point, and I've actually convinced you that Donald J. Trump purposefully committed a large-scale, horrifying atrocity against the United States. Congratulations. You are alarmed, and probably a little depressed.

So what do we do about it?

"What exactly to do about Trump, Bill Barr, Mike Pompeo, and their epic corruption will be a defining question of the Joe Biden presidency," wrote Alexander Sammon of *The American Prospect*,[19] about three weeks after Biden decisively defeated Trump in the 2020 election.

I can't answer all of the questions about the administration's "epic corruption." At least not in this forum. But after living in the hellscape of Trump's biological attack on America for the duration of my researching and writing this book, I feel qualified to say that he should, and must, be held to account for the death and devastation he caused.

To do that, to bring a criminal action against him — which I believe is not only justifiable but necessary — his intent needs to be clearly established. My whole argument in this book is that his intent was clear from the start, and only became more clear as the pandemic dragged on. But the open-source evidence compiled in these pages can be only a starting point.

South Carolina congressional rep Jim Clyburn's idea would be the next step — a "9/11-like commission" that would fully, and in non-partisan fashion (if that's even possible anymore), gather all the facts,[20] including those facts that are now classified, sitting on secret servers, or even deep inside Trump's head.

My expectation is that those facts would prove, even more definitively, what I've argued in this volume — that Trump had intent to inflict harm, even massive harm, by allowing the deadly virus to ravage, or "wash over" the country.

And then, assuming the COVID Commission finds what I believe it will find after an investigation that I expect could take two or even three years, Trump needs to be prosecuted. I expect he would be convicted, and the penalty would be up to the legal authorities.

Making an example of Trump would not only serve justice and bring some small sense of rightness to the millions of Americans affected by his malfeasance, but perhaps more importantly, act as deterrent to stop future Trumps, who could otherwise include Trump himself, from committing similar atrocities.

On the day that I wrote this concluding piece of *Close To Zero*, America passed yet another macabre milestone - 350,000 deaths from COVID-19. That's more than one of every 1,000 Americans who were alive in February 2020 — dead from the coronavirus pandemic. It goes without saying that making Trump pay a price won't bring those people back to life.

But it may help, at least to some extent, to bring the country back to life. The lacerations of 2020 are going to take years to heal. If there's one lesson I take from the experience of assembling *Close To Zero*, it's that as a country, we cannot let them open up and bleed again.

On March 10, 2020, from his Florida post-election defeat convalescence, Trump — banned from Twitter — released a typically absurdist and rather pathetic "statement."[21]

"I hope everyone remembers when they're getting the COVID-19 (often referred to as the China Virus) Vaccine, that if I wasn't President, you wouldn't be getting that beautiful 'shot' for 5 years, at best, and probably wouldn't be getting it at all," he wrote. "I hope everyone remembers!"

Oh, everyone remembers all right.

. . . .

THE PANDEMIC PUTSCH

"You can either go down in history as a patriot, or you can go down in history as a pussy."

— *Donald Trump*
January 6, 2021[1]

Donald Trump committed an exhaustive litany of offenses and atrocities during his four years installed at the helm of the United States government's executive branch. The death toll of about 410,000 Americans in the coronavirus pandemic by the day he finally shuffled off the White House coil ranks as the worst and most appalling.

But just two weeks before his January 20 departure date, Trump committed yet another outrage, and while this one killed "only" five people, it was so far beyond the pale, even for him, that it allowed him to set a record — it got him impeached a second time.

Let's think about that for a moment. The House of Representatives — this time with 10 Republicans joining in — impeached Donald Trump with just one short week remaining in his term.[2] It seems almost incomprehensible that any Congress, especially one that already impeached him once, would take the effort to impeach any president who would be out of office anyway in seven days. Yet somehow, Trump managed to commit a "high crime" so utterly inexcusable, he cleared that extremely high bar.

What he did, of course, was to incite a riot that became an insurrection,[3] and in reality a coup attempt. Thousands of his ardent fans invaded the United States Capitol building as Congress was going through the formality of ratifying the 2020 Electoral College votes to officially, once and for all, make Trump's election opponent Joe Biden the next president.

I'm not going to go over the details of that grim affair here. I want only to note that the Capitol coup was quite literally a war against America waged by Trump. The coronavirus pandemic was his biological war against America. But while Congress and a majority of the public wasted little time holding Trump to account for his act of insurrection,[4] the American legal and governmental apparatus showed no sign — at least as of this writing in mid-January, 2021 — of inflicting any consequences on Trump for deliberately causing the worst death toll in any single year of American history[5] — or at least since the 1918-1919 flu pandemic.

The Capitol insurrection and the COVID pandemic are part of the same Trump program. The Trumpian Capitol siege would never have happened without the pandemic. His biological war and actual, paramilitary war are the same war.

As we covered in Chapter Five, throughout the 2020 presidential campaign, Trump did nothing that any candidate, even an incumbent, would normally do if he were actually trying to win the election. He never tried to expand his voter base, and did worse than nothing to solve the most acute and defining crisis of his presidency — the pandemic.

What he did do was rail and rant against the use of mail-in ballots.

Remote voting became a necessity when it was made clear that large numbers of people were not going to risk their health and lives at indoor polling places where they could easily catch the virus. But his own supporters, indoctrinated by his pro-COVID propaganda would be much more likely to vote in person, on election day.

The pandemic became integral to Trump's plan to seize power and hold it — to take the presidency without actually doing anything to win the election. If he could discredit and invalidate mail-in ballots, he would win by suppressing the votes of Americans correctly wary of the out-of-control coronavirus.

Failing to suppress as many as necessary, Trump planned to declare mail-in ballots illegal, a theme that became the centerpiece of his campaign.[6] That way, as mail-in ballots and other early votes were counted, in almost all cases after the election night tally of same-day voting was wrapped up, Trump would declare himself the winner, in effect dismissing all votes except those for himself as illegal.

Trump planned this scam well in advance,[7] even acting out a "victory speech" three weeks in before election night, a speech in which he plotted to declare himself the winner of the election, even if he was losing.

And that is exactly what he did, in an election-night diatribe that *CNN* called "the most dishonest speech of his presidency."[8]

Even that horrifying speech wasn't horrifying enough to get him impeached, however.

Trump challenged the election results in court, losing dozens of times without a win. He tried to threaten and extort the secretary of state of Georgia into "finding" enough votes to give him a victory there, two months after he lost that state and the presidency.[9]

Trump refused to abandon his "big lie" about the election[10] — a lie that would not have been possible without his biological attack on America to set it up. On January 6, after summoning a few thousand of his most devoted followers to Washington, D.C., Trump delivered a rambling, two-hour diatribe in which he told them that Biden (who won the election by 7 million votes, 4.4 percentage points, and 74 Electoral College votes[11]) would be an "illegitimate president"[12] and exhorted them to march to the Capitol building and "fight like hell."[13]

"If you don't fight like hell you're not going to have a country anymore," he told them, among other insane exhortations and amped-up versions of the same old lies about his election "landslide" win.

His biological attack on America made his big lie possible. It appears he really believed it would work — that he would be able to ride the lie to a second term. After he was defeated over and over again in court, in recounts, and state legislatures — pathetically refusing to take his loss like a grown-up — he went to his last resort. He attempted a violent takeover of the United States Congress.

Donald Trump's Pandemic Putsch failed.

He succeeded in undermining American democracy at turn after turn throughout his four years. He succeeded at crippling the country physically and economically. He could not, however, achieve the ultimate goal that he must have set for himself, the goal that his patron Vladimir Putin had already achieved — installing himself as president for life.

There is nothing good to say about the absolute and epic disaster that was the Trump era. Except perhaps that, despite his best and most horrifying efforts — it's over.

For at least that one small blessing, we can be thankful.

ACKNOWLEDGEMENTS

Researching and writing a book about an ongoing crisis in real time is a bit of a head-spinning task. The entire four years of Donald Trump's presidency was a time-warping experience, with new outrages, horrors, and absurdities dropping from the sky on a daily, even hourly basis, causing a sort of vertigo in which time appears to accelerate and elongate simultaneously.

Once the coronavirus pandemic hit, the disorientation only got worse. Keeping up with the relentless madness while attempting simultaneously to assemble it all into some sort of coherent narrative was possible only with the work of the dedicated reporters whose work I cite throughout CLOSE TO ZERO.

I don't know any of them personally, and I'm rather critical of the media in general in this book for missing the overall story of Trump's deliberate malfeasance — what I call his biological warfare attack on America. But that does not in any way detract from their extraordinary, fearless work in covering and uncovering the facts about what Trump did, and the terrible consequences of his actions.

For that reason, my deepest gratitude goes out to all of those reporters. Without them, this book would not exist.

An extremely special thanks to my longtime pal and oft-time collaborator John Whalen who designed and created the book's cover, and in my eyes could not have produced more striking work.

Another great friend and editor, Sharan Street, did me the honor of editing the text of CLOSE TO ZERO. My utmost thanks to Sharan for taking that bullet. And deep thanks as well to my best pal from a very early age, Daniel Reichert, who took on the estimable task of taking my author photos, and pulled it off beautifully.

My literary agent, Jennifer Unter, has been there for me on this project and others for many years, for which I can't thank her enough. Thanks also go to Ina Tuamola who commendably assembled the copious, all-important endnotes to the book, as well as to Noemi Jakab for her stellar work formatting the manuscript for final publication.

Thanks as always to my mom, Jean F. Vankin, still rocking at 90, who powered her way through the pandemic and even spent some weekends delivering meals on wheels to people who were probably 10 or 15 years younger than she is.

And last but most, to my amazing and beautiful wife Kirsten Holly Smith, who remained cooped up with me throughout the whole period of pandemic isolation and managed not to go totally crazy. My unlimited love and gratitude to her. For everything.

About the Author

Photo by Daniel Reichert

JONATHAN VANKIN is a journalist, author and screenwriter whose work has received numerous awards and honors, while his books have been translated into over 20 languages.

Vankin's first book, *Conspiracies, Cover-Ups and Crimes*, was the first comprehensive, journalistic investigation of America's conspiracy-theory underground, foreshadowing the current state of sociopolitical affairs by two decades. That book and its follow-up, the *Greatest Conspiracies* series co-authored with John Whalen, went on to become the most influential books on the subject and led to Vankin's numerous media appearances on such networks as CNN, MSNBC, CNBC, FOX, the BBC and the CBC as well as hundreds of radio stations.

ALSO BY JONATHAN VANKIN

Conspiracies, Cover-Ups and Crimes: From Dallas to Waco (Paragon House/Dell/IllumiNet Press)

The 50/60/70/80 Greatest Conspiracies of all Time (Citadel Press – co-author with John Whalen)

Based on a True Story (But With More Car Crashes): Fact and Fantasy in 100 Favorite Movies (Chicago Review Press – co-author with John Whalen)

Graphic Novels / Comics

Tokyo Days, Bangkok Nights (DC/Vertigo)

The Big Book of Scandal (DC/Paradox Press)

The Big Book of the '70s (DC/Paradox Press)

The Big Book of Grimm (DC/Paradox Press)

Tasty Bullet (Image – with Arnold Pander)

The Witching (DC/Vertigo)

Theater

Forever Dusty: The Dusty Springfield Musical (book, with Kirsten Holly Smith)

ENDNOTES

Introduction

[1] Liptak, Kevin. "Trump's latest call with Putin raises more questions than it answers." *CNN.com*. December 30, 2019. https://www.cnn.com/2019/12/30/politics/trump-call-putin-readout-terror-attack/index.html

[2] Taylor, Adam. "Trump has spoken privately with Putin at least 16 times. Here's what we know about the conversations." *The Washington Post*. October 4, 2019. https://www.washingtonpost.com/world/2019/10/04/trump-has-spoken-privately-with-putin-least-times-heres-what-we-know-about-conversations/

[3] Trump Golf Count. https://trumpgolfcount.com

[4] Ma, Josephine. "Coronavirus: China's first confirmed Covid-19 case traced back to November 17." *South China Morning Post*. March 13, 2020. https://www.scmp.com/news/china/society/article/3074991/coronavirus-chinas-first-confirmed-covid-19-case-traced-back

[5] Yong, Ed. "Why the Coronavirus Is So Confusing." *Atlantic*. April 29, 2020. https://www.theatlantic.com/health/archive/2020/04/pandemic-confusing-uncertainty/610819/

[6] Worldometer. https://www.worldometers.info/coronavirus/country/us/

[7] Philips, Matt, Horowitz, Jason and Choe, Sang-Hun. "U.S. Stocks Plunge as Coronavirus Crisis Spreads." *New York Times*. February 24, 2020. https://www.nytimes.com/2020/02/24/business/stock-market-coronavirus.html

[8] Tappe, Anneken. "30 million Americans have filed initial unemployment claims since mid-March." *CNN.com*. April 30, 2020. https://www.cnn.com/2020/04/30/economy/unemployment-benefits-coronavirus/index.html

[9] "Gross Domestic Product, 2nd Quarter 2020 (Advance Estimate) and Annual Update." Bureau of Economic Analysis. July 30, 2020. https://www.bea.gov/news/2020/gross-domestic-product-2nd-quarter-2020-advance-estimate-and-annual-update

[10] Cox, Jeff. "Second-quarter GDP plunged by worst-ever 32.9% amid virus-induced shutdown." *CNBC.com*. July 30, 2020. https://www.cnbc.com/2020/07/30/us-gdp-q2-2020-first-reading.html

[11] Johns Hopkins University. *Global Health Security Index*. Johns Hopkins University Bloomberg School of Public Health. October, 2019. https://www.ghsindex.org/wp-content/uploads/2019/10/2019-Global-Health-Security-Index.pdf

[12] Wilson, Christopher. "Coronavirus infections appear to spike in U.S. even as they decline elsewhere." *Yahoo! News*. June 10, 2020. https://news.yahoo.com/covid-case-spike-united-states-texas-arizona-north-carolina-coronavirus-201958682.html

[13] Gangel, Jamie, Herb, Jeremy and Stuart, Elizabeth. "'Play it down': Trump admits to concealing the true threat of coronavirus in new Woodward book." *CNN.com*. September 10, 2020. https://edition.cnn.com/2020/09/09/politics/bob-woodward-rage-book-trump-coronavirus/index.html

[14] Costa, Robert and Rucker, Philip. "Woodward book: Trump says he knew coronavirus was 'deadly' and worse than the flu while intentionally misleading Americans." *The Washington Post*. September 9, 2020. https://www.washingtonpost.com/politics/bob-woodward-rage-book-trump/2020/09/09/0368fe3c-efd2-11ea-b4bc-3a2098fc73d4_story.html

[15] Cohen, Michael. *Disloyal: A Memoir: The True Story of the Former Personal Attorney to President Donald J. Trump* (p. 158). Skyhorse. Kindle Edition.

[16] Singer, Emily. "Trump Always Seeks Calm! (Except These 22 Times When He Stoked Baseless Fear)." *National Memo*. September 11, 2020. https://www.nationalmemo.com/trump-always-seeks-calm-except-these-22-times-when-he-stoked-baseless-fear

[17] Kamisar, Ben. "RNC chairwoman says history will vindicate Trump's coronavirus handling." *NBCNews.com*. September 13, 2020. https://www.nbcnews.com/politics/meet-the-press/rnc-chairwoman-says-history-will-vindicate-trump-s-coronavirus-handling-n1239977

[18] Murphy, Chris. *Twitter*. August 29, 2020. https://twitter.com/ChrisMurphyCT/status/1299701890322706432

[19] Reston, Maeve. "Birx shares her chilling conclusion as America arrives at a moment of introspection on the coronavirus." *CNN.com*. March 27, 2021. https://www.cnn.com/2021/03/27/politics/covid-war-deaths-preventable/index.html

[20] Parker, Ashley, Abutaleb, Yasmeen and Dawsey, Josh. "Trump administration has many task forces — but still no plan for beating covid-19." *The Washington Post*. April 11, 2020. https://www.washingtonpost.com/politics/trump-task-forces-coronavirus-pandemic/2020/04/11/5cc5a30c-7a77-11ea-a130-df573469f094_story.html

[21] Ibid.

[22] Eban, Katherine. "How Jared Kushner's Secret Testing Plan 'Went Poof Into Thin Air.'" *Vanity Fair*. July 30, 2020. https://www.vanityfair.com/news/2020/07/how-jared-kushners-secret-testing-plan-went-poof-into-thin-air

[23] Bump, Philip. "Trump blames blue states for the coronavirus death toll — but most recent deaths have been in red states." *The Washington Post*. September 16, 2020. https://www.washingtonpost.com/politics/2020/09/16/trump-blames-blue-states-coronavirus-death-toll-but-most-recent-deaths-have-been-red-states/

[24] Abutaleb, Yasmeen and Dawsey, Josh. "New Trump pandemic adviser pushes controversial 'herd immunity' strategy, worrying public health officials." *The Washington Post*. August 31, 2020. https://www.washingtonpost.com/politics/trump-coronavirus-scott-atlas-herd-immunity/2020/08/30/925e68fe-e93b-11ea-970a-64c73a1c2392_story.html?utm_campaign=wp_main

[25] Zhang, Sharon. "Trump's New COVID Adviser Is Pushing Herd Immunity, Which Some Liken to Eugenics." *Truthout.org*. August 31, 2020. https://truthout.org/articles/trumps-new-covid-adviser-is-pushing-herd-immunity-which-some-liken-to-eugenics/

[26] Diamond, Dan. "'We want them infected': Trump appointee demanded 'herd immunity' strategy, emails reveal." *Politico*. December 16, 2020. https://www.politico.com/news/2020/12/16/trump-appointee-demanded-herd-immunity-strategy-446408

[27] "Donald Trump Laura Ingraham Interview Transcript August 31: Says People 'in the Dark Shadows' Controlling Biden." *Rev.com*. September 1, 2020. https://www.rev.com/blog/transcripts/donald-trump-laura-ingraham-interview-transcript-august-31-says-people-in-the-dark-shadows-controlling-biden

[28] Diamond, Jeremy and Liptak, Kevin. "Internal tensions and a resignation to virus' spread govern President Trump's pandemic response." *CNN.com*. September 1, 2020. https://www.cnn.com/2020/09/01/politics/white-house-coronavirus-response-atlas-fauci/index.html

[29] Rupar, Aaron. "Trump's ABC town hall revealed a president disconnected from reality." *Vox.com*. September 16, 2020. https://www.vox.com/2020/9/16/21439460/trump-abc-town-hall-stephanopoulos

[30] "Remarks by President Trump, Vice President Pence, and Members of the Coronavirus Task Force in Press Conference." White House Archives. February 27, 2020. https://trumpwhitehouse.archives.gov/briefings-statements/remarks-president-trump-vice-president-pence-members-coronavirus-task-force-press-conference/

[31] Costa and Rucker. "Woodward book: Trump says he knew coronavirus was 'deadly' and worse than the flu while intentionally misleading Americans."

[32] Lockwood, Devi. "What a Trump Rally Looks Like From the Inside." *New York Times*. February 10, 2020. https://www.nytimes.com/2020/02/10/opinion/trump-rally-new-hampshire.html

[33] Grenoble, Ryan. "Trump Knew COVID-19 Was Airborne And 'Deadly,' Held Crowded Rallies Anyway." *HuffPost*. September 10, 2020. https://www.huffpost.com/entry/trump-covid-coronavirus-rallies-deadly_n_5f5a4c29c5b6b48507fd3302

[34] Benen, Steve. "Newly released audio shows COVID message Trump didn't share with US." *MSNBC.com*. September 15, 2020. https://www.msnbc.com/rachel-maddow-show/newly-released-audio-shows-covid-message-trump-didn-t-share-n1240122

[35] Trump, Donald. *Twitter*. April 10, 2020. https://www.thetrumparchive. com/?searchbox=%22The+Invisible+Enemy+will+soon+be+in+full+retreat%22

[36] Rupar, Aaron. "New Woodward audio is the starkest illustration yet of how Trump misled about coronavirus." *Vox.com*. September 15, 2020. https://www.vox. com/2020/9/15/21437802/trump-woodward-audio-coronavirus-killer

[37] Garrett, Laurie. "Trump Is Guilty of Pandemicide." *Foreign Policy*. February 18, 2021. https://foreignpolicy.com/2021/02/18/trump-is-guilty-of-pandemicide/

[38] Worldometer. https://www.worldometers.info/coronavirus/country/us/

[39] Boehlert, Eric. "Memo to media: We still don't know why Trump is doing this." *Press Run*. April 8, 2020. https://pressrun.media/p/we-still-dont-know-why-trump-is-doing

[40] Ibid.

[41] Beutler, Brian. "The Donald Trump Incompetence Dodge." *Crooked Media*. May 21, 2020. https://crooked.com/articles/trump-incompetence-dodge/

[42] Baker, Peter. "In Commuting Stone's Sentence, Trump Goes Where Nixon Would Not." *New York Times*. July 11, 2020. https://www.nytimes.com/2020/07/11/us/ politics/trump-roger-stone-nixon.html

[43] "National Guard officer says police suddenly moved on Lafayette Square protesters, used 'excessive force' before Trump visit." *The Washington Post*. July 27, 2020. https://www.washingtonpost.com/nation/2020/07/27/national-guard-commander-says-police-suddenly-moved-lafayette-square-protesters-used-excessive-force-clear-path-trump/

[44] Conway, George. "Blaming Trump's virus failures on impeachment is gaslighting of the highest order." *The Washington Post*. March 31, 2020. https://www. washingtonpost.com/opinions/2020/03/31/impeachment-didnt-distract-coronavirus-preparations-trump-did/

[45] Lipton, Eric et al. "Despite Timely Alerts, Trump Was Slow To Act." *New York Times*. April 12, 2020. https://static01.nyt.com/images/2020/04/12/nytfrontpage/ scan.pdf

[46] Lemire, Jonathan et al. "Signs missed and steps slowed in Trump's pandemic response." *AP News*. April 12, 2020. https://apnews. com/6a8f85aad99607f313cca6ab1398e04d

[47] Keith, Tamara and Romo, Vanessa. "Trump's Gut Collides With Science On Coronavirus Messaging." *NPR.org*. March 5, 2020. https://www.npr. org/2020/03/05/812519679/trumps-gut-collides-with-science-on-coronavirus-messaging

[48] Lipton, Eric et al. "He Could Have Seen What Was Coming: Behind Trump's Failure on the Virus." *New York Times*. April 11, 2020 (updated October 2). https://www.nytimes.com/2020/04/11/us/politics/coronavirus-trump-response. html

[49] Da Silva, Chantal. "GOP Senators Fear Trump Use of 'Secret Police' Is Unconstitutional: Merkley." *Newsweek.* July 22, 2020. https://www.newsweek.com/gop-senators-fear-trump-use-secret-police-unconstitutional-merkley-1519623

[50] Savage, Charlie. "Painting Bleak Portrait of Urban Crime, Trump Sends More Agents to Chicago and Other Cities." *New York Times.* July 22, 2020 (updated July 30). https://www.nytimes.com/2020/07/22/us/politics/trump-federal-agents-cities.html

[51] Cooper, Ryan. "Why Trump's invasion of Portland is textbook fascism." *The Week.* July 28, 2020. https://theweek.com/articles/927661/why-trumps-invasion-portland-textbook-fascism

[52] Bogage, Jacob. "Trump says Postal Service needs money for mail-in voting, but he'll keep blocking funding." *The Washington Post.* August 12, 2020. https://www.washingtonpost.com/business/2020/08/12/postal-service-ballots-dejoy/

[53] Millheiser, Ian. "Trump admits he's stalling pandemic relief to make it harder to vote." *Vox.com.* August 13, 2020. https://www.vox.com/2020/8/13/21366319/trump-post-office-vote-by-mail-fox-sabotage-pandemic-covid-19-coronavirus

[54] Swan, Jonathan and Basu, Zachary. "Episode 1: A premeditated lie lit the fire." *Axios.com.* January 16, 2021. https://www.axios.com/trump-election-premeditated-lie-ebaf4a1f-46bf-4c37-ba0d-3ed5536ef537.html?utm_source=twitter

[55] Boot, Max. "The worst president. Ever." *The Washington Post.* April 5, 2020. https://www.washingtonpost.com/opinions/2020/04/05/worst-president-ever/

[56] Kaszeta, Dan. "No, the coronavirus is not a biological weapon." *The Washington Post.* April 27, 2020. https://www.washingtonpost.com/outlook/2020/04/26/no-coronavirus-is-not-biological-weapon/

[57] Saey, Tina Hesman. "No, the coronavirus wasn't made in a lab. A genetic analysis shows it's from nature." *Science News.* March 26, 2020. https://www.sciencenews.org/article/coronavirus-covid-19-not-human-made-lab-genetic-analysis-nature

[58] Lithwick, Dahlia. "We're Now Living the American Carnage Trump Promised Would End at His Inauguration." *Slate.com.* April 9, 2020. https://slate.com/news-and-politics/2020/04/trump-coronavirus-american-carnage.html

[59] Perez, Matt. "Trump On Healthcare Workers: 'They're Running Into Death Just Like Soldiers Run Into Bullets.'" *Forbes.* May 14, 2020. https://www.forbes.com/sites/mattperez/2020/05/14/trump-on-healthcare-workers-theyre-running-into-death-just-like-soldiers-run-into-bullets/#f6cb51c4a00c

[60] Jewett, Christina and Szabo, Liz. "Coronavirus is killing far more US health workers than official data suggests." *Guardian.* April 15, 2020. https://www.theguardian.com/us-news/2020/apr/15/coronavirus-us-health-care-worker-death-toll-higher-official-data-suggests

[61] DeVega, Chauncey. "Psychologist John Gartner: Trump is a 'sexual sadist' who

is 'actively engaging in sabotage.'" *Salon.* April 25, 2020. https://www.salon.com/2020/04/25/psychologist-john-gartner-trump-is-a-sexual-sadist-who-is-actively-engaging-in-sabotage/

62 Krugman, Paul. *Twitter.* January 1, 2021. https://twitter.com/paulkrugman/status/1345020807911714816?s=20

63 Miller, Greg and Nakashima, Ellen. "President's intelligence briefing book repeatedly cited virus threat." *The Washington Post.* April 27, 2020. https://www.washingtonpost.com/national-security/presidents-intelligence-briefing-book-repeatedly-cited-virus-threat/2020/04/27/ca66949a-8885-11ea-ac8a-fe9b8088e101_story.html

64 Trump later claimed via a May 3, 2020, post on his Twitter account that the intelligence briefers "did NOT bring up the CoronaVirus subject matter until late into January," and that "they only spoke of the Virus in a very non-threatening, or matter of fact, manner." Trump, Donald. *Twitter.* May 3, 2020. https://www.thetrumparchive.com/?searchbox=did+NOT+bring+up+the+CoronaVirus+subject+matter+until+late+into+January

65 Rascoe, Ayesha and Dwyer, Colin. "Trump Received Intelligence Briefings On Coronavirus Twice In January." *NPR.com.* May 2, 2020. https://www.npr.org/sections/coronavirus-live-updates/2020/05/02/849619486/trump-received-intelligence-briefings-on-coronavirus-twice-in-january

66 Eder, Steve et al. "430,000 People Have Traveled From China to U.S. Since Coronavirus Surfaced." *New York Times.* April 4, 2020 (updated April 15). https://www.nytimes.com/2020/04/04/us/coronavirus-china-travel-restrictions.html

67 Higgins-Dunn, Noah and Kimball, Spencer. "Trump backs off quarantine of New York region as CDC advises against nonessential travel." *CNBC.com.* March 29, 2020. https://www.cnbc.com/2020/03/28/trump-considering-quarantine-in-new-york-new-jersey-and-connecticut.html

68 Kanno-Youngs, Zolan and Nicas, Jack. "'Swept Up by FEMA': Complicated Medical Supply System Sows Confusion." *New York Times.* April 6, 2020. https://www.nytimes.com/2020/04/06/us/politics/coronavirus-fema-medical-supplies.html

69 Swan, Jonathan and Muller, Joann. "Inside the start of the great virus airlift." *Axios.com.* March 29, 2020. https://www.axios.com/coronavirus-airlift-masks-medical-supplies-1d1913bf-744e-41cf-895c-d8934afa2c36.html

70 "Coronavirus Disease 2019 (COVID-19) Situation Report 37." World Health Organization. https://www.who.int/docs/default-source/coronaviruse/situation-reports/20200226-sitrep-37-covid-19.pdf?sfvrsn=2146841e_2

71 "CDC Confirms Possible Instance of Community Spread of COVID-19 in U.S." Centers for Disease Control and Prevention. February 26, 2020. https://www.cdc.gov/media/releases/2020/s0226-Covid-19-spread.html

[72] "Remarks by President Trump, Vice President Pence, and Members of the Coronavirus Task Force in Press Conference."

[73] Lopez, German. "The Trump administration's botched coronavirus response, explained." *Vox.com*. April 2, 2020. https://www.vox.com/policy-and-politics/2020/3/14/21177509/coronavirus-trump-covid-19-pandemic-response

[74] Yong. "Why the Coronavirus Is So Confusing."

[75] Diamond, Dan. "Feuds, fibs and finger-pointing: Trump officials say coronavirus response was worse than known." *Washington Post*. March 29, 2021. https://www.washingtonpost.com/health/2021/03/29/trump-officials-tell-all-coronavirus-response/

[76] The COVID Tracking Project. https://covidtracking.com/data/us-daily

[77] Moran, Lee. "Epidemiologist Slams U.S. Coronavirus Response: 'Close To Genocide By Default.'" *Huffington Post*. May 6, 2020. https://www.huffingtonpost.co.uk/entry/epidemiologist-coronavirus-genocide-by-default_n_5eb2a5ebc5b63e6bd96f5d81?ri18n=true

[78] Boehlert. "Memo to media: We still don't know why Trump is doing this."

[79] Knutson, Jacob. "Obama rips Trump's coronavirus response as 'absolute chaotic disaster.'" *Axios.com*. May 10, 2020. https://www.axios.com/obama-trump-coronavirus-2f0f5386-9949-4b7c-8563-82c7d2463a8d.html

[80] Fandos, Nicholas and Barnes, Julian E. "Republican-Led Review Backs Intelligence Findings on Russian Interference." *New York Times*. April 22, 2020. https://www.nytimes.com/2020/04/21/us/politics/russian-interference-senate-intelligence-report.html

[81] Unger, Craig. *American Kompromat: How the KGB Cultivated Donald Trump, and Related Tales of Sex, Greed, Power, and Treachery*. Penguin Publishing Group, 2021. Kindle Edition.

[82] Gaouette, Nicole, Cohen, Marshall and Conte, Michael. "Putin leverages coronavirus chaos to make a direct play to Trump." *CNN.com*. April 18, 2020. https://www.cnn.com/2020/04/18/politics/trump-putin-unprecedented-contacts/index.html

[83] McFaul, Michael. *Twitter*. July 5, 2020. https://twitter.com/McFaul/status/1279818813882548230

[84] Taylor, Adam. "Trump has spoken privately with Putin at least 16 times. Here's what we know about the conversations." *The Washington Post*. October 4, 2019. https://www.washingtonpost.com/world/2019/10/04/trump-has-spoken-privately-with-putin-least-times-heres-what-we-know-about-conversations/

[85] Savage, Charlie, Schmitt, Eric and Schwirtz, Michael. "Russia Secretly Offered Afghan Militants Bounties to Kill U.S. Troops, Intelligence Says." *New York Times*. June 26, 2020 (updated July 29). https://www.nytimes.com/2020/06/26/us/politics/russia-afghanistan-bounties.html

86 President of Russia. "Telephone conversation with US President Donald Trump." June 1, 2020. http://www.kremlin.ru/events/president/news/63444

87 Crowley, Michael and Barnes, Julian E. "Trump Plans to Withdraw Some U.S. Troops From Germany, a Key NATO Ally." *New York Times.* June 5, 2020. https://www.nytimes.com/2020/06/05/world/europe/trump-troops-europe-nato-germany.html

88 Brown, Ryan and Cohen, Zachary. "US to withdraw nearly 12,000 troops from Germany in move that will cost billions and take years." *CNN.com.* July 29, 2020. https://www.cnn.com/2020/07/29/politics/us-withdraw-troops-germany/index.html

89 Hjelmgaard, Kim. "Pentagon to pull 12,000 US troops from Germany following Trump demands, slammed as 'gift to Russia.'" *USA Today News.* July 29, 2020. https://www.usatoday.com/story/news/world/2020/07/29/us-troops-leave-germany-following-trump-demands-costly-move/5534462002/

90 Cooper, Helene. "Biden Freezes Trump's Withdrawal of 12,000 Troops From Germany." *New York Times.* February 4, 2021. https://www.nytimes.com/2021/02/04/us/politics/biden-germany-troops-trump.html

91 President of Russia. "Telephone conversation with US President Donald Trump." http://www.kremlin.ru/events/president/news/63444

92 Waldman, Paul. "Even Republicans on the Intelligence Committee admit that Putin helped Trump get elected." *The Washington Post.* April 21, 2020. https://www.washingtonpost.com/opinions/2020/04/21/even-republicans-intelligence-committee-admit-putin-helped-trump-get-elected/

93 Marshall, Josh. "Did President Trump Dictate the False Statement? Or Was It President Putin?" *Talking Points Memo.* August 1, 2017. https://talkingpointsmemo.com/edblog/did-president-trump-dictate-the-false-statement-or-was-it-president-putin

94 "Who's Ahead in the National Polls?" *FiveThirtyEight.com.* July 8, 2020. https://projects.fivethirtyeight.com/polls/president-general/national/

95 Takala, Rudy. "Trump Has 91 Percent Chance of Winning Reelection: Political Science Professor." *MediaIte.* July 8, 2020. https://www.mediaite.com/news/trump-has-91-percent-chance-of-winning-reelection-political-science-professor/

96 Edelman, K.J. "FiveThirtyEight's Nate Silver Says Trump Has a Chance Despite Huge Current Poll Deficit: He Can 'Absolutely Win.'" *MediaIte.* June 22, 2020. https://www.mediaite.com/politics/fivethirtyeights-nate-silver-says-trump-has-a-chance-despite-huge-current-poll-deficit-he-can-absolutely-win/

97 Tsvetkova, Maria and Ivanova, Polina. "Sharp increase in Moscow pneumonia cases fuels fears over coronavirus statistics." *Reuters.* March 19, 2020. https://www.reuters.com/article/us-coronavirus-health-russia/sharp-increase-in-moscow-pneumonia-cases-fuels-fears-over-coronavirus-statistics-idUSKBN216305

[98] Titova, Irina. "Doctors in Russia are accusing the government of covering up its coronavirus outbreak and denying them protective equipment." *Business Insider.* March 20, 2020. https://www.businessinsider.com/coronavirus-russia-doctors-say-government-is-covering-up-cases-2020-3

[99] "Russia's Top Coronavirus Doctor Who Met Putin Tests Positive." *Moscow Times.* March 31, 2020 (updated April 6). https://www.themoscowtimes.com/2020/03/31/russias-top-coronavirus-doctor-who-met-putin-tests-positive-a69815

[100] Rainsford, Sarah. "Coronavirus crisis tests Putin's grip on power in Russia." *BBC.* April 22, 2020. https://www.bbc.com/news/world-europe-52370414

[101] Harris, Shane et al. "U.S. intelligence reports from January and February warned about a likely pandemic." *The Washington Post.* March 20, 2020. https://www.washingtonpost.com/national-security/us-intelligence-reports-from-january-and-february-warned-about-a-likely-pandemic/2020/03/20/299d8cda-6ad5-11ea-b5f1-a5a804158597_story.html

[102] DeYoung, Karen et al. "Americans at World Health Organization transmitted real-time information about coronavirus to Trump administration." *The Washington Post.* April 19, 2020. https://www.washingtonpost.com/world/national-security/americans-at-world-health-organization-transmitted-real-time-information-about-coronavirus-to-trump-administration/2020/04/19/951c77fa-818c-11ea-9040-68981f488eed_story.html

[103] Lipton, Eric et al. "He Could Have Seen What Was Coming: Behind Trump's Failure on the Virus."

[104] Keith and Romo. "Trump's Gut Collides With Science On Coronavirus Messaging."

[105] Taylor, Marisa and Roston, Aram. "Exclusive: Pressed by Trump, U.S. pushed unproven coronavirus treatment guidance." *Reuters.* April 4, 2020. https://www.reuters.com/article/us-health-coronavirus-usa-guidance-exclu/exclusive-pressed-by-trump-u-s-pushed-unproven-coronavirus-treatment-guidance-idUSKBN21M0R2

[106] Barnes, Julian E. et al. "White House Classified Computer System Is Used to Hold Transcripts of Sensitive Calls." *New York Times.* September 27, 2019 (updated September 29). https://www.nytimes.com/2019/09/27/us/politics/nsc-ukraine-call.html

[107] Galeotti, Mark. *We Need To Talk About Putin: Why the West Gets Him Wrong, and How to Get Him Right* (pp. 25-26). London: Ebury Publishing, 2019. Kindle edition.

[108] Page, Jeremy. "China's Progress Against Coronavirus Used Draconian Tactics Not Deployed in the West." *Wall Street Journal.* March 24, 2020. https://www.wsj.com/articles/the-west-is-misinterpreting-wuhans-coronavirus-progressand-drawing-the-wrong-lessons-11585074966

[109] Wadhams, Nick and Jacobs, Jennifer. *"China Concealed Extent of Virus Outbreak, U.S. Intelligence Says."* *Bloomberg News.* April 1, 2020. https://www.bloomberg.com/news/articles/2020-04-01/china-concealed-extent-of-virus-outbreak-u-s-intelligence-says

[110] Thiessen, Marc A. *"China should be legally liable for the pandemic damage it has done."* *The Washington Post.* April 9, 2020. https://www.washingtonpost.com/opinions/2020/04/09/china-should-be-legally-liable-pandemic-damage-it-has-done/

[111] Rogin, Josh. "State Department cables warned of safety issues at Wuhan lab studying bat coronaviruses." *The Washington Post.* April 14, 2020. https://www.washingtonpost.com/opinions/2020/04/14/state-department-cables-warned-safety-issues-wuhan-lab-studying-bat-coronaviruses/

[112] Miller, Greg and Nakashima, Ellen. "President's intelligence briefing book repeatedly cited virus threat." *The Washington Post.* April 27, 2020. https://www.washingtonpost.com/national-security/presidents-intelligence-briefing-book-repeatedly-cited-virus-threat/2020/04/27/ca66949a-8885-11ea-ac8a-fe9b8088e101_story.html

[113] Finnegan, Conor and Margolin, Josh. "Pompeo changes tune on Chinese lab's role in virus outbreak, as intel officials cast doubt." *Abcnews.go.com.* May 7, 2020. https://abcnews.go.com/Politics/pompeo-tune-chinese-labs-role-virus-outbreak-intel/story?id=70559769

[114] "Facilitated Group Discussion Pandemic Response." 2016 Presidential Transition. https://www.politico.com/f/?id=00000170-e50c-d588-ab77-ed5ff3310000

[115] Harris, Shane et al. "U.S. intelligence reports from January and February warned about a likely pandemic." *The Washington Post.* March 21, 2020. https://www.washingtonpost.com/national-security/us-intelligence-reports-from-january-and-february-warned-about-a-likely-pandemic/2020/03/20/299d8cda-6ad5-11ea-b5f1-a5a804158597_story.html

[116] Pérez-Peña, Richard and McNeil, Donald G., Jr. "W.H.O., Now Trump's Scapegoat, Warned About Coronavirus Early and Often." *New York Times.* May 7, 2020. https://www.nytimes.com/2020/04/16/health/WHO-Trump-coronavirus.html

[117] Biden, Joe. "FLASHBACK by Joe Biden: Trump is worst possible leader to deal with coronavirus outbreak." *USA Today Opinion.* January 27, 2020. https://eu.usatoday.com/story/opinion/2020/01/27/coronavirus-donald-trump-made-us-less-prepared-joe-biden-column/4581710002/

[118] Harris et al. "U.S. intelligence reports from January and February warned about a likely pandemic."

[119] Reyes, Raul A. "The real reason Trump treats meatpacking workers as disposable." *CNN.com.* April 30, 2020. https://www.cnn.com/2020/04/29/opinions/trump-treats-meatpacking-workers-as-disposable-reyes/index.html

[120] "Centers for Disease Control and Prevention Situation Update." Department

of Health and Human Services and Federal Emergency Management Agency. https://int.nyt.com/data/documenthelper/6926-mayhhsbriefing/af7319f4a55fd0ce5dc9/optimized/full.pdf#page=1

121 Trump, Donald via Rupar, Aaron. *Twitter*. May 5, 2020. https://twitter.com/atrupar/status/1257778264241844224

122 Gabbat, Adam. "Thousands of Americans backed by rightwing donors gear up for protests." *Guardian*. April 18, 2020. https://www.theguardian.com/us-news/2020/apr/18/coronavirus-americans-protest-stay-at-home

123 Gabbat, Adam. "Why the DeVos family's backing of the Michigan protests is no surprise." *Guardian*. April 26, 2020. https://www.theguardian.com/us-news/2020/apr/26/devos-family-michigan-protest-rightwing-donors

124 Shear, Michael D. and Mervosh, Sarah. "Trump Encourages Protest Against Governors Who Have Imposed Virus Restrictions." *New York Times*. April 17, 2020. https://www.nytimes.com/2020/04/17/us/politics/trump-coronavirus-governors.html

125 Trump, Donald. *Twitter*. April 17, 2020. https://www.thetrumparchive.com/?searchbox=%22LIBERATE%22&dates=%5B%222020-04-17%22%2C%222020-04-18%22%5D

126 Gertz, Matt. *Twitter*. September 14, 2020. https://twitter.com/MattGertz/status/1305673823207948288?s=20

127 Gearan, Anne and Wagner, John. "Trump expresses support for angry anti-shutdown protesters as more states lift coronavirus lockdowns." *The Washington Post*. May 1, 2020. https://www.washingtonpost.com/politics/trump-expresses-support-for-angry-anti-shutdown-protesters-as-more-states-lift-coronavirus-lockdowns/2020/05/01/25570dbe-8b9f-11ea-8ac1-bfb250876b7a_story.html

128 Reid, Shannon and Valasik, Matthew. "Why are white supremacists protesting to 'reopen' the US economy?" *Conversation*. April 28, 2020. https://theconversation.com/why-are-white-supremacists-protesting-to-reopen-the-us-economy-137044

129 Vogel, Kenneth P. et al. "The Quiet Hand of Conservative Groups in the Anti-Lockdown Protests." *New York Times*. April 21, 2020. https://www.nytimes.com/2020/04/21/us/politics/coronavirus-protests-trump.html

130 Dearan, Jason and Stobbe, Mike. "Trump administration buries detailed CDC advice on reopening." *AP News*. May 6, 2020. https://apnews.com/7a00d5fba3249e573d2ead4bd323a4d4

131 "Donald Trump's 2014 Political Predictions." *YouTube*. February 10, 2014. https://youtu.be/K7c_-EipVKs

132 Kendzior, Sarah. "We're heading into dark times. This is how to be your own light in the Age of Trump." *Correspondent*. November 18, 2016. https://thecorrespondent.com/5696/were-heading-into-dark-times-this-is-how-to-be-your-own-light-in-the-age-of-trump/1611114266432-e23ea1a6

133 DeVega, Chauncey. "Psychologist John Gartner: Trump is a 'sexual sadist' who is

'actively engaging in sabotage.'"

[134] Haltiwanger, John. "All the times Trump risked exposing himself to coronavirus as his advisers urge people his age to be extremely cautious." *Business Insider.* March 16, 2020. https://www.businessinsider.com/coronavirus-all-the-times-trump-was-potentially-exposed-covid-19-2020-3

Chapter One: Bio-war, What Is It Good For?

[1] Harris, Sheldon H. *Factories of Death: Japanese Biological Warfare, 1932-45, and the American Cover-up.* New York: Routledge, 2002.

[2] Kelly, John. *The Great Mortality: An Intimate History of the Black Death, the Most Devastating Plague of All Time.* New York: Harper Perennial, 2005. Kindle Edition.

[3] Wheelis, Mark. "Biological Warfare at the 1346 Siege of Caffa." *Emerg Infect Dis.* September, 2002. https://www.ncbi.nlm.nih.gov/pmc/articles/PMC2732530/

[4] Horrox, Rosemay. *The Black Death.* Manchester: Manchester University Press, 1994. https://www.google.com/books/edition/The_Black_Death/1O_PX2wVD0sC?hl=en&gbpv=0

[5] Kelly. *The Great Mortality.*

[6] Howard, Jenny. "Plague was one of history's deadliest diseases—then we found a cure." *National Geographic.* July 6, 2020. https://www.nationalgeographic.com/science/health-and-human-body/human-diseases/the-plague/

[7] Black, Winston. "What Was the Black Death." *Livescience.com.* December 12, 2019. https://www.livescience.com/what-was-the-black-death.html

[8] Butler, T. "Plague history: Yersin's discovery of the causative bacterium in 1894 enabled, in the subsequent century, scientific progress in understanding the disease and the development of treatments and vaccines." *Clin Microbiol Infect.* March, 2014. https://pubmed.ncbi.nlm.nih.gov/24438235/ (https://pubmed.ncbi.nlm.nih.gov/24438235/)

[9] "Secrets of the Dead: Mystery of the Black Death." *Pbs.org.* May 29, 2014. https://www.pbs.org/wnet/secrets/mystery-black-death-background/1488/

[10] Frischknecht, Friedrich. "The history of biological warfare." *EMBO Rep.* June, 2003. https://www.ncbi.nlm.nih.gov/pmc/articles/PMC1326439/

[11] Bryner, Jeanna. "Wuhan lab says there's no way coronavirus originated there. Here's the science." *Livescience.com.* April 18, 2020.

https://www.livescience.com/coronavirus-wuhan-lab-complicated-origins.html

[12] Rupar, Aaron. "Trump seems to think there'd be no coronavirus if there was no testing. It doesn't work like that." *Vox.com.* May 15, 2020. https://www.vox.com/2020/5/15/21259888/trump-coronavirus-testing-very-few-cases

[13] Margolin, Josh and Meek, James G. "Intelligence report warned of coronavirus crisis as early as November: Sources." *Abcnews.go.com*. April 9, 2020. https://abcnews.go.com/Politics/intelligence-report-warned-coronavirus-crisis-early-november-sources/story?id=70031273

[14] Diamond, Jeremy. "Trump's visit to Walter Reed 'not protocol' for routine visit, source says." *CNN.com*. November 17, 2019. https://www.cnn.com/2019/11/17/politics/trump-physical-walter-reed-protocol-routine-presidential-visit/index.html

[15] Liptak, Kevin. "White House releases results of Trump's annual physical." *CNN.com*. June 4, 2020. https://www.cnn.com/2020/06/03/politics/donald-trump-annual-physical/index.html

[16] Office of the Director of National Intelligence. "Deputy Director of National Intelligence for Mission Integration: Beth Sanner." https://www.dni.gov/index.php/who-we-are/leadership/deputy-dni-for-mission-integration

[17] Office of the Director of National Intelligence. "What is the PDB?" https://www.intelligence.gov/publics-daily-brief/presidents-daily-brief

[18] Barnes, Julian E. and Goldman, Adam. "For Spy Agencies, Briefing Trump Is a Test of Holding His Attention." *New York Times*. May 21, 2020 (updated May 28). https://www.nytimes.com/2020/05/21/us/politics/presidents-daily-brief-trump.html

[19] Eder, et. al. "430,000 People Have Traveled From China to U.S. Since Coronavirus Surfaced."

[20] Aratani, Lori and Miroff, Nick. "Passengers flying to the U.S. from 26 countries in Europe will face enhanced screening." *The Washington Post*. March 13, 2020. https://www.washingtonpost.com/transportation/2020/03/13/travelers-europe-will-face-additional-scrutiny/

[21] Worldometer. https://www.worldometers.info/coronavirus/

In terms of cases per million in countries with at least 1 million population.

[22] Hirsch, Lauren. "Trump says, 'Anybody who wants a test gets a test' after Pence says US can't meet coronavirus testing demand." *CNBC.com*. March 6, 2020 (updated March 9). https://www.cnbc.com/2020/03/06/trump-anybody-who-wants-a-test-gets-a-test-amid-shortage-for-coronavirus.html

[23] Segers, Grace. "Trump says coronavirus "will go away" and urges Americans to "just stay calm"." *CBSnews.com*. March 10, 2020. https://www.cbsnews.com/news/trump-says-coronavirus-will-go-away-and-urges-americans-to-just-stay-calm-2020-03-10/

[24] Harris, Robert and Paxman, Jeremy. *A Higher Form of Killing: The Secret History of Chemical and Biological Warfare*. New York: Random House Publishing Group, 2007. Kindle Edition.

[25] Ibid.

26 Timberg, Craig, Dwoskin, Elizabeth and Balingit, Moriah. "Protests spread, fueled by economic woes and Internet subcultures." *The Washington Post*. May 1, 2020. https://www.washingtonpost.com/technology/2020/05/01/anti-stay-home-protests/

27 Pilkington, Ed. "Black Americans dying of Covid-19 at three times the rate of white people." *Guardian*. May 20, 2020. https://www.theguardian.com/world/2020/may/20/black-americans-death-rate-covid-19-coronavirus

28 Centers for Disease Control and Prevention. "The Tuskegee Timeline." https://www.cdc.gov/tuskegee/timeline.htm

29 Frischknecht. "The history of biological warfare."

30 Reardon, Sara. "US military accidentally ships live anthrax to labs." *Nature*. May 28, 2015. https://www.nature.com/news/us-military-accidentally-ships-live-anthrax-to-labs-1.17653

31 Ibid.

32 Loftus, John. *America's Nazi Secret: An Insider's History*. Independent Publishers Group, 2011. Kindle Edition. (Originally, *The Belarus Secret*. New York: Alfred A. Knopf, 1982.)

33 Intramural Research Program. "Discovery of the disease agent causing Lyme disease." https://irp.nih.gov/accomplishments/discovery-of-the-disease-agent-causing-lyme-disease (https://irp.nih.gov/accomplishments/discovery-of-the-disease-agent-causing-lyme-disease)

34 Centers for Disease Control and Prevention. "Lyme Disease: Data and Surveillance." https://www.cdc.gov/lyme/datasurveillance/index.html

35 Donnelly, John M. "House orders Pentagon to say if it weaponized ticks and released them." *Roll Call*. July 15, 2019. https://www.rollcall.com/2019/07/15/house-orders-pentagon-to-say-if-it-weaponized-ticks-and-released-them/

36 Olivier, Jonathan. "'Bitten' Explores a Lyme Disease Conspiracy." *Outside*. May 29, 2019. https://www.outsideonline.com/2395909/bitten-kris-newby-book-review

37 Nakashima, Ellen. "Trump removes inspector general who was to oversee $2 trillion stimulus spending." *The Washington Post*. April 7, 2020. https://www.washingtonpost.com/national-security/trump-removes-inspector-general-who-was-to-oversee-2-trillion-stimulus-spending/2020/04/07/2f0c6cb8-78ea-11ea-9bee-c5bf9d2e3288_story.html

38 Telford, Sam. "No, Lyme disease is not an escaped military bioweapon, despite what conspiracy theorists say." *The Washington Post*. August 11, 2019. https://www.washingtonpost.com/health/no-lyme-diease-is-not-an-escaped-military-bioweapon-despite-what-conspiracy-theorists-say/2019/08/09/5bbd85fa-afe4-11e9-8e77-03b30bc29f64_story.html

39 Olivier. "'Bitten' Explores a Lyme Disease Conspiracy."

40 Péres, Louis A., Jr. "The Cost of Covert Operations in Cuba." *NACLA*. December

16, 2016. https://nacla.org/news/2016/12/16/cost-covert-operations-cuba (https://nacla.org/news/2016/12/16/cost-covert-operations-cuba)

[41] Richards, Bill. "Report Suggests CIA Involvement In Fla. Illnesses." *The Washington Post*. December 17,1979. https://www.washingtonpost.com/archive/politics/1979/12/17/report-suggests-cia-involvement-in-fla-illnesses/5b10205e-170b-4e38-b64e-2e9bca8f50df/

[42] Loria, Kevin. "Over and over again, the military has conducted dangerous bio-warfare experiments on Americans." *Business Insider*. September 25, 2016. https://www.businessinsider.com/military-government-secret-experiments-biological-chemical-weapons-2016-9?r=US&IR=T

[43] Kiger, Patrick J. "Did Colonists Give Infected Blankets to Native Americans as Biological Warfare?" *History.com*. November 15, 2018 (updated November 25, 2019). https://www.history.com/news/colonists-native-americans-smallpox-blankets

[44] Brown, Thomas. *Did the U.S. Army Distribute Smallpox Blankets to Indians? Fabrication and Falsification in Ward Churchill's Genocide Rhetoric*. Ann Arbor: MPublishing, 2006. http://hdl.handle.net/2027/spo.5240451.0001.009

[45] "Covid Deaths by Race." APM Research Lab. https://www.apmresearchlab.org/covid/deaths-by-race

[46] Centers for Disease Control and Prevention. "Health Equity Considerations and Racial and Ethnic Minority Groups." https://www.cdc.gov/coronavirus/2019-ncov/need-extra-precautions/racial-ethnic-minorities.html

[47] Serwer, Adam. "The Coronavirus Was an Emergency Until Trump Found Out Who Was Dying." *Atlantic*. May 8, 2020. https://www.theatlantic.com/ideas/archive/2020/05/americas-racial-contract-showing/611389/

[48] Eligon, John et. al. "Black Americans Face Alarming Rates of Coronavirus Infection in Some States." *New York Times*. April 7, 2020 (updated April 14). https://www.nytimes.com/2020/04/07/us/coronavirus-race.html

[49] Broad, William J. "Suspect's Manifesto Points to Planned Anthrax Use, but Also to a Lack of Expertise." *New York Times*. July 26, 2011. https://www.nytimes.com/2011/07/27/science/27anthrax.html

[50] Parker, Abutaleb and Dawsey. "Trump administration has many task forces."

[51] Wessely, Simon. "Psychological implications of chemical and biological weapons: Long term social and psychological effects may be worse than acute ones." *BMJ*. October, 2001. https://www.ncbi.nlm.nih.gov/pmc/articles/PMC1121425/

[52] "Led to the noose in diapers: the strange life and death of Shoko Asahara, murderous guru behind Tokyo sarin attack." *South China Morning Post*. July 6, 2018. https://www.scmp.com/news/asia/east-asia/article/2154051/led-noose-diapers-strange-life-and-death-shoko-asahara-murderous

[53] Fletcher, Holly. "Aum Shinrikyo." *Council on Foreign Relations*. June 19, 2012. https://www.cfr.org/backgrounder/aum-shinrikyo

54 Bleek, Philipp C. "Revisiting Aum Shinrikyo: New Insights into the Most Extensive Non-State Biological Weapons Program to Date." *Nti.org.* December 11, 2011. https://www.nti.org/analysis/articles/revisiting-aum-shinrikyo-new-insights-most-extensive-non-state-biological-weapons-program-date-1/

55 Ibid.

56 Ibid.

Chapter Two: American Carnage

1 Bet, Martina. "Donald Trump news: Do resurfaced videos prove tycoon ALWAYS wanted to become US President?" *Daily Express.* February 13, 2019. https://www.express.co.uk/news/world/1086632/donald-trump-news-white-house-us-president-latest-spt

2 Goldberger, Paul. "TRUMP ANNOUNCES PLAN TO CONSTRUCT WORLD'S TALLEST BUILDING." *New York Times.* November 19, 1985. https://www.nytimes.com/1985/11/19/nyregion/trump-announces-plan-to-construct-worlds-tallest-building.html

3 Roberts, Sam. "Ed Koch's Epic Feud With Trump Survives the Mayor's Death." *New York Times.* February 27, 2017. https://www.nytimes.com/2017/02/27/nyregion/trump-koch-feud-letters-new-york-city.html

4 Chua-Eoan, Howard. "Crimes of the Century: The Son of Sam, 1977." *Time.* March 1, 2007. http://content.time.com/time/specials/packages/article/0,28804,1937349_1937350_1937438,00.html

5 Flood, Joe. "Why the Bronx burned." *New York Post.* May 16, 2010. https://nypost.com/2010/05/16/why-the-bronx-burned/

6 Bagli, Charles V. "Trump Sells Hyatt Share To Pritzkers." *New York Times.* October 8, 1996. https://www.nytimes.com/1996/10/08/business/trump-sells-hyatt-share-to-pritzkers.html

7 Cohen, Michael. *Disloyal: A Memoir.* (p. 6).

8 Matthews, Dylan. "Andrew Jackson was a slaver, ethnic cleanser, and tyrant. He deserves no place on our money." *Vox.com.* April 20, 2016. https://www.vox.com/2016/4/20/11469514/andrew-jackson-indian-removal

9 Johnson, Jenna and Tumulty, Karen. "Trump cites Andrew Jackson as his hero — and a reflection of himself." *The Washington Post.* March 15, 2017. https://www.washingtonpost.com/politics/trump-cites-andrew-jackson-as-his-hero--and-a-reflection-of-himself/2017/03/15/4da8dc8c-0995-11e7-a15f-a58d4a988474_story.html

10 Boot. "Opinion: The worst president. Ever."

11 "How (un)popular is Donald Trump?" *FiveThirtyEight.com.* January 20, 2021. https://projects.fivethirtyeight.com/trump-approval-ratings/

[12] Umbrasas, Karl. "The Life Course of Apocalyptic Groups." *Journal of Strategic Security*. August, 2018. https://scholarcommons.usf.edu/cgi/viewcontent. cgi?article=1653&context=jss (https://scholarcommons.usf.edu/cgi/viewcontent. cgi?article=1653&context=jss)

[13] Fletcher. "Aum Shinrikyo."

[14] Pitts, Gordon. "Trump touts soft markets in cities like Toronto." *Globe and Mail*. March 20, 2007. https://www.theglobeandmail.com/report-on-business/trump-touts-soft-markets-in-cities-like-toronto/article17993211/

[15] Jones, Samuel Milton. *The New Right: A Plea for Fair Play Through a More Just Social Order*. New York: Eastern Book Concern, 1899. Page 61.

[16] Hirsh, Michael. "How Russian Money Helped Save Trump's Business." *Foreign Policy*. December 21, 2018. https://foreignpolicy.com/2018/12/21/how-russian-money-helped-save-trumps-business/

[17] "Donald Trump's 2014 Political Predictions."

[18] Rosenbaum, Ron. "Trump's Nuclear Experience." *Slate*. March 1, 2016. http://www.slate.com/articles/news_and_politics/the_spectator/2016/03/trump_s_nuclear_experience_advice_for_reagan_in_1987.html

[19] Trump, Donald. *Twitter*. May 30, 2020. https://www.thetrumparchive.com/?results=1&dates=%5B%222020-05-30%22%2C%222020-05-31%22%5D

[20] "Latest Polls." *FiveThirtyEight.com*. https://projects.fivethirtyeight.com/polls/president-general/national/

[21] Hill, Evan et al. "How the Fatal Shooting at a Portland Protest Unfolded." *New York Times*. August 31, 2020 (updated September 3). https://www.nytimes.com/2020/08/31/video/portland-protests-shooting-investigation.html

[22] Hill, Evan et al. "'Straight to Gunshots': How a U.S. Task Force Killed an Antifa Activist." *New York Times*. October 13, 2020 (updated December 4). https://www.nytimes.com/2020/10/13/us/michael-reinoehl-antifa-portland-shooting.html

[23] Bernstein, Maxine. "President Trump on fatal police shooting of Portland homicide suspect Michael Reinoehl: 'That's the way it has to be. There has to be retribution.'" *Oregonian*. September 13, 2020. https://www.oregonlive.com/crime/2020/09/president-trump-on-fatal-police-shooting-of-portland-killing-suspect-michael-reinoehl-thats-the-way-it-has-to-be-there-has-to-be-retribution.html

[24] Hanna, Jason and Campbell, Josh. "Trump gloats about US Marshals' killing of Portland 'antifa' suspect." *CNN.com*. October 16, 2020. https://edition.cnn.com/2020/10/15/politics/trump-fugitive-shooting/index.html

[25] Ibid.

[26] "Trump Administration Insider: President Wanted to 'Maim' Migrants." *Daily Beast*. August 25, 2020. https://www.thedailybeast.com/trump-administration-insider-president-wanted-to-maim-immigrants?ref=scroll

[27] Shear, Michael D. and Hirschfeld Davis, Julie. "Shoot Migrants' Legs, Build Alligator Moat: Behind Trump's Ideas for Border." *New York Times*. October 1, 2019 (updated October 2). https://www.nytimes.com/2019/10/01/us/politics/trump-border-wars.html

[28] "Trump Administration Insider: President Wanted to 'Maim' Migrants."

[29] Goodman, Ryan, Dugas, Mari and Tonckens, Nicholas. "Incitement Timeline: Year of Trump's Actions Leading to the Attack on the Capitol." *Just Security*. January 11, 2021. https://www.justsecurity.org/74138/incitement-timeline-year-of-trumps-actions-leading-to-the-attack-on-the-capitol/

[30] Collins, Kaitlan. *Twitter*. January 7, 2021. https://twitter.com/kaitlancollins/status/1347023890959228933

[31] Wagner, Meg and Macaya, Melissa. "Fallout intensifies over Trump's response to Capitol riot." *CNN.com*. January 9, 2021. https://edition.cnn.com/politics/live-news/washington-dc-riots-trump-news-friday/h_3b3d237d139679d425ef2e0a54ddfca7

[32] Miller, Joshua Rhett. "Video shows Capitol rioter hit officer with fire extinguisher." *New York Post*. January 11, 2021. https://nypost.com/2021/01/11/video-shows-capitol-rioter-hit-officer-with-fire-extinguisher/

[33] Griffin, Kyle. *Twitter*. January 8, 2021. https://twitter.com/kylegriffin1/status/1347595193101348864?s=20

[34] Parker, Ashley, Dawsey, Josh and Rucker, Philip. "Six hours of paralysis: Inside Trump's failure to act after a mob stormed the Capitol." *The Washington Post*. January 12, 2021. https://www.washingtonpost.com/politics/trump-mob-failure/2021/01/11/36a46e2e-542e-11eb-a817-e5e7f8a406d6_story.html

[35] Trump, Donald. *Twitter*. January 6, 2021. https://www.thetrumparchive.com/?results=1&searchbox=%22Go+home+with+love+%26+in+peace%22

[36] Fried, Ina. "Twitter locks Trump out over election fraud tweets amid Capitol siege." *Axios.com*. January 6, 2021. https://www.axios.com/twitter-removes-trump-tweets-f198f970-c9f8-469d-9b34-13429aa26320.html

[37] Trump, Donald. *Twitter*. April 18, 2020. https://www.thetrumparchive.com/?results=1&searchbox=%22People+are+dropping+off+like+flies%22

[38] Worldometer. https://www.worldometers.info/coronavirus/country/us/

[39] Fuller, Thomas and Baker, Mike. "Coronavirus Death in California Came Weeks Before First Known U.S. Death." *New York Times*. April 22, 2020 (updated May 7). https://www.nytimes.com/2020/04/22/us/coronavirus-first-united-states-death.html

[40] Gopinath, Gita. "The Great Lockdown: Worst Economic Downturn Since the Great Depression." *IMF Blog*. April 14, 2020. https://blogs.imf.org/2020/04/14/the-great-lockdown-worst-economic-downturn-since-the-great-depression/ (https://blogs.imf.org/2020/04/14/the-great-lockdown-worst-economic-downturn-since-the-great-depression/)

[41] Kendzior, Sarah. *Twitter*. April 5, 2020. https://twitter.com/sarahkendzior/status/1246580809273876483?s=20

[42] Kendzior, Sarah. "Trump and Putin: The worst case scenario." *Quartz (qz.com)*. December 23, 2016. https://qz.com/871436/donald-trump-nuclear-weapons-putin-and-trump-release-statements-that-hint-at-increased-nuclear-armament/

[43] Romano, Lois. "Donald Trump, Holding All The Cards The Tower! The Team! The Money! The Future!" *The Washington Post*. November 15, 1984. https://www.washingtonpost.com/archive/lifestyle/1984/11/15/donald-trump-holding-all-the-cards-the-tower-the-team-the-money-the-future/8be79254-7793-4812-a153-f2b88e81fa54/

[44] Belvedere, Matthew J. "Trump asks why US can't use nukes: MSNBC." *CNBC.com*. August 3, 2016. https://www.cnbc.com/2016/08/03/trump-asks-why-us-cant-use-nukes-msnbcs-joe-scarborough-reports.html

[45] Crowley, Michael. "Trump's nuclear nightmare." *Politico*. August 3, 2016. https://www.politico.com/story/2016/08/donald-trump-nuclear-weapons-226639

[46] Mecklin, John. "It is now two minutes to midnight: 2018 Doomsday Clock Statement." *Bulletin of the Atomic Scientists*. January 25, 2018. https://thebulletin.org/doomsday-clock/2018-doomsday-clock-statement/ (https://thebulletin.org/doomsday-clock/2018-doomsday-clock-statement/)

[47] Gerson, Joseph. "Doomsday and the Apocalyptic Trump Nuclear War Fighting Doctrine." *Truthout*. January 26, 2018. https://truthout.org/articles/doomsday-and-the-apocalyptic-trump-nuclear-war-fighting-doctrine/ (https://truthout.org/articles/doomsday-and-the-apocalyptic-trump-nuclear-war-fighting-doctrine/)

[48] Mehta, Aaron. "Mattis: No such thing as a 'tactical' nuclear weapon, but new cruise missile needed." *Defense News*. February 6, 2018. https://www.defensenews.com/space/2018/02/06/mattis-no-such-thing-as-a-tactical-nuclear-weapon-but-new-cruise-missile-needed/

[49] Gerson. "Doomsday and the Apocalyptic Trump Nuclear War Fighting Doctrine."

[50] Lopez, Todd C. "U.S. Withdraws From Intermediate-Range Nuclear Forces Treaty." U.S. Department of Defense. August 2, 2019. https://www.defense.gov/Explore/News/Article/Article/1924779/us-withdraws-from-intermediate-range-nuclear-forces-treaty/

[51] Costa and Rucker. "Woodward book: Trump says he knew coronavirus was 'deadly' and worse than the flu while intentionally misleading Americans."

[52] Mizokami, Kyle. "What Is Trump's New Nuclear Weapon?" *Popular Mechanics*. September 10, 2020. https://www.popularmechanics.com/military/weapons/a33982748/what-is-trumps-new-nuclear-weapon/

[53] Perry, William J. and Collina, Tom Z. "How to Starve Trump's Lust for Nukes: The president can launch a missile, but he can't buy one. Only Congress can." *Politico*. September 10, 2019. https://www.politico.com/magazine/story/2019/09/10/donald-trump-nuclear-arms-race-228058

54 Plaskin, Glenn. "The Playboy Interview With Donald Trump." *Playboy Magazine*. March 1, 1990. https://www.playboy.com/read/playboy-interview-donald-trump-1990

55 Hudson, John and Sonne, Paul. "Trump administration discussed conducting first U.S. nuclear test in decades." *The Washington Post*. May 23, 2020. https://www.washingtonpost.com/national-security/trump-administration-discussed-conducting-first-us-nuclear-test-in-decades/2020/05/22/a805c904-9c5b-11ea-b60c-3be060a4f8e1_story.html

56 Kendzior. "Trump and Putin: The worst case scenario."

57 Appelbaum, Yoni. "I Alone Can Fix It." *Atlantic*. July 22, 2016. https://www.theatlantic.com/politics/archive/2016/07/trump-rnc-speech-alone-fix-it/492557/

58 Collins, Eliza. "Trump: I consult myself on foreign policy." *Politico*. March 16, 2016. https://www.politico.com/blogs/2016-gop-primary-live-updates-and-results/2016/03/trump-foreign-policy-adviser-220853

59 Britzky, Haley. "Everything Trump says he knows 'more about than anybody.'" *Axios.com*. January 5, 2019. https://www.axios.com/everything-trump-says-he-knows-more-about-than-anybody-b278b592-cff0-47dc-a75f-5767f42bcf1e.html

60 Illing, Sean. "Is Trumpism a cult?" *Vox.com*. January 26, 2020. https://www.vox.com/policy-and-politics/2019/12/13/20992370/trump-republican-party-cult-steven-hassan

61 Warren, Katie. "I visited Trump's childhood neighborhood on the outskirts of NYC, and it didn't take long to see why he's called it an 'oasis.'" *Business Insider*. August 19, 2020. https://www.businessinsider.com/donald-trump-childhood-neighborhood-queens-new-york-city-photos-2018-11?r=US&IR=T

62 Blair, Gwenda. "How Norman Vincent Peale Taught Donald Trump to Worship Himself." *Politico*. October 6, 2015. https://www.politico.com/magazine/story/2015/10/donald-trump-2016-norman-vincent-peale-213220

63 Schreckinger, Ben. "Donald Trump: 'This is a movement.'" *Politico*. August 29, 2015 (updated August 30). https://www.politico.com/story/2015/08/donald-trump-2016-movement-213160

64 Cillizza, Chris. "Donald Trump just said something truly terrifying." *CNN.com*. July 25, 2018. https://edition.cnn.com/2018/07/25/politics/donald-trump-vfw-unreality/index.html

65 Superville, Darlene. "Trump says getting rid of "bad" people made him successful." *AP News*. February 29, 2020. https://apnews.com/article/69a306253b3d02f18b4c68fbfe44c80e

66 Illing. "Is Trumpism a cult?"

67 Pierce, Charles P. "The President* Has Gone as Soft as Church Music." *Esquire*. August 21, 2019. https://www.esquire.com/news-politics/politics/a28772482/donald-trump-twitter-king-of-israel-wayne-allyn-root/

[68] Melendez, Pilar. "Donald Trump Defends Trade War With China: 'I Am the Chosen One.'" *Daily Beast.* August 21, 2019. https://www.thedailybeast.com/donald-trump-defends-trade-war-with-china-i-am-the-chosen-one

[69] Wade, Peter. "Trump's History With the Word Sarcasm Is Littered with Excuses and Ignorance." *Rolling Stone.* April 28, 2020. https://www.rollingstone.com/politics/politics-news/trump-sarcasm-history-990750/

[70] Martínez, Jessica and Smith, Gregory A. "How the faithful voted: A preliminary 2016 analysis." *Pew Research Center.* November 9, 2016. https://www.pewresearch.org/fact-tank/2016/11/09/how-the-faithful-voted-a-preliminary-2016-analysis/

[71] Worldometer. https://www.worldometers.info/coronavirus/country/us/

[72] Smith, Gregory A. "White evangelicals among groups with slipping confidence in Trump's handling of COVID-19." *Pew Research Center.* May 14, 2020. https://www.pewresearch.org/fact-tank/2020/05/14/white-evangelicals-among-groups-with-slipping-confidence-in-trumps-handling-of-covid-19/

[73] Maza, Christina. "Trump Will Start the End of the World, Claim Evangelicals Who Support Him." *Newsweek.* January 12, 2018. https://www.newsweek.com/trump-will-bring-about-end-worldevangelicals-end-times-779643

[74] Thiel, Bob. *Donald Trump and America's Apocalypse* (p. 172). Nazarene Books. Kindle Edition.

[75] Maza. "Trump Will Start the End of the World, Claim Evangelicals Who Support Him."

[76] Timmons, Heather. "Trump's foreign policy looks a lot like Rapture Christians' plan to welcome the apocalypse." *Quartz (qz.com).* May 15, 2018. https://qz.com/1270516/jerusalem-embassy-trumps-foreign-policy-looks-like-rapture-christians-plan-to-trigger-apocalypse/

[77] Umbrasas. "The Life Course of Apocalyptic Groups."

[78] Woodward, Bob and Costa, Bob. "Interview with Donald Trump, Corey Lewandowski, press secretary Hope Hicks and Donald Trump, Jr." *The Washington Post.* March 31, 2016. https://www.washingtonpost.com/wp-stat/graphics/politics/trump-archive/docs/donald-trump-interview-with-bob-woodward-and-robert-costa.pdf?itid=lk_inline_manual_3

[79] "Full text: 2017 Donald Trump inauguration speech transcript." *Politico.* January 20, 2017. https://www.politico.com/story/2017/01/full-text-donald-trump-inauguration-speech-transcript-233907

Chapter Three: A Very Different Thing

[1] "Transcript: Donald Trump Visits CDC, Calls Jay Inslee a 'Snake.'" *Rev.com.* March 6, 2020. https://www.rev.com/blog/transcripts/transcript-donald-trump-visits-

cdc-calls-jay-inslee-a-snake

[2] Eaton, Sabrina. "Presidential vacations: Which commander in chief took the most time off?" *Cleveland.* August 9, 2017 (updated May 19, 2019). https://www.cleveland.com/nation/2017/08/presidential_vacations_who_too.html

[3] "1918 Pandemic (H1N1 virus)." Centers for Disease Control and Prevention. https://www.cdc.gov/flu/pandemic-resources/1918-pandemic-h1n1.html

[4] Mosk, Matthew. "George W. Bush in 2005: 'If we wait for a pandemic to appear, it will be too late to prepare.'" *Abc.go.com.* April 5, 2020. https://abcnews.go.com/Politics/george-bush-2005-wait-pandemic-late-prepare/story?id=69979013

[5] Ibid.

[6] Diamond, Dan. "Inside America's 2-Decade Failure to Prepare for Coronavirus." *Politico.* April 11, 2020. https://www.politico.com/news/magazine/2020/04/11/america-two-decade-failure-prepare-coronavirus-179574

[7] "Implementation of the National Strategy for Pandemic Influenza." White House Archives. November 1, 2005. https://georgewbush-whitehouse.archives.gov/infocus/pandemicflu/ (https://georgewbush-whitehouse.archives.gov/infocus/pandemicflu/)

[8] Charatan, Fred. "Bush announces US plan for flu pandemic." *BMJ.* November 12, 2005. https://www.ncbi.nlm.nih.gov/pmc/articles/PMC1283304/

[9] Parker, Abutaleb and Dawsey. "Trump administration has many task forces."

[10] Mosk. "George W. Bush in 2005."

[11] Seitz, Amanda. "Few sickened when Obama declared 2009 flu a health emergency." *AP News.* March 6, 2020. https://apnews.com/article/8603491796

[12] Francis, David. "Ebola's Toll Was Horrific. It Could Have Been Much Worse." *Foreign Policy.* February 11, 2015. https://foreignpolicy.com/2015/02/11/epidemic-ebola-pentagon-obama-outbreak-africa/

[13] "2014-2016 Ebola Outbreak in West Africa." Centers for Disease Control and Prevention. https://www.cdc.gov/vhf/ebola/history/2014-2016-outbreak/

[14] Trump, Donald. *Twitter.* October 16, 2014. (https://www.thetrumparchive.com/)https://www.thetrumparchive.com/?results=1&searchbox=%22wrong+with+President+Obama%27s+mental+health%22

[15] Karlawish, Jason. "A pandemic plan was in place. Trump abandoned it — and science — in the face of Covid-19." *Stat News.* May 17, 2020. https://www.statnews.com/2020/05/17/the-art-of-the-pandemic-how-donald-trump-walked-the-u-s-into-the-covid-19-era/

[16] Executive Office of the President of the United States. "Playbook for early response to high-consequence emerging infectious disease threats and biological incidents." https://www.documentcloud.org/documents/6819703-WH-Pandemic-Playbook.html#document/p2

[17] The COVID Tracking Project. https://covidtracking.com/data/national

[18] Rieder, Rem. "Contrary to Trump's Claim, A Pandemic Was Widely Expected at Some Point." *Factcheck.org*. March 20, 2020. https://www.factcheck.org/2020/03/contrary-to-trumps-claim-a-pandemic-was-widely-expected-at-some-point/

[19] Boehlert, Eric. "History will judge media's refusal to call Trump a liar." *Press Run*. June 15, 2020. https://pressrun.media/p/historians-will-never-understand (https://pressrun.media/p/historians-will-never-understand)

[20] "Remarks by President Trump, Vice President Pence, and Members of the Coronavirus Task Force in a Fox News Virtual Town Hall." White House Archives. March 24, 2020. https://trumpwhitehouse.archives.gov/briefings-statements/remarks-president-trump-vice-president-pence-members-coronavirus-task-force-fox-news-virtual-town-hall/ (https://trumpwhitehouse.archives.gov/briefings-statements/remarks-president-trump-vice-president-pence-members-coronavirus-task-force-fox-news-virtual-town-hall/)

[21] Graff, Garrett M. "An Oral History of the Pandemic Warnings Trump Ignored." *Wired*. April 17, 2020. https://www.wired.com/story/an-oral-history-of-the-pandemic-warnings-trump-ignored/

[22] Dawsey, Josh. "Trump asked China's Xi to help him win reelection, according to Bolton book." *The Washington Post*. June 18, 2020. (https://www.washingtonpost.com/politics/trump-asked-chinas-xi-to-help-him-win-reelection-according-to-bolton-book/2020/06/17/d4ea601c-ad7a-11ea-868b-93d63cd833b2_story.html) https://www.washingtonpost.com/politics/trump-asked-chinas-xi-to-help-him-win-reelection-according-to-bolton-book/2020/06/17/d4ea601c-ad7a-11ea-868b-93d63cd833b2_story.htm

[23] Diamond, Dan and Toosi, Nahal. "Trump team failed to follow NSC's pandemic playbook." *Politico*. March 25, 2020. https://www.politico.com/news/2020/03/25/trump-coronavirus-national-security-council-149285

[24] Toosi, Nahal, Lippman, Daniel and Diamond, Dan. "Before Trump's inauguration, a warning: 'The worst influenza pandemic since 1918.'" *Politico*. March 16, 2020. https://www.politico.com/news/2020/03/16/trump-inauguration-warning-scenario-pandemic-132797

[25] Tracy, Abigail. "How Trump Gutted Obama's Pandemic-Preparedness Systems." *Vanity Fair*. May 1, 2020. https://www.vanityfair.com/news/2020/05/trump-obama-coronavirus-pandemic-response

[26] Papenfuss, Mary. "Trump Slams 'Nasty' Question As PBS Reporter Challenges Him On Shutdown Of Pandemic Unit." *Huffington Post*. March 14, 2020. https://www.huffingtonpost.co.uk/entry/yamiche-alcindor-pbs-donald-trump-nsc-global-health-security_n_5e6bfe8bc5b6dda30fc8f955

[27] Drash, Wayne. "Cuts to CDC epidemic programs will endanger Americans, former chief says." *CNN.com*. February 5, 2018. https://edition.cnn.com/2018/02/03/health/cdc-slashes-global-epidemic-programs-outrage/index.html

[28] Gore, D'Angelo. "False Claim About CDC's Global Anti-Pandemic Work." *Factcheck.org*. March 12, 2020. https://www.factcheck.org/2020/03/false-claim-about-cdcs-global-anti-pandemic-work/

[29] Mackey, Robert. "Trump Says He Had No Idea His Pandemic Response Team Was Disbanded. What If That's True?" *Intercept*. March 14, 2020. https://theintercept.com/2020/03/14/trump-says-no-idea-pandemic-response-team-disbanded-thats-true/

[30] "Remarks by President Trump, Vice President Pence, and Members of the Coronavirus Task Force in Press Conference." White House Archives. February 27, 2020. https://trumpwhitehouse.archives.gov/briefings-statements/remarks-president-trump-vice-president-pence-members-coronavirus-task-force-press-conference/ (https://trumpwhitehouse.archives.gov/briefings-statements/remarks-president-trump-vice-president-pence-members-coronavirus-task-force-press-conference/)

[31] Oprysko, Caitlin. "'I don't take responsibility at all': Trump deflects blame for coronavirus testing fumble." *Politico*. March 13, 2020. https://www.politico.com/news/2020/03/13/trump-coronavirus-testing-128971

[32] Diamond and Toosi. "Trump team failed to follow NSC's pandemic playbook."

[33] "Remarks by President Trump After Tour of the Centers for Disease Control and Prevention | Atlanta, GA." White House Archives. March 7, 2020. https://trumpwhitehouse.archives.gov/briefings-statements/remarks-president-trump-tour-centers-disease-control-prevention-atlanta-ga/ (https://trumpwhitehouse.archives.gov/briefings-statements/remarks-president-trump-tour-centers-disease-control-prevention-atlanta-ga/)

[34] Dale, Daniel et al. "Fact check: Trump falsely claims, again, that anybody who wants a test can get one." *CNN.com*. May 12, 2020. https://edition.cnn.com/2020/05/11/politics/trump-fact-check-may-11/index.html

[35] Knowles, Hannah et al. "Californians required to cover their faces in 'most settings outside the home.'" *The Washington Post*. June 19, 2020. https://www.washingtonpost.com/nation/2020/06/18/coronavirus-live-updates-us/

[36] "Transcript of President Trump's Interview With The Wall Street Journal." *Wall Street Journal*. June 18, 2020. https://www.wsj.com/articles/transcript-of-president-trumps-interview-with-the-wall-street-journal-11592501000

[37] Sebenius, Isaac and Sebenius, James K. "How many needless Covid-19 deaths were caused by delays in responding? Most of them." *Stat News*. June 19, 2020. https://www.statnews.com/2020/06/19/faster-response-prevented-most-us-covid-19-deaths/

[38] "Cumulative number of COVID-19 tests performed in the U.S. from March 1 to July 30, 2020." *Statista*. https://www.statista.com/statistics/1111631/cumulative-number-of-covid19-tests-carried-out-in-the-us/

[39] "About MERS." Centers for Disease Control and Prevention. https://www.cdc.gov/

coronavirus/mers/about/index.html

40 Engelberg, Stephen, Song, Lisa and DePillis, Lydia. "How South Korea Scaled Coronavirus Testing While the U.S. Fell Dangerously Behind." *ProPublica.* March 15, 2020. https://www.propublica.org/article/how-south-korea-scaled-coronavirus-testing-while-the-us-fell-dangerously-behind

41 Oh, Myoung-Don et al. "Middle East respiratory syndrome: what we learned from the 2015 outbreak in the Republic of Korea." *Korean J Intern Med.* March, 2018. https://www.ncbi.nlm.nih.gov/pmc/articles/PMC5840604/

42 Terhune, Chad et al. "Special Report: How Korea trounced U.S. in race to test people for coronavirus." *Reuters.* March 18, 2020. https://www.reuters.com/article/us-health-coronavirus-testing-specialrep/special-report-how-korea-trounced-u-s-in-race-to-test-people-for-coronavirus-idUSKBN2153BW

43 "Coronavirus: President Trump's testing claims fact-checked." *BBC.* May 15, 2020. https://www.bbc.co.uk/news/world-us-canada-52493073

44 Taylor, Marisa. "Exclusive: U.S. axed CDC expert job in China months before virus outbreak." *Reuters.* March 22, 2020. https://www.reuters.com/article/us-health-coronavirus-china-cdc-exclusiv-idUSKBN21910S

45 Soucheray, Stephanie. "Coroner: First US COVID-19 death occurred in early February." *CIDRAP News.* April 22, 2020. https://www.cidrap.umn.edu/news-perspective/2020/04/coroner-first-us-covid-19-death-occurred-early-february

46 Wittes, Benjamin. "Trump as National Security Threat." *Lawfare.* March 2, 2016. https://www.lawfareblog.com/trump-national-security-threat

47 "Timeline of the Muslim Ban." ACLU Washington. https://www.aclu-wa.org/pages/timeline-muslim-ban

48 Barnes, Julian E. and Cooper, Helene. "Trump Discussed Pulling U.S. From NATO, Aides Say Amid New Concerns Over Russia." *New York Times.* January 14, 2019. https://www.nytimes.com/2019/01/14/us/politics/nato-president-trump.html

49 Mallin, Alexander and Rogin, Ali. "Lawmakers, experts doubt Trump could unilaterally pull US from NATO." *Abcnews.go.com.* July 12, 2018. https://abcnews.go.com/Politics/lawmakers-experts-doubt-trump-unilaterally-pull-us-nato/story?id=56552444

50 Harding, Luke. "Could Trump pull US out of Nato and what would happen if he did?" *Guardian.* July 12, 2018. https://www.theguardian.com/world/2018/jul/12/trump-nato-threat-withdraw-what-would-happen

51 Unger, Craig. *House of Trump, House of Putin* (p. 49). Penguin Publishing Group. Kindle Edition.

52 Smith, David. "Trump 'treasonous' after siding with Putin on election meddling." *Guardian.* July 16, 2018. https://www.theguardian.com/us-news/2018/jul/16/trump-finds-putin-denial-of-election-meddling-powerful

53 Corn, David. "John Bolton Provides a Harrowing Portrait of Trump's Surrender to Putin." *Mother Jones*. June 18, 2020. https://www.motherjones.com/politics/2020/06/john-bolton-provides-a-harrowing-portrait-of-trumps-surrender-to-putin/

54 Trump, Donald. *Twitter*. June 18, 2013. https://www.thetrumparchive.com/?results=1&searchbox=%22Do+you+think+Putin+will+be+going%22

55 Yourish, Karen and Griggs, Troy. "8 U.S. Intelligence Groups Blame Russia for Meddling, but Trump Keeps Clouding the Picture." *New York Times*. August 2, 2018. https://www.nytimes.com/interactive/2018/07/16/us/elections/russian-interference-statements-comments.html

56 "Read the Mueller Report: Searchable Document and Index." *New York Times*. April 18, 2019. https://www.nytimes.com/interactive/2019/04/18/us/politics/mueller-report-document.html

57 Hill, Fiona and Gaddy, Clifford G. *Mr. Putin (Geopolitics in the 21st Century)* (p. 384). Brookings Institution Press, 2012. Kindle Edition.

58 Dugyala, Rishika. "Kremlin: Putin calls to thank Trump for help on terrorism." *Politico*. December 29, 2019. https://www.politico.com/news/2019/12/29/kremlin-putin-calls-to-thank-trump-for-help-on-terrorism-090430

59 Wee, Sui-Lee and Wang, Vivian. "China Grapples With Mystery Pneumonia-Like Illness." *New York Times*. January 6, 2020 (updated January 21). https://www.nytimes.com/2020/01/06/world/asia/china-SARS-pneumonialike.html?auth=login-email&login=email

60 Page, Jeremy, Fan, Wenxin and Khan, Natasha. "How It All Started: China's Early Coronavirus Missteps." *Wall Street Journal*. March 6, 2020. https://www.wsj.com/articles/how-it-all-started-chinas-early-coronavirus-missteps-11583508932

61 Wang, Chi. "Russia is no friend to China. In fact, Xi's friendship with Putin is a betrayal of the Chinese people." *South China Morning Post*. December 10, 2019. https://www.scmp.com/comment/opinion/article/3041246/russia-no-friend-china-fact-xis-friendship-putin-betrayal-chinese

62 Dobbins, James, Shatz, Howard J. and Wyne, Ali. "A Warming Trend in China–Russia Relations." *RAND Corporation*. April 18, 2019. https://www.rand.org/blog/2019/04/a-warming-trend-in-china-russia-relations.html

63 Cohen, Zachary et al. "US intelligence agencies started tracking coronavirus outbreak in China as early as November." *CNN.com*. April 9, 2020. https://edition.cnn.com/2020/04/08/politics/intel-agencies-covid-november/index.html

64 Walcott, John. "'Willful Ignorance.' Inside President Trump's Troubled Intelligence Briefings." *Time*. February 2, 2019 (updated February 5). https://time.com/5518947/donald-trump-intelligence-briefings-national-security/

65 Blake, Aaron. "6 times Trump has sided with a foreign country over the U.S. government." *The Washington Post*. January 10, 2019. https://www.washingtonpost.com/politics/2019/01/10/times-trump-has-sided-with-foreign-

country-over-his-own-government/

[66] Haque, Umair. "America Surrendered to Coronavirus — the Result is a Tidal Wave of Death." *Eudaimonia & Co.* June 18, 2020. https://eand.co/america-surrendered-to-coronavirus-the-result-is-a-tidal-wave-of-death-b47c20d6597f (https://eand.co/america-surrendered-to-coronavirus-the-result-is-a-tidal-wave-of-death-b47c20d6597f)

Chapter Four: Totally Under Control

[1] "Timeline - In his own words: Trump and the coronavirus." *Reuters.* October 2, 2020. https://www.reuters.com/article/us-health-coronavirus-usa-trump-comments/timeline-in-his-own-words-trump-and-the-coronavirus-idUKKBN26N0U5

[2] "Previous U.S. COVID-19 Case Data." Centers for Disease Control and Prevention. https://www.cdc.gov/coronavirus/2019-ncov/cases-updates/previouscases.html

[3] Biden. "FLASHBACK by Joe Biden: Trump is worst possible leader to deal with coronavirus outbreak."

[4] Liptak, Kevin and Collins, Kaitlan. "Measures to protect Trump from coronavirus scale up even as he seeks to move on." *CNN.com.* June 26, 2020. https://edition.cnn.com/2020/06/26/politics/donald-trump-coronavirus-protocols/index.html

[5] Vazques, Maegan and Malloy, Allie. "Trump says he's 'all for masks,' but believes coronavirus will 'disappear.'" *CNN.com.* July 1, 2020. https://edition.cnn.com/2020/07/01/politics/donald-trump-masks-coronavirus/index.html

[6] Liptak and Collins. "Measures to protect Trump from coronavirus scale up even as he seeks to move on."

[7] Oprysko, Caitlin et al. "Trump hits back at Biden's accusation of 'darkness in America': Key moments." Politico. August 27, 2020. https://www.politico.com/news/2020/08/27/rnc-thursday-key-moments-403972

[8] Ibid.

[9] "President Donald J. Trump's Acceptance of the Republican Nomination for President of the United States of America: Guest Guidance." Politico. https://www.politico.com/f/?id=00000174-30aa-d006-a7f4-f0af007b0000

[10] Boehlert, Eric. "Russian bounties — Trump threatens the American experiment." *Press Run.* July 2, 2020. https://pressrun.media/p/russian-bounties-trump-threatens (https://pressrun.media/p/russian-bounties-trump-threatens)

[11] Harris et al. "U.S. intelligence reports from January and February warned about a likely pandemic."

[12] "Proclamation on Suspension of Entry as Immigrants and Nonimmigrants of Persons who Pose a Risk of Transmitting 2019 Novel Coronavirus." White House Archives. January 31, 2020. https://trumpwhitehouse.archives.gov/presidential-

actions/proclamation-suspension-entry-immigrants-nonimmigrants-persons-pose-risk-transmitting-2019-novel-coronavirus/ (https://trumpwhitehouse.archives.gov/presidential-actions/proclamation-suspension-entry-immigrants-nonimmigrants-persons-pose-risk-transmitting-2019-novel-coronavirus/)

13 Kessler, Glenn. "Trump's claim that he imposed the first 'China ban.'" *The Washington Post.* April 7, 2020. https://www.washingtonpost.com/politics/2020/04/07/trumps-claim-that-he-imposed-first-china-ban/

14 Greenberg, Jon et al. "'We have it totally under control.' A timeline of President Donald Trump's response to the coronavirus pandemic." *Poynter.* March 24, 2020. https://www.poynter.org/fact-checking/2020/we-have-it-totally-under-control-a-timeline-of-president-donald-trumps-response-to-the-coronavirus-pandemic/

15 James, Erin and Omer, Saad B. "Why a Travel Ban Won't Stop the Coronavirus." *National Interest.* February 3, 2020. https://nationalinterest.org/blog/buzz/why-travel-ban-won%E2%80%99t-stop-coronavirus-119681 (https://nationalinterest.org/blog/buzz/why-travel-ban-won%E2⬚t-stop-coronavirus-119681)

16 Eder et al. "430,000 People Have Traveled From China to U.S. Since Coronavirus Surfaced."

17 Robertson, Lori. "Trump's Snowballing China Travel Claim." *Factcheck.org.* April 10, 2020 (updated April 15). https://www.factcheck.org/2020/04/trumps-snowballing-china-travel-claim/

18 Levin, Bess. "Of Course the Trump Administration Ignored a Step-by-Step Guide to Fighting a Coronavirus-esque Pandemic." *Vanity Fair.* March 26, 2020. https://www.vanityfair.com/news/2020/03/donald-trump-obama-pandemic-playbook

19 Biesecker, Michael. "US 'wasted' months before preparing for coronavirus pandemic." *AP News.* April 5, 2020. https://apnews.com/article/090600c299a8cf07f5b44d92534856bc

20 Worldometer. https://www.worldometers.info/coronavirus/usa/new-york/

21 Peters, Jeremy W., Plott, Elaina and Haberman, Maggie. "260,000 Words, Full of Self-Praise, From Trump on the Virus." *New York Times.* April 26, 2020. https://www.nytimes.com/interactive/2020/04/26/us/politics/trump-coronavirus-briefings-analyzed.html

22 Collins, Sean. "Trump could help solve the mask problem. Instead he's making baseless attacks on New York nurses." *Vox.com.* March 30, 2020. https://www.vox.com/policy-and-politics/2020/3/30/21199538/coronavirus-mask-trump-new-york-hospital-stealing

23 Falzone, Diana. "'Like a Bully at the Lunchroom': How the Federal Government Took Control of the PPE Pipeline." *Vanity Fair.* May 6, 2020. https://www.vanityfair.com/news/2020/05/how-the-federal-government-took-control-of-the-ppe-pipeline

24 Kanno-Youngs and Nicas. "'Swept Up by FEMA': Complicated Medical Supply System Sows Confusion."

[25] Biesecker. "US 'wasted' months before preparing for coronavirus pandemic."

[26] Watson, Kathryn. "Trump invokes Defense Production Act to require GM to produce ventilators." *CBSnews.com*. March 27, 2020. https://www.cbsnews.com/news/trump-invokes-defense-production-act-to-require-gm-to-produce-ventilators-2020-03-27/

[27] Ellyatt, Holly. "US sends 200 ventilators to Russia as crisis deepens, hopes for 'better relationship.'" *CNBC.com*. May 20, 2020. https://www.cnbc.com/2020/05/20/us-sends-200-ventilators-to-russia-as-coronavirus-crisis-deepens.html

[28] Callahan, Patricia, Rotella, Sebastian and Golden, Tim. "Taxpayers Paid Millions to Design a Low-Cost Ventilator for a Pandemic. Instead, the Company Is Selling Versions of It Overseas." *ProPublica*. March 30, 2020. https://www.propublica.org/article/taxpayers-paid-millions-to-design-a-low-cost-ventilator-for-a-pandemic-instead-the-company-is-selling-versions-of-it-overseas-

[29] "COVID-19 Among Workers in Meat and Poultry Processing Facilities ⊠ 19 States, April 2020." Centers for Disease Control and Prevention. https://www.cdc.gov/mmwr/volumes/69/wr/mm6918e3.htm?s_cid=mm6918e3_w

[30] Molteni, Megan. "Why Meatpacking Plants Have Become Covid-19 Hot Spots." *Wired*. May 7, 2020. https://www.wired.com/story/why-meatpacking-plants-have-become-covid-19-hot-spots/

[31] Collins, Kaitlan and Vazquez, Maegan. "Trump orders meat processing plants to stay open." *CNN.com*. April 28, 2020. https://edition.cnn.com/2020/04/28/politics/defense-production-act-executive-order-food-supply/index.html

[32] "Meatpacking union: 44 COVID-19 deaths among workers." *AP News*. May 28, 2020. https://apnews.com/article/f332a2d38e693b25a82a846bf7337a40

[33] Godoy, Maria and Wood, Daniel. "What Do Coronavirus Racial Disparities Look Like State By State?" *NPR.org*. May 30, 2020. https://www.npr.org/sections/health-shots/2020/05/30/865413079/what-do-coronavirus-racial-disparities-look-like-state-by-state

[34] "Occupational Employment and Wages, May 2018: 51-3023 Slaughterers and Meat Packers." U.S. Bureau of Labor Statistics. https://www.bls.gov/oes/2018/may/oes513023.htm

[35] Fremstad, Shawn, Rho, Hye Jin and Brown, Hayley. "Meatpacking Workers are a Diverse Group Who Need Better Protections." *Center for Economic and Policy Research*. April 29, 2020. https://cepr.net/meatpacking-workers-are-a-diverse-group-who-need-better-protections/ (https://cepr.net/meatpacking-workers-are-a-diverse-group-who-need-better-protections/)

[36] Johnson, Akilah and Buford, Talia. "Early Data Shows African Americans Have Contracted and Died of Coronavirus at an Alarming Rate." *ProPublica*. April 3, 2020. https://www.propublica.org/article/early-data-shows-african-americans-have-contracted-and-died-of-coronavirus-at-an-alarming-rate

[37] Jeffery, Adam. "Scenes of protests across the country demanding states reopen the economy amid coronavirus pandemic." *CNBC.com.* April 18, 2020 (updated April 20). https://www.cnbc.com/2020/04/18/coronavirus-scenes-of-protests-across-the-country-demanding-states-reopen-the-economy.html

[38] Stanley-Becker, Isaac and Romm, Tony. "The anti-quarantine protests seem spontaneous. But behind the scenes, a powerful network is helping." *The Washington Post.* April 22, 2020. https://www.washingtonpost.com/politics/inside-the-conservative-networks-backing-anti-quarantine-protests/2020/04/22/da75c81e-83fe-11ea-a3eb-e9fc93160703_story.html

[39] Ibid.

[40] Karni, Annie and McNeil, Donald G., Jr. "Trump Wants U.S. 'Opened Up' by Easter, Despite Health Officials' Warnings." *New York Times.* March 24, 2020. https://www.nytimes.com/2020/03/24/us/politics/trump-coronavirus-easter.html

[41] Trump, Donald. *Twitter.* April 17, 2020. https://www.thetrumparchive.com/?results=1&searchbox=%22LIBERATE%22

[42] Ibid.

[43] Ibid.

[44] The COVID Tracking Project. https://covidtracking.com/data/national

[45] Hawkins, Derek et al. "Arizona, Florida, Texas are latest coronavirus epicenters." *The Washington Post.* June 29, 2020. https://www.washingtonpost.com/nation/2020/06/28/coronavirus-live-updates-us/

[46] "COVID-19: Oklahoma numbers continue to spike, with 450 new cases, 2 more Oklahomans' deaths announced Thursday." *Tulsa World.* June 19, 2020. https://www.tulsaworld.com/news/covid-19-oklahoma-numbers-continue-to-spike-with-450-new-cases-2-more-oklahomans-deaths/article_c7bd2ce0-292f-5c3c-bb12-2e4c4efe11b5.html

[47] Mena, Kelly. "Washington Post: Trump campaign had social distancing stickers removed before Tulsa rally." *CNN.com.* June 28, 2020. https://edition.cnn.com/2020/06/27/politics/social-distancing-stickers-trump-campaign-tulsa-rally

[48] "The Latest: Tulsa reports record spike in COVID-19 cases." *AP News.* June 24, 2020. https://apnews.com/article/245057f1c2211c7ea2fc7b0e9d6e5686

[49] The COVID Tracking Project. https://covidtracking.com/data/state/oklahoma

[50] Ibid.

[51] Worldometer. https://www.worldometers.info/coronavirus/country/us/

[52] Olorunnipa, Toluse, Witte, Griff and Bernstein, Lenny. "Trump cheers on governors even as they ignore White House coronavirus guidelines in race to reopen." *The Washington Post.* May 5, 2020. https://www.washingtonpost.com/politics/trump-cheers-on-governors-as-they-ignore-white-house-coronovirus-guidelines-in-race-to-reopen/2020/05/04/bedc6116-8e18-11ea-a0bc-4e9ad4866d21_story.html

[53] Worldometer. https://www.worldometers.info/coronavirus/country/us/

[54] "Interview: David Brody of CBN News Interviews Donald Trump at The White House - June 22, 2020." *Youtube.* June 24, 2020. https://youtu.be/SNFFHLnxArU (https://youtu.be/SNFFHLnxArU)

[55] Ornstein, Charles and Ngu, Ash. "No, President Trump, Testing Is Not Causing Case Counts to Rise. The Virus Is Just Spreading Faster." *ProPublica.* June 25, 2020. https://www.propublica.org/article/state-coronavirus-data-doesnt-support-trumps-misleading-testing-claims

[56] Bengel, Chris. "What KBO's Opening Day looked like with no fans in the stands." *CBSSports.com.* May 5, 2020. https://www.cbssports.com/mlb/news/what-kbos-opening-day-looked-like-with-no-fans-in-the-stands/

[57] Irfan, Umair. "The case for ending the Covid-19 pandemic with mass testing." *Vox.com.* April 13, 2020. https://www.vox.com/2020/4/13/21215133/coronavirus-testing-covid-19-tests-screening

[58] Feuer, Will. "Trump blames rise in coronavirus cases on increased testing, despite evidence of more spread." *CNBC.com.* June 23, 2020. https://www.cnbc.com/2020/06/23/trump-blames-rise-in-coronavirus-cases-on-testing-despite-signs-of-spread.html

[59] Weixel, Nathaniel. "Trump on coronavirus: 'If we stop testing right now, we'd have very few cases, if any.'" *Hill.* June 15, 2020. https://thehill.com/policy/healthcare/502819-trump-on-coronavirus-if-we-stop-testing-right-now-wed-have-very-few-cases

[60] Bender, Michael C. "Trump Talks Juneteenth, John Bolton, Economy in WSJ Interview." *Wall Street Journal.* June 19, 2020. https://www.wsj.com/articles/trump-talks-juneteenth-john-bolton-economy-in-wsj-interview-11592493771?shareToken=st1351778119cb4a0a8ce1222d0d949e83

[61] Worldometer. https://www.worldometers.info/coronavirus/country/us/

[62] Behrmann, Savannah. "Senate Dems ask HHS watchdog to investigate Trump's 'slow the testing down' comment." *USA Today News.* June 23, 2020. https://eu.usatoday.com/story/news/politics/2020/06/23/dems-want-investigation-trumps-slow-testing-down-comment/3239642001/

[63] Abutaleb, Yasmeen, Telford, Taylor and Dawsey, Josh. "Democrats, public health experts decry Trump for saying he asked officials to slow down coronavirus testing." *The Washington Post.* June 22, 2020. https://www.washingtonpost.com/politics/2020/06/21/democrats-public-health-experts-decry-trump-saying-he-asked-officials-slow-down-coronavirus-testing/

[64] Forgey, Quint. "'I don't kid': Trump says he wasn't joking about slowing coronavirus testing." *Politico.* June 23, 2020. https://www.politico.com/news/2020/06/23/trump-joking-slowing-coronavirus-testing-335459

[65] "Researchers Develop First Diagnostic Test for Novel Coronavirus in China." *Technology Networks.* January 20, 2020. https://www.technologynetworks.

com/diagnostics/news/researchers-develop-first-diagnostic-test-for-novel-coronavirus-in-china-329537

66 Patel, Neel V. "Why the CDC botched its coronavirus testing." *MIT Technology Review.* March 5, 2020. https://www.technologyreview.com/2020/03/05/905484/why-the-cdc-botched-its-coronavirus-testing/

67 Nazaryan, Alexander. "After months of being silenced, CDC is easing back into public view." *Yahoo! News.* July 2, 2020. https://news.yahoo.com/after-months-of-being-silenced-the-cdc-is-easing-back-into-public-view-090053863.html?soc_src=hl-viewer&soc_trk=tw

68 Ibid.

69 Dale, Daniel. "Fact check: Trump falsely claims he 'inherited' the faulty coronavirus test. It was developed this year." *CNN.com.* April 7, 2020. https://edition.cnn.com/2020/04/07/politics/fact-check-trump-inherited-broken-obsolete-coronavirus-tests/index.html

70 Wilkie, Christina and Mangan, Dan. "Trump blames Obama for lack of coronavirus tests: 'I don't take responsibility at all.'" *CNBC.com.* March 13, 2020 (updated March 14). https://www.cnbc.com/2020/03/13/coronavirus-trump-says-i-dont-take-responsibility-at-all-for-lack-of-tests.html

71 Joseph, Andrew. "Contact tracing could help avoid another lockdown. Can it work in the U.S.?" *Stat News.* May 29, 2020. https://www.statnews.com/2020/05/29/contact-tracing-can-it-help-avoid-more-lockdowns/

72 Eban. "How Jared Kushner's Secret Testing Plan 'Went Poof Into Thin Air.'"

73 Stein, Rob. "As Coronavirus Surges, How Much Testing Does Your State Need To Subdue The Virus?" *NPR.org.* June 30, 2020. https://www.npr.org/sections/health-shots/2020/06/30/883703403/as-coronavirus-surges-how-much-testing-does-your-state-need-to-subdue-the-virus

74 The COVID Tracking Project. https://covidtracking.com/data/national

75 Siddarth, Divya and Weyl, Glen E. "Why We Must Test Millions a Day." *Edmond J. Safra Center for Ethics.* April 8, 2020. https://ethics.harvard.edu/files/center-for-ethics/files/white_paper_6_testing_millions_final.pdf (https://ethics.harvard.edu/files/center-for-ethics/files/white_paper_6_testing_millions_final.pdf)

76 "July 6, 2020 | State Testing Targets." Pandemics Explained. https://globalepidemics.org/july-6-2020-state-testing-targets/ (https://globalepidemics.org/july-6-2020-state-testing-targets/)

77 Ibid.

78 Worldometer. https://www.worldometers.info/coronavirus/country/us/

79 Haque, Umair. "How Bad is America's Coronavirus Surge? Really, Really Bad." *Eudaimonia & Co.* June 30, 2020. https://eand.co/how-bad-is-americas-coronavirus-surge-really-really-bad-65407d6585de (https://eand.co/how-bad-is-americas-coronavirus-surge-really-really-bad-65407d6585de)

[80] The COVID Tracking Project. https://covidtracking.com/data/national

[81] Worldometer. https://www.worldometers.info/coronavirus/country/us/

[82] Brown, Emma, Reinhard, Beth and Davis, Aaron C. "Coronavirus death toll: Americans are almost certainly dying of covid-19 but being left out of the official count." *The Washington Post.* April 5, 2020. https://www.washingtonpost.com/ investigations/coronavirus-death-toll-americans-are-almost-certainly-dying-of-covid-19-but-being-left-out-of-the-official-count/2020/04/05/71d67982-747e-11ea-87da-77a8136c1a6d_story.html

[83] Trump, Donald. *Twitter.* June 23, 2020. https://www.thetrumparchive.com/ ?results= 1&searchbox=%22by+far+the+most%2C+and+best%2C+in+ the+World

[84] Trump, Donald. *Twitter.* June 30, 2020. https://www.thetrumparchive. com/?results=1&searchbox=%22leads+the+world+in+coronavirus+testing%22

[85] Worldometer. https://www.worldometers.info/coronavirus/

[86] Gross, Terry. "Reporter: White House Knew Of Coronavirus' 'Major Threat,' But Response Fell Short." *NPR.org.* March 12, 2020. https://www.npr. org/2020/03/12/814881355/white-house-knew-coronavirus-would-be-a-major-threat-but-response-fell-short

[87] Worldometer. https://www.worldometers.info/coronavirus/country/us/

[88] Wolfe, Daniel and Dale, Daniel. "'It's going to disappear': A timeline of Trump's claims that Covid-19 will vanish." *CNN.com.* October 31, 2020. https://edition. cnn.com/interactive/2020/10/politics/covid-disappearing-trump-comment-tracker/

[89] Diamond, Dan. "Trump's mismanagement helped fuel coronavirus crisis." *Politico.* March 7, 2020. https://www.politico.com/news/2020/03/07/trump-coronavirus-management-style-123465

[90] Gabbatt, Adam. "Trump plan to cut federal support for Covid-19 testing sites sparks alarm." *Guardian.* June 25, 2020. https://www.theguardian.com/us-news/2020/jun/25/us-coronavirus-testing-sites-federal-support-cut-officials-alarm

[91] Grieder, Erica. "Greg Abbott's Trump Problem." *Texas Monthly.* June 3, 2016. https://www.texasmonthly.com/burka-blog/greg-abbotts-trump-problem/

[92] Svitek, Patrick. "Gov. Greg Abbott expresses regret over reopening Texas bars during coronavirus." *Texas Tribune.* June 26, 2020. https://www.texastribune. org/2020/06/26/greg-abbott-texas-bars-regret/

[93] Gabbatt. "Trump plan to cut federal support for Covid-19 testing sites sparks alarm."

[94] Clemons, Steve. "Coronavirus Report: The Hill's Steve Clemons interviews Rep. Sean Patrick Maloney." *Hill.* June 16, 2020. https://thehill.com/homenews/ coronavirus-report/502963-coronavirus-report-the-hills-steve-clemons-interviews-rep-sean

95 Winfield Cunningham, Paige. "Democratic senators say Trump administration has been slow to use coronavirus testing funds." *The Washington Post*. June 22, 2020. https://www.washingtonpost.com/politics/democratic-senators-say-trump-administration-has-been-slow-to-use-coronavirus-testing-funds/2020/06/21/d9868c66-b3f3-11ea-a510-55bf26485c93_story.html

96 Worldometer. https://www.worldometers.info/coronavirus/country/us/

97 Gumbrecht, Jamie, Fox, Maggie and Nedelman, Michael. "Updated CDC guidelines now say people exposed to coronavirus may not need to be tested." *CNN.com*. August 26, 2020. https://edition.cnn.com/2020/08/26/health/cdc-guidelines-coronavirus-testing/index.html

98 Valencia, Nick, Murray, Sara and Holmes, Kristen. "CDC was pressured 'from the top down' to change coronavirus testing guidance, official says." *CNN.com*. August 27, 2020. https://edition.cnn.com/2020/08/26/politics/cdc-coronavirus-testing-guidance/index.html

99 Edwards, Erika. "CDC director walks back testing guidance, but does not alter recommendations on website." *NBCNews.com*. August 27, 2020. https://www.nbcnews.com/health/health-news/cdc-director-walks-back-testing-guidance-does-not-alter-recommendations-n1238428

100 "White House, Under Fire for Discouraging Coronavirus Testing, Says It Will Buy Millions of Test Kits." *New York Times*. August 27, 2020 (updated August 28). https://www.nytimes.com/2020/08/27/world/covid-19-coronavirus.html#link-63a48e9d

101 Ibid.

102 Pradhan, Rachana. "Problems With Trump-Touted COVID-19 Test Pile Up." *Daily Beast*. June 19, 2020. https://www.thedailybeast.com/problems-with-trump-touted-abbott-rapid-covid-19-test-pile-up

103 Axe, David. "Donald Trump Is Buying 150 Million COVID Tests. What Could Possibly Go Wrong?" *Daily Beast*. August 28, 2020. https://www.thedailybeast.com/trumps-150-million-covid-19-antigen-tests-from-abbott-could-be-a-game-changer-or-a-mess

104 Owermohle, Sarah. "Trump cuts U.S. research on bat-human virus transmission over China ties." *Politico*. April 27, 2020. https://www.politico.com/news/2020/04/27/trump-cuts-research-bat-human-virus-china-213076

105 Mack, Eric. "Obama Gave $3.7M Grant to Sketchy China Virology Lab." *Newsmax*. April 18, 2020. https://www.newsmax.com/t/newsmax/article/963512/18

106 Brown, Matthew and Hjelmgaard, Kim. "Fact check: Obama administration did not send $3.7 million to Wuhan lab." *USA Today News*. May 4, 2020. https://eu.usatoday.com/story/news/factcheck/2020/05/04/fact-check-obama-administration-did-not-send-3-7-m-wuhan-lab/3061490001/

107 Mole, Beth. "White House ordered NIH to cancel coronavirus research funding,

Fauci says." *Ars Technica*. June 25, 2020. https://arstechnica.com/science/2020/06/white-house-ordered-nih-to-cancel-coronavirus-research-funding-fauci-says/

[108] Parker, Abutaleb and Dawsey. "Trump administration has many task forces."

[109] Worldometer. https://www.worldometers.info/coronavirus/country/us/

[110] Parker, Abutaleb and Dawsey. "Trump administration has many task forces."

[111] Tilove, Jonathan. "Chanting 'Let us work!', 'Fire Fauci!', protesters at Capitol decry virus restrictions." *Austin American-Statesman*. April 18, 2020. https://www.statesman.com/news/20200418/chanting-rsquolet-us-workrsquo-rsquofire-faucirsquo-protesters-at-capitol-decry-virus-restrictions

[112] Orr, Gabby and Levine, Marianne. "Trump's #FireFauci retweet spurs a cycle of outrage and a White House denial." *Politico*. April 13, 2020. https://www.politico.com/news/2020/04/13/trump-fauci-fire-tweet-coronavirus-183907

[113] LeBlanc, Paul. "Can Trump fire Fauci? Technically, no." *CNN.com*. July 13, 2020 (updated July 14). https://edition.cnn.com/2020/07/13/politics/can-trump-fire-fauci/index.html

[114] Abutaleb, Yasmeen, Dawsey, Josh and McGinley, Laurie. "Fauci is sidelined by the White House as he steps up blunt talk on pandemic." *The Washington Post*. July 11, 2020. https://www.washingtonpost.com/politics/2020/07/11/fauci-trump-coronavirus/

[115] Ibid.

[116] Holland, Steve and Alper, Alexander. "Trump advises voluntary mask use against coronavirus but won't wear one himself." *Reuters*. April 3, 2020. https://www.reuters.com/article/us-usa-health-coronavirus-masks/trump-advises-voluntary-mask-use-against-coronavirus-but-wont-wear-one-himself-idUSKBN21L39K

[117] Chu, Derek K. et al. "Physical distancing, face masks, and eye protection to prevent person-to-person transmission of SARS-CoV-2 and COVID-19: a systematic review and meta-analysis." *Lancet*. June 27, 2020. https://www.thelancet.com/journals/lancet/article/PIIS0140-6736(20)31142-9/fulltext

[118] "Widespread facemask use could shrink the 'R' number and prevent a second COVID-19 wave: study." *Medical Xpress*. June 9, 2020. https://medicalxpress.com/news/2020-06-widespread-facemask-covid-.html

[119] Blake, Aaron. "Trump's dumbfounding refusal to encourage wearing masks." *The Washington Post*. June 25, 2020. https://www.washingtonpost.com/politics/2020/06/25/trumps-dumbfounding-refusal-encourage-wearing-masks/

[120] Liptak, Kevin. "Trump says he won't wear a mask in front of cameras." *CNN.com*. May 21, 2020. https://edition.cnn.com/2020/05/21/politics/donald-trump-michigan-masks/index.html

[121] Glick, Peter. "Masks and Emasculation: Why Some Men Refuse to Take Safety Precautions." *Scientific American*. April 30, 2020. https://blogs.scientificamerican.

com/observations/masks-and-emasculation-why-some-men-refuse-to-take-safety-precautions/

[122] North, Anna. "What Trump's refusal to wear a mask says about masculinity in America." *Vox.com.* May 12, 2020. https://www.vox.com/2020/5/12/21252476/masks-for-coronavirus-trump-pence-honeywell-covid-19

[123] Ibid.

[124] Lemire, Jonathan. "Trump wears mask in public for first time during pandemic." *AP News.* July 12, 2020. https://apnews.com/article/7651589ac439646e5cf873d021f1f4b6

[125] Diamond, Jeremy and Liptak, Kevin. "'Pleading' from aides led to Trump agreeing -- after months -- to wear a mask." *CNN.com.* July 10, 2020. https://edition.cnn.com/2020/07/10/politics/trump-mask-walter-reed-coronavirus/index.html

[126] Shear, Michael D. and Haberman, Maggie. "Health Dept. Official Says Doubts on Hydroxychloroquine Led to His Ouster." *New York Times.* April 22, 2020 (updated May 14). https://www.nytimes.com/2020/04/22/us/politics/rick-bright-trump-hydroxychloroquine-coronavirus.html

[127] Peryer, Marisa. "US prescriptions for hydroxychloroquine skyrocketed from February to March, study finds." *CNN.com.* July 7, 2020. https://edition.cnn.com/2020/07/06/health/hydroxychloroquine-prescription-increase-coronavirus-study/index.html

[128] Worldometer. https://www.worldometers.info/coronavirus/country/us/

[129] Ibid.

[130] Klein, Betsy and Vazquez, Maegan. "Trump says he will pressure governors over school reopenings even as virus surges." *CNN.com.* July 7, 2020. https://edition.cnn.com/2020/07/07/politics/trump-education-schools-reopening/index.html

[131] Trump, Donald. *Twitter.* July 6, 2020. https://www.thetrumparchive.com/?results=1&searchbox=%22SCHOOLS+MUST+OPEN+IN+THE+FALL%22

[132] Smith-Schoenwalder, Cecelia. "Trump: We Will Pressure Schools to Reopen in Fall." *U.S. News.* July 7, 2020. https://www.usnews.com/news/national-news/articles/2020-07-07/trump-we-will-pressure-schools-to-reopen-in-fall

[133] Khazan, Olga. "The School Reopeners Think America Is Forgetting About Kids." *Atlantic.* June 25, 2020. https://www.theatlantic.com/health/archive/2020/06/will-schools-reopen-fall/613468/

[134] Estrin, Daniel. "After Reopening Schools, Israel Orders Them To Shut If COVID-19 Cases Are Discovered." *NPR.org.* June 3, 2020. https://www.npr.org/sections/coronavirus-live-updates/2020/06/03/868507524/israel-orders-schools-to-close-when-covid-19-cases-are-discovered

[135] Buckley, Chris. "Schools Shut in Beijing as Coronavirus Flares." *New York Times.* June 16, 2020. https://www.nytimes.com/2020/06/16/world/asia/Beijing-coronavirus-flareup.html

[136] Khazan. "The School Reopeners Think America Is Forgetting About Kids."

[137] Van Beusekom, Mary. "Studies profile lung changes in asymptomatic COVID-19, viral loads in patient samples." *CIDRAP News*, February 25, 2020. https://www. cidrap.umn.edu/news-perspective/2020/02/studies-profile-lung-changes-asymptomatic-covid-19-viral-loads-patient

[138] Kapur, Sahil. "Trump's trying to end Obamacare but there's emerging evidence it could undo him." *NBCNews.com*. July 3, 2020. https://www.nbcnews.com/politics/2020-election/trump-s-trying-end-obamacare-there-s-emerging-evidence-it-n1232883

[139] Rizzo, Salvador. "Bottomless Pinocchio: Trump's claim that he will 'always' protect those with preexisting conditions." *The Washington Post*. June 29, 2020. https://www.washingtonpost.com/politics/2020/06/29/bottomless-pinocchio-trumps-claim-that-he-will-always-protect-those-with-preexisting-conditions/

[140] Trump, Donald. *Twitter*. June 27, 2020. https://www.thetrumparchive.com/?results=1&searchbox=%22I+will+ALWAYS+PROTECT+PEOPLE%22

Chapter Five: Words That Nobody Ever Heard Of Before

[1] Rahman, Khaleda. "Trump Says U.S. Economy After COVID-19 Will Soar 'Like a Rocket Ship.'" *Newsweek*. April 12, 2020. https://www.newsweek.com/trump-says-economy-will-soar-rocket-ship-1497458

[2] Weise, Karen, Harmon, Amy and Fink, Sheri. "Why Washington State? How Did It Start? Questions Answered on the U.S. Coronavirus Outbreak." *New York Times*. March 4, 2020 (updated March 6). https://www.nytimes.com/2020/03/04/us/coronavirus-in-washington-state.html

[3] Read, Richard. "To slow coronavirus spread in Seattle area, state bans gatherings of more than 250 people." *Los Angeles Times*. March 11, 2020. https://www.latimes.com/world-nation/story/2020-03-11/inslee-restricts-gatherings-seattle

[4] Lutz, Rachel. "Slowing the Coronavirus Spread: President Trump Presents New Guidelines for Next 15 Days." *Contagion Live*. March 17, 2020. https://www.contagionlive.com/news/slowing-the-coronavirus-spread-president-trump-presents-new-guidelines-for-next-15-days

[5] "The President's Coronavirus Guidelines for America." White House Archives. March 16, 2020. https://trumpwhitehouse.archives.gov/wp-content/uploads/2020/03/03.16.20_coronavirus-guidance_8.5x11_315PM.pdf (https://trumpwhitehouse.archives.gov/wp-content/uploads/2020/03/03.16.20_coronavirus-guidance_8.5x11_315PM.pdf)

[6] Lutz. "Slowing the Coronavirus Spread."

[7] "President Trump's proposed guidelines for relaxing social distancing guidance." *The Washington Post*. April 16, 2020. https://www.washingtonpost.com/context/

president-trump-s-proposed-guidelines-for-relaxing-social-distancing-guidance/
b7768600-7906-408c-89a3-06fd5a47aa26/

8 "Washington Gov. Inslee bans large gatherings in greater Seattle area." *Ktvz.com.*
March 11, 2020. https://ktvz.com/health/2020/03/11/washington-gov-inslee-
bans-large-gatherings-in-greater-seattle-area/

9 Feinsand, Mark. "Opening Day delayed; Spring games canceled." *MLB News.* March
12, 2020. https://www.mlb.com/news/mlb-2020-season-delayed

10 Quinn, Sam. "Rudy Gobert touched every microphone at Jazz media availability
Monday, now reportedly has coronavirus." *CBSSports.com.* March 12, 2020.
https://www.cbssports.com/nba/news/rudy-gobert-touched-every-microphone-
at-jazz-media-availability-monday-now-reportedly-has-coronavirus/

11 "NHL to pause season due to coronavirus." *NHL.* March 13, 2020. https://www.
nhl.com/news/nhl-coronavirus-to-provide-update-on-concerns/c-316131734

12 Reynolds, Tim. "MLS shutting down for 30 days due to coronavirus." *AP News.*
March 12, 2020. https://apnews.com/article/36359214c3d5b244ac1d502542ccf4a5

13 Seifert, Kevin. "XFL cancels regular-season games, 'committed' to playing in 2021."
ESPN.com. March 13, 2020. https://www.espn.com/xfl/story/_/id/28894247/xfl-
cancels-regular-season-games-committed-playing-2021

14 Kerr, Jeff. "XFL suspends operations and lays off employees, currently has no
plans to return in 2021, per report." *CBSSports.com.* April 10, 2020. https://
www.cbssports.com/xfl/news/xfl-suspends-operations-and-lays-off-employees-
currently-has-no-plans-to-return-in-2021-per-report/

15 Epstein, Adam. "Coronavirus is forcing the biggest global sports shutdown since
World War II." *Quartz (qz.com).* March 11, 2020. https://qz.com/1816538/
coronavirus-is-shutting-down-sports-from-soccer-to-ncaa-basketball/

16 Gopinath. "The Great Lockdown: Worst Economic Downturn Since the Great
Depression."

17 "Global Economic Prospects." The World Bank. https://www.worldbank.org/en/
publication/global-economic-prospects

18 "Great Depression History." *Sky History.* https://www.history.com/topics/great-
depression/great-depression-history

19 Sassoon, Donald. "To understand this crisis we can look to the Long
Depression too." *Guardian.* April 29, 2012. https://www.theguardian.com/
commentisfree/2012/apr/29/long-depression-crashes-capitalism-history

20 Irwin, Neil. "Coronavirus Shows the Problem With Trump's Stock Market
Boasting." *New York Times.* February 26, 2020 (updated February 27). https://
www.nytimes.com/2020/02/26/upshot/coronavirus-trump-stock-market.html

21 Trump, Donald. *Twitter.* February 26, 2020. https://www.thetrumparchive.com/
?results=1&searchbox=%22Low+Ratings+Fake+News+MSDNC+%28Comcast
%29+%26+CNN%22

[22] Franck, Thomas. "Dow briefly wipes out gains under Trump's presidency, remains slightly positive since his election." *CNBC.com*. March 18, 2020 (updated March 19). https://www.cnbc.com/2020/03/18/dow-wipes-out-gains-under-trumps-presidency-still-slightly-positive-since-his-election.html

[23] Nussbaum, Matthew. "Before drop, Trump boasted about the stock market once every 35 hours." *Politico*. February 6, 2018. https://www.politico.com/story/2018/02/06/trump-stock-market-boasts-395193

[24] Pitofsky, Marina. "WaPo: Trump allegedly asked Fauci if officials could let coronavirus 'wash over' US." *Hill*. April 11, 2020. https://thehill.com/homenews/administration/492390-wapo-trump-allegedly-asked-fauci-if-officials-could-let-coronavirus

[25] Peters, Plott and Haberman. "260,000 Words, Full of Self-Praise, From Trump on the Virus."

[26] The COVID Tracking Project. https://covidtracking.com/data/us-daily

[27] Kessler, Glenn, Rizzo, Salvador and Kelly, Meg. "President Trump made 19,127 false or misleading claims in 1,226 days." *The Washington Post*. June 1, 2020. https://www.washingtonpost.com/politics/2020/06/01/president-trump-made-19127-false-or-misleading-claims-1226-days/

[28] Rapfogel, Nicole and Gee, Emily. "The Health Care Repeal Lawsuit Could Strip Coverage from 23 Million Americans." *Center for American Progress*. June 24, 2020. https://www.americanprogress.org/issues/healthcare/news/2020/06/24/486768/health-care-repeal-lawsuit-strip-coverage-23-million-americans/

[29] Dale, Daniel. *Twitter*. July 19, 2020. https://twitter.com/ddale8/status/1284843766084505600?s=20

[30] Westwood, Sarah and Luhby, Tami. "Conservative Republicans unveil Obamacare replacement plan." *CNN.com*. October 22, 2019. https://edition.cnn.com/2019/10/22/politics/republican-conservatives-unveil-obamacare-replacement-plan/index.html

[31] Trump, Mary L., *Too Much and Never Enough* (p. 205). Simon & Schuster. Kindle Edition.

[32] Moffatt, Mike. "Presidential Elections and the Economy." *Thought Co*. July 3, 2019. https://www.thoughtco.com/presidential-elections-and-the-economy-1146241

[33] Watts, William. "Why the stock market rally is actually signaling an 'abnormal' economic recovery, not a V-shaped coronavirus rebound." *Market Watch*. May 16, 2020. https://www.marketwatch.com/story/why-the-stock-markets-stay-at-home-rally-isnt-really-signaling-a-v-shaped-coronavirus-recovery-2020-05-11

[34] "Labor Force Statistics from the Current Population Survey." U.S. Bureau of Labor Statistics. https://data.bls.gov/timeseries/LNS14000000

[35] "Remarks by President Trump on the Jobs Numbers Report." White House Archives. June 8, 2020. https://trumpwhitehouse.archives.gov/briefings-

statements/remarks-president-trump-jobs-numbers-report/ (https://trumpwhitehouse.archives.gov/briefings-statements/remarks-president-trump-jobs-numbers-report/)

[36] "News Release: Unemployment Insurance Weekly Claims." Department of Labor. July 9, 2020. https://www.dol.gov/sites/dolgov/files/OPA/newsreleases/ui-claims/20201364.pdf

[37] Casselman, Ben and Hsu, Tiffany. "Continued Layoffs Signal an 'Economic Scarring.'" *New York Times*. June 18, 2020 (updated June 24). https://www.nytimes.com/2020/06/18/business/economy/coronavirus-unemployment-claims.html

[38] Ibid

[39] Phillips, Amber. "Trump now says he knew the virus 'could be horrible' when he was saying things like 'it's going to disappear.'" *The Washington Post*. April 1, 2020. https://www.washingtonpost.com/politics/2020/04/01/trump-now-says-he-knew-virus-could-be-horrible-when-he-was-saying-things-like-its-going-disappear/

[40] Smith, Allan. "Trump defends erroneous coronavirus predictions in wide-ranging interview: 'I will be right eventually.'" *NBCNews.com*. July 19, 2020. https://www.nbcnews.com/politics/donald-trump/trump-defends-erroneous-coronavirus-predictions-wide-ranging-interview-i-will-n1234307

[41] Baragona, Justin. "Trump Shrugs Off COVID Death Toll in Fox News Interview: 'It Is What It Is.'" *Daily Beast*. July 19, 2020. https://www.thedailybeast.com/trump-shrugs-off-covid-death-toll-in-interview-with-fox-news-chris-wallace-it-is-what-it-is

[42] Ecarma, Caleb. "The Media Once Again Heralds Trump's New Somber 'Tone.'" *Vanity Fair*. April 1, 2020. https://www.vanityfair.com/news/2020/04/media-once-again-heralds-donald-trump-coronavirus-tone

[43] Phillips. "Trump now says he knew the virus 'could be horrible' when he was saying things like 'it's going to disappear.'"

[44] Bartlett, Bruce. "He Is Even Dumber Than We Thought." *New Republic*. June 8, 2020. https://newrepublic.com/article/158069/donald-trump-not-smart-polls

[45] Cillizza, Chris. "Donald Trump can't face the stubborn reality: He was wrong about coronavirus." *CNN.com*. March 31, 2020. https://edition.cnn.com/2020/03/31/politics/donald-trump-coronavirus/index.html

[46] Rahman. "Trump Says U.S. Economy After COVID-19 Will Soar 'Like a Rocket Ship.'"

[47] Werner, Erica and Stein, Jeff. "Trump administration pushing to block new money for testing, tracing and CDC in upcoming coronavirus relief bill." *The Washington Post*. July 19, 2020. https://www.washingtonpost.com/us-policy/2020/07/18/white-house-testing-budget-cdc-coronavirus/

[48] Behrmann. "Senate Dems ask HHS watchdog to investigate Trump's 'slow the testing down' comment."

[49] Werner, Erica, Kane, Paul and DeBonis, Mike. "Trump signs $2 trillion coronavirus bill into law as companies and households brace for more economic pain." *The Washington Post*. March 28, 2020. https://www.washingtonpost.com/us-policy/2020/03/27/congress-coronavirus-house-vote/

[50] Long, Heather, Still, Ashlyn and Shapiro, Leslie. "Calculate how much you would get from the $600 (or more) coronavirus checks." *The Washington Post*. December 28, 2020. https://www.washingtonpost.com/graphics/business/coronavirus-stimulus-check-calculator/?itid=lk_inline_manual_9

[51] Werner, Kane and DeBonis. "Trump signs $2 trillion coronavirus bill into law as companies and households brace for more economic pain."

[52] Rein, Lisa. "In unprecedented move, Treasury orders Trump's name printed on stimulus checks." *The Washington Post*. April 15, 2020. https://www.washingtonpost.com/politics/coming-to-your-1200-relief-check-donald-j-trumps-name/2020/04/14/071016c2-7e82-11ea-8013-1b6da0e4a2b7_story.html

[53] Buchwald, Elisabeth. "The Paycheck Protection Program is poised to get an additional $300 billion, but it's not the only option to keep some small businesses afloat." *Market Watch*. April 21, 2020. https://www.marketwatch.com/story/the-paycheck-protection-program-has-run-out-of-money-but-its-not-the-only-option-to-keep-some-small-businesses-afloat-2020-04-20

[54] Cheney, Kyle and O'Brien, Connor. "Trump removes independent watchdog for coronavirus funds, upending oversight panel." *Politico*. April 7, 2020. https://www.politico.com/news/2020/04/07/trump-removes-independent-watchdog-for-coronavirus-funds-upending-oversight-panel-171943

[55] Gillum, Jack et al. "Trump Friends and Family Cleared for Millions in Small Business Bailout." *ProPublica*. July 6, 2020. https://www.propublica.org/article/trump-friends-and-family-cleared-for-millions-in-small-business-bailout

[56] Popken, Ben and Lehren, Andrew W. "Release of PPP loan recipients' data reveals troubling patterns." *NBCNews.com*. December 2, 2020. https://www.nbcnews.com/business/business-news/release-ppp-loan-recipients-data-reveals-troubling-patterns-n1249629

[57] "Consumption Effects of Unemployment Insurance during the COVID-19 Pandemic." JPMorgan Chase & Co. https://www.jpmorganchase.com/institute/research/labor-markets/unemployment-insurance-covid19-pandemic

[58] Menton, Jessica. "Are Trump and the GOP right that the $600 unemployment bonus is discouraging work?" *USA Today*. July 24, 2020. https://eu.usatoday.com/story/money/2020/07/24/coronavirus-stimulus-package-600-unemployment-discouraging-work-covid-19/5496727002/

[59] Telford, Taylor, Kindy, Kimberly and Bogage, Jacob. "Trump orders meat plants to stay open in pandemic." *The Washington Post*. April 29, 2020. https://www.washingtonpost.com/business/2020/04/28/trump-meat-plants-dpa/

[60] Rosenberg, Gabriel N. "The government must pay people to stay home."

The Washington Post. March 29, 2020. https://www.washingtonpost.com/outlook/2020/03/29/government-must-pay-people-stay-home

61 "Investigating and responding to COVID-19 cases in non-healthcare work settings." Centers for Disease Control and Prevention. https://www.cdc.gov/coronavirus/2019-ncov/php/open-america/non-healthcare-work-settings.html

62 "48 active COVID-19 workplace outbreaks in Oregon." *KGW.com*. July 8, 2020 (updated July 9). https://www.kgw.com/article/news/health/coronavirus/here-are-the-48-active-covid-19-workplace-outbreaks-in-oregon/283-30eb69d0-04a8-4c5a-9cfd-7d331e867d9f

63 Menton. "Are Trump and the GOP right that the $600 unemployment bonus is discouraging work?"

64 "U.S. cost of living: Statistics and facts." *Statista*. https://www.statista.com/topics/768/cost-of-living/

65 Lambert, Lance. "Republican plan for $200 weekly unemployment extension would mean a benefit cut for 30 million Americans." *Fortune*. July 27, 2020 (updated July 28). https://fortune.com/2020/07/27/unemployment-600-extra-benefits-extension-cut-republican-plan-stimulus-package-bill-200-per-week-how-much-update/

66 "Employment in the United States from 2011 to 2021." *Statista*. https://www.statista.com/statistics/269959/employment-in-the-united-states/

67 Fandos, Nicholas and Cochrane, Emily. "Trump Officials Float Idea of Narrow Bill to Extend Unemployment Benefits." *New York Times*. July 26, 2020. https://www.nytimes.com/2020/07/26/us/politics/coronavirus-stimulus-bill-unemployment.html

68 "US 2020 election: The economy under Trump in six charts." *BBC*. November 3, 2020. https://www.bbc.co.uk/news/world-45827430

69 "SATURDAY, FEBRUARY 7, 1981; The Economy." *New York Times*. February 7, 1981. https://www.nytimes.com/1981/02/07/business/saturday-february-7-1981-the-economy.html

70 Trump. *Too Much and Never Enough* (p. 99).

71 Ibid., (p. 43).

72 Waldman, Paul. "Opinion: Why isn't Trump trying to win?" *The Washington Post*. June 25, 2020. https://www.washingtonpost.com/opinions/2020/06/25/why-isnt-trump-trying-win/

73 Parker, Ashley and Rucker, Philip. "One question still dogs Trump: Why not try harder to solve the coronavirus crisis?" *The Washington Post*. July 27, 2020. https://www.washingtonpost.com/politics/trump-not-solve-coronavirus-crisis/2020/07/26/7fca9a92-cdb0-11ea-91f1-28aca4d833a0_story.html

74 "Putin and Trump discussed arms control, Iran in phone call: Kremlin." *Reuters*. July 23, 2020. https://www.reuters.com/article/us-russia-usa-putin-trump/

putin-and-trump-discussed-arms-control-iran-in-phone-call-kremlin-idUSKCN24O2KL

[75] Williams, Pete and Via y Rada, Nicole. "Trump's election fight includes over 50 lawsuits. It's not going well." *NBCNews.com*. November 23, 2020 (updated December 10). https://www.nbcnews.com/politics/2020-election/trump-s-election-fight-includes-over-30-lawsuits-it-s-n1248289

[76] Rainey, Rebecca and Mueller, Eleanor. "Trump opposed to extending $600 unemployment boost." *Politico*. May 20, 2020. https://www.politico.com/newsletters/morning-shift/2020/05/20/trump-opposed-to-extending-600-unemployment-boost-787765

[77] Levin, Bess. "Republicans Are Worried Coronavirus Stimulus Bill Is Too Generous to the Unemployed." *Vanity Fair*. March 25, 2020. https://www.vanityfair.com/news/2020/03/lindsey-graham-coronavirus-stimulus-bill

Chapter Six: Red Dawn

[1] Lipton et al. "He Could Have Seen What Was Coming: Behind Trump's Failure on the Virus."

[2] Holshue, Michelle L. et al. "First Case of 2019 Novel Coronavirus in the United States." *The New England Journal of Medicine*. January 31, 2020. https://www.nejm.org/doi/pdf/10.1056/NEJMoa2001191

[3] Blake Aaron and Rieger, JM. "Timeline: The 201 times Trump has downplayed the coronavirus threat." *The Washington Post*. November 3, 2020. https://www.washingtonpost.com/politics/2020/03/12/trump-coronavirus-timeline/

[4] "40 times Trump said the coronavirus would go away." *The Washington Post*. November 2, 2020. https://www.washingtonpost.com/video/politics/40-times-trump-said-the-coronavirus-would-go-away/2020/04/30/d2593312-9593-4ec2-aff7-72c1438fca0e_video.html

[5] Mosk, Matthew, Folmer, Kaitlyn and Margolin, Josh. "As coronavirus threatened invasion, a new 'Red Dawn' team tried to save America." *Abcnews.go.com*. July 28, 2020. https://abcnews.go.com/Health/coronavirus-threatened-invasion-red-dawn-team-save-america/story?id=72000727

[6] Blake and Rieger. "Timeline: The 201 times Trump has downplayed the coronavirus threat."

[7] Mosk, Folmer and Margolin. "As coronavirus threatened invasion, a new 'Red Dawn' team tried to save America."

[8] Haberman, Maggie. "Trade Adviser Warned White House in January of Risks of a Pandemic." *New York Times*. April 6, 2020 (updated April 17). https://www.nytimes.com/2020/04/06/us/politics/navarro-warning-trump-coronavirus.html

[9] Ibid.

10 "Remarks by President Trump, Vice President Pence, and Members of the Coronavirus Task Force in Press Briefing | April 7, 2020." White House Archives. April 7, 2020. https://trumpwhitehouse.archives.gov/briefings-statements/ remarks-president-trump-vice-president-pence-members-coronavirus-task-force-press-briefing-april-7-2020/ (https://trumpwhitehouse.archives.gov/ briefings-statements/remarks-president-trump-vice-president-pence-members-coronavirus-task-force-press-briefing-april-7-2020/)

11 Margolin and Meek. "Intelligence report warned of coronavirus crisis as early as November."

12 Garrett, Laurie. "Why Trump's new CDC director is an abysmal choice." *CNN.com.* May 14, 2018. https://edition.cnn.com/2018/05/13/opinions/trumps-terrible-choice-for-cdc-redfield-garrett/index.html

13 "Remarks by President Trump, Vice President Pence, and Members of the Coronavirus Task Force in Press Briefing." White House Archives. March 20, 2020. https://trumpwhitehouse.archives.gov/briefings-statements/remarks-president-trump-vice-president-pence-members-c-oronavirus-task-force-press-briefing/ (https://trumpwhitehouse.archives.gov/briefings-statements/ remarks-president-trump-vice-president-pence-members-c-oronavirus-task-force-press-briefing/)

14 "Remarks by President Trump in Press Briefing | July 30, 2020." White House Archives. July 30, 2020. https://trumpwhitehouse.archives.gov/briefings-statements/remarks-president-trump-press-briefing-july-30-2020/ (https:// trumpwhitehouse.archives.gov/briefings-statements/remarks-president-trump-press-briefing-july-30-2020/)

15 Smith, Chris. "Scientists warn that Trump is wrong: Warm weather won't kill coronavirus." *BGR.* April 9, 2020. https://bgr.com/2020/04/09/coronavirus-usa-warmer-weather-wont-reduce-covid-19-transmission/

16 "Remarks by President Trump at the White House Business Session with our Nation's Governors." White House Archives. February 10, 2020. https:// trumpwhitehouse.archives.gov/briefings-statements/remarks-president-trump-white-house-business-session-nations-governors/ (https://trumpwhitehouse. archives.gov/briefings-statements/remarks-president-trump-white-house-business-session-nations-governors/)

17 "US 2020 election: The economy under Trump in six charts."

18 Saletan, William. "The Trump Pandemic." *Slate.* August 9, 2020. https://slate.com/ news-and-politics/2020/08/trump-coronavirus-deaths-timeline.html

19 Biden, Joe. "My Statement on John Bolton's Revelations." *Medium.* June 18, 2020. https://medium.com/@JoeBiden/my-statement-on-john-boltons-revelations-61f90477d555

20 Bernstein, Andrea. "Where Trump Learned the Art of the Quid Pro Quo." *Atlantic.* January 20, 2020. https://www.theatlantic.com/ideas/archive/2020/01/trumps-brand-of-transactional-politics/604978/

[21] Waldman. "Opinion: Why isn't Trump trying to win?"

[22] Kendzior, Sarah. *Twitter*. July 25, 2020. https://twitter.com/sarahkendzior/status/1287033658692575234

[23] "Fact Checking President Trump: 'Zero Evidence That Election Is Being Rigged' | MTP Daily | MSNBC." *YouTube*. August 24, 2020. https://www.youtube.com/watch?v=tVlqlZeGz30&feature=youtu.be

[24] "2016 Presidential Election Results." *New York Times*. August 9, 2017. https://www.nytimes.com/elections/2016/results/president

[25] Bump, Philip. "Donald Trump will be president thanks to 80,000 people in three states." *The Washington Post*. December 1, 2016. https://www.washingtonpost.com/news/the-fix/wp/2016/12/01/donald-trump-will-be-president-thanks-to-80000-people-in-three-states/

[26] Wasserman, David. "2016 National Popular Vote Tracker." *Cook Political Report*. https://docs.google.com/spreadsheets/d/133Eb4qQmOxNvtesw2hdVns073R68EZx4SfCnP4IGQf8/edit#gid=19

[27] Trump, Donald. *Twitter*. August 19, 2020. https://www.thetrumparchive.com/?results=1&searchbox=%22Don%E2%80%99t+buy+GOODYEAR+TIRES%22

[28] Hlavaty, Kaylyn. "Goodyear responds after president calls for boycott of Akron's 4th-largest employer." *News5cleveland.com*. August 19, 2020. https://www.news5cleveland.com/news/local-news/akron-canton-news/goodyear-responds-after-president-calls-for-boycott-of-akrons-4th-largest-employer-over-maga-hat-ban

[29] Foer, Franklin. "How Donald Trump Is Killing Politics." *Atlantic*. August 31, 2020. https://www.theatlantic.com/ideas/archive/2020/08/donald-trump-attacking-politics-itself/615886/

[30] "Latest Polls." *FiveThirtyEight.com*. https://projects.fivethirtyeight.com/polls/president-general/national/

[31] "Election Center 2008." *CNN.com*. https://edition.cnn.com/ELECTION/2008/results/president/

[32] Giles, Christopher. "Hydroxychloroquine being 'discarded prematurely', say scientists." *BBC*. August 6, 2020. https://www.bbc.co.uk/news/health-53679498

[33] Andrews, Travis M. and Paquette, Danielle. "Trump retweeted a video with false covid-19 claims. One doctor in it has said demons cause illnesses." *The Washington Post*. July 29, 2020. https://www.washingtonpost.com/technology/2020/07/28/stella-immanuel-hydroxychloroquine-video-trump-americas-frontline-doctors/

[34] Leary, Alex and Needleman, Sarah E. "Trump Retweets Attacks Against Fauci on Coronavirus Policy." *Wall Street Journal*. July 28, 2020. https://www.wsj.com/articles/trump-revives-attacks-against-fauci-on-coronavirus-policy-11595948672

[35] "My Interview with Dave Portnoy of Barstool Sports!" *Youtube*. July 24, 2020.

https://www.youtube.com/watch?v=vRWr9dI8-Jw&feature=youtu.be

36 Worldometer. https://www.worldometers.info/coronavirus/

37 Collins, Kaitlan. "Trump adds coronavirus adviser who echoes his unscientific claims." *CNN.com*. August 12, 2020. https://edition.cnn.com/2020/08/12/politics/scott-atlas-donald-trump-coronavirus/index.html

38 Perez, Matt. "Who Is Dr. Scott Atlas? Trump's New Covid Health Adviser Seen As Counter To Fauci And Birx." *Forbes*. August 12, 2020. https://www.forbes.com/sites/mattperez/2020/08/12/who-is-dr-scott-atlas-trumps-new-covid-health-adviser-seen-as-counter-to-fauci-and-birx/?sh=11d2e66e20a4

39 Trump, Donald. *Twitter*. July 6, 2020. (https://www.thetrumparchive.com)https://www.thetrumparchive.com/?results=1&searchbox=%22SCHOOLS+MUST+OPEN+IN+THE+FALL%21%21%21%22

40 Kershner, Isabel and Belluck, Pam. "When Covid Subsided, Israel Reopened Its Schools. It Didn't Go Well." *New York Times*. August 4, 2020. https://www.nytimes.com/2020/08/04/world/middleeast/coronavirus-israel-schools-reopen.html

41 Strauss, Valerie. "No, Trump and DeVos can't withhold funding from schools whenever they want. Here's what they can do." *The Washington Post*. July 13, 2020. https://www.washingtonpost.com/education/2020/07/13/no-trump-devos-cant-withhold-funding-schools-whenever-they-want-heres-what-they-can-do/

42 Diamond. "'We want them infected': Trump appointee demanded 'herd immunity' strategy, emails reveal."

43 "97,000 children reportedly test positive for coronavirus in two weeks as schools gear up for instruction." *CBSnews.com*. August 10, 2020. https://www.cbsnews.com/news/covid-19-kids-school-children-positive-tests-coronavirus-reopening/

44 "Provisional COVID-19 Death Counts by Sex, Age, and State." Centers for Disease Control and Prevention. https://data.cdc.gov/NCHS/Provisional-COVID-19-Death-Counts-by-Sex-Age-and-S/9bhg-hcku/data (https://data.cdc.gov/NCHS/Provisional-COVID-19-Death-Counts-by-Sex-Age-and-S/9bhg-hcku/data)

45 Heald-Sargent, Taylor et al. "Age-Related Differences in Nasopharyngeal Severe Acute Respiratory Syndrome Coronavirus 2 (SARS-CoV-2) Levels in Patients With Mild to Moderate Coronavirus Disease 2019 (COVID-19)." *JAMA Network*. July 30, 2020. https://jamanetwork.com/journals/jamapediatrics/fullarticle/2768952

46 Joon Park, Young et al. "Contact Tracing during Coronavirus Disease Outbreak, South Korea, 2020." *Emerg Infect Dis*. October, 2020. https://wwwnc.cdc.gov/eid/article/26/10/20-1315_article (https://wwwnc.cdc.gov/eid/article/26/10/20-1315_article)

47 "For Parents: Multisystem Inflammatory Syndrome in Children (MIS-C) associated with COVID-19." Centers for Disease Control and Prevention. https://www.cdc.gov/coronavirus/2019-ncov/daily-life-coping/children/mis-c.html

[48] Slisco, Aila. "Child COVID Cases up 90% Last Month as Trump Says Kids Are 'Almost Immune.'" *Newsweek*. August 11, 2020. https://www.newsweek.com/child-covid-cases-90-last-month-trump-says-kids-are-almost-immune-1524488

[49] Corey, Rebecca. "Trump says children are 'almost immune' to COVID-19. Doctors say that's false." *Yahoo! News*. October 17, 2020. https://news.yahoo.com/trump-says-children-are-almost-immune-to-covid-doctors-dont-agree-123542125.html

[50] Dennis, Brady and Dupree, Jacqueline. "U.S. reports highest number of covid-19 deaths in one day since mid-May." *The Washington Post*. August 13, 2020. https://www.washingtonpost.com/politics/us-reports-highest-number-of-covid-19-deaths-in-one-day-since-mid-may/2020/08/12/4cafe146-dcae-11ea-8051-d5f887d73381_story.html

[51] Ibid.

[52] Holpuch, Amanda. "'They're dying … it is what it is': key takeaways from Trump's shocking interview." *Guardian*. August 4, 2020. https://www.theguardian.com/us-news/2020/aug/04/donald-trump-interview-axios-covid-19-epstein-john-lewis

[53] Baragona. "Trump Shrugs Off COVID Death Toll in Fox News Interview."

[54] Charbonneau, Madeline. "9 People Test Positive at Georgia School After Viral Photo of Packed Hallways." *Daily Beast*. August 9, 2020. https://www.thedailybeast.com/9-people-test-positive-at-georgia-school-with-photo-of-crowded-hallway

[55] Walker, Christina, Grayer, Annie and Stuart, Elizabeth. "More than 2,000 students, teachers and staff quarantined in several schools." *CNN.com*. August 17, 2020. https://edition.cnn.com/2020/08/13/us/schools-quarantined-coronavirus/index.html

[56] "President Donald J. Trump Is Working to Give Students and Parents Flexibility and Schools the Support They Need to Reopen This Fall." White House Archives. July 23, 2020. https://trumpwhitehouse.archives.gov/briefings-statements/president-donald-j-trump-working-give-students-parents-flexibility-schools-support-need-reopen-fall/ (https://trumpwhitehouse.archives.gov/briefings-statements/president-donald-j-trump-working-give-students-parents-flexibility-schools-support-need-reopen-fall/)

[57] Christensen, Jen et al. "There has been a 90% increase in Covid-19 cases in US children in the last four weeks, report says." *CNN.com*. August 11, 2020. https://edition.cnn.com/2020/08/11/health/covid-19-children-cases-rising-wellness/index.html

[58] Worldometer. https://www.worldometers.info/coronavirus/country/us/

[59] O'Grady, Siobhán et al. "Trump dismisses coronavirus cases in children, says they're a 'tiny fraction' of deaths." *The Washington Post*. August 11, 2020. https://www.washingtonpost.com/nation/2020/08/10/coronavirus-covid-live-updates-us/

[60] "10 years. 180 school shootings. 356 victims." *CNN.com*. July, 2019. https://edition.cnn.com/interactive/2019/07/us/ten-years-of-school-shootings-trnd/

[61] Peel, Michael and Burn-Murdoch, John. "How to avoid the virus as the world reopens | Free to read." *Financial Times.* June 10, 2020. https://www.ft.com/content/2418ff87-1d41-41b5-b638-38f5164a2e94

[62] Westwood, Sarah, Brown, Pamela and Liptak, Kevin. "Trump's school reopening push a gamble aimed at White suburban voters." *CNN.com.* July 17, 2020. https://edition.cnn.com/2020/07/17/politics/donald-trump-schools-strategy-2020/index.html

[63] Reston, Maeve. "Donald Trump's mind-bending logic on school reopenings." *CNN.com.* July 25, 2020. https://edition.cnn.com/2020/07/25/politics/donald-trump-schools-reopening-coronavirus/index.html

[64] Werner, Erica and Stein, Jeff. "Relief talks stumble again as Trump asserts a deal is 'not going to happen.'" *The Washington Post.* August 13, 2020. https://www.washingtonpost.com/us-policy/2020/08/12/trump-coronavirus-relief-congress/

[65] Tompkins, Al. "As schools reopen, more quarantines are ordered." *Poynter.* August 19, 2020. https://www.poynter.org/reporting-editing/2020/as-schools-reopen-more-quarantines-are-ordered/

[66] Nierenberg, Amelia and Pasick, Adam. "Schools Briefing: University Outbreaks and Parental Angst." *New York Times.* August 19, 2020. https://www.nytimes.com/2020/08/19/us/colleges-closing-covid.html

[67] Community Interventions and Critical Populations Task Force CDC COVID-19 Emergency Response. "CRAFT Schools Briefing Packet." July 8, 2019. https://int.nyt.com/data/documenthelper/7072-school-reopening-packet/b70172f2cc13c9cf0e6a/optimized/full.pdf#page=1

[68] Higgins-Dunn, Noah. "Infectious disease experts warn against reopening schools in Florida, Texas and other states where coronavirus cases are surging." *CNBC.com.* July 23, 2020. https://www.cnbc.com/2020/07/23/coronavirus-infectious-disease-experts-warn-against-reopening-schools-in-florida-texas.html

[69] Lipton. "He Could Have Seen What Was Coming."

[70] Mecher, Carter. *Emails.* January 28, 2020. https://int.nyt.com/data/documenthelper/6879-2020-covid-19-red-dawn-rising/66f590d5cd41e11bea0f/optimized/full.pdf#page=1

[71] Lipton. "He Could Have Seen What Was Coming."

[72] Egan, Lauren. "Trump calls coronavirus Democrats' 'new hoax.'" *NBCNews.com.* February 29, 2020. https://www.nbcnews.com/politics/donald-trump/trump-calls-coronavirus-democrats-new-hoax-n1145721

[73] "Trump calls Ukraine allegations a 'hoax' at news conference." *CBSnews.com.* September 25, 2019. https://www.cbsnews.com/video/trump-calls-ukraine-allegations-a-hoax-at-news-conference/

[74] Epstein, Reid J. "How the Iowa Caucuses Became an Epic Fiasco for Democrats." *New York Times.* February 9, 2020 (updated February 11). https://www.nytimes.com/2020/02/09/us/politics/iowa-democratic-caucuses.html

[75] Rieder, Rem. "Democratic Ad Twists Trump's 'Hoax' Comment." *Factcheck.org.* April 14, 2020. https://www.factcheck.org/2020/04/democratic-ad-twists-trumps-hoax-comment/

[76] Sherfinski, David. "Trump slams Democrats over virus lockdowns: 'Everything will open up' after the election." *Washington Times.* July 23, 2020. https://www.washingtontimes.com/news/2020/jul/23/donald-trump-slams-democrats-over-virus-lockdowns-/

[77] Cook, Nancy and Choi, Matthew. "Trump rallies his base to treat coronavirus as a 'hoax.'" *Politico.* February 2, 2020. https://www.politico.com/news/2020/02/28/trump-south-carolina-rally-coronavirus-118269

[78] Lee, Carol E. and Kube, Courtney. "Trump eyes Putin meeting before November election, say four people familiar with discussions." *NBCNews.com.* August 16, 2020. https://www.nbcnews.com/politics/national-security/trump-eyes-putin-meeting-november-election-say-four-people-familiar-n1236861

Chapter Seven: Will He Be My New Best Friend?

[1] Isachenkov, Vladimir and De Pury, Kate. "Putin says Trump foes harm US with Russia collusion probes." *AP News.* December 14, 2017. https://apnews.com/article/7d3b8ea669494eb598d16fd15a32409c

[2] Trump, Donald. *Twitter.* October 26, 2012. https://www.thetrumparchive.com/?results=1&searchbox=%22I+knew+last+year+that+TIME+Magazine%22

[3] Trump, Donald. *Twitter.* December 9, 2015. https://www.thetrumparchive.com/ ?results=1&searchbox=%22I+told+you+TIME+Magazine+would+never+pick+me%22

[4] Ross, Jamie. "Trump Flips Out at Greta Thunberg After She Beats Him to Time Person of the Year." *Daily Beast.* December 12, 2019. https://www.thedailybeast.com/trump-flips-out-at-greta-thunberg-after-she-beats-him-to-time-person-of-the-year

[5] Trump, Donald. *Twitter.* December 12, 2019. https://www.thetrumparchive.com/?results=1&searchbox=%22Chill+Greta%2C+Chill%22

[6] "Time Magazine: Trump's Person of the Year Boast Is 'Total BS.'" *Daily Beast.* November 25, 2017. https://www.thedailybeast.com/time-magazine-trumps-person-of-the-year-boast-is-total-bs

[7] Fahrenthold, David A. "A Time magazine with Trump on the cover hangs in his golf clubs. It's fake." *The Washington Post.* June 27, 2017. https://www.washingtonpost.com/politics/a-time-magazine-with-trump-on-the-cover-hangs-in-his-golf-clubs-its-fake/2017/06/27/0adf96de-5850-11e7-ba90-f5875b7d1876_story.html?utm_term=.f991b3840849

[8] Alexander, Dan. "Trump Wrote Putin To Congratulate Him On Being Named

TIME Person Of The Year." *Forbes*. August 18, 2020. https://www.forbes.com/sites/danalexander/2020/08/18/trump-wrote-putin-to-congratulate-him-on-being-named-time-person-of-the-year/?sh=5dcb5796485b

9 United States Senate. "Senate Intelligence Counterintelligence Searchable Volume 5 Report_volume5." https://www.scribd.com/document/472924573/Senate-Intelligence-Counterintelligence-Searchable-Volume-5-Report-volume5#

10 Colson, Thomas. "Trump told Putin 'I'm a big fan of yours' and asked him to be the guest of honor at a Miss Universe pageant, in a series of fawning letters." *Business Insider*. August 19, 2020. https://www.businessinsider.com/revealed-donald-trump-letters-to-vladimir-putin-miss-universe-russia-2020-8?r=US&IR=T

11 Trump, Donald. *Twitter*. June 18, 2013. https://www.thetrumparchive.com/?results=1&searchbox=%22if+so%2C+will+he+become+my+new+best+friend%22

12 Harris, Shane, Helderman, Rosalind S. and Demirjian, Karoun. "In a personal letter, Trump invited Putin to the 2013 Miss Universe pageant." *The Washington Post*. March 10, 2018. https://www.washingtonpost.com/world/national-security/in-a-personal-letter-trump-invited-putin-to-the-2013-miss-universe-pageant/2018/03/09/a3404358-23d2-11e8-a589-763893265565_story.html

13 Colvin, Jill. "Have Trump and Putin Met Before? Depends When You Asked." *NBCNewYork.com*. July 7, 2017. https://www.nbcnewyork.com/news/national-international/trump-putin-first-meeting-or-is-it/2083074/

14 Massie, Christopher. "Trump And Putin Appeared On '60 Minutes' Together... From Different Continents." *BuzzFeed News*. November 10, 2015. https://www.buzzfeednews.com/article/christophermassie/tick-tick-tick-tick

15 "'This Week' Transcript: Donald Trump, Vice President Joe Biden, and Ret. Gen. John Allen." *Abcnews.go.com*. July 31, 2016. https://abcnews.go.com/Politics/week-transcript-donald-trump-vice-president-joe-biden/story?id=41020870

16 Nakashima, Ellen. "Cyber researchers confirm Russian government hack of Democratic National Committee." *The Washington Post*. June 20, 2016. https://www.washingtonpost.com/world/national-security/cyber-researchers-confirm-russian-government-hack-of-democratic-national-committee/2016/06/20/e7375bc0-3719-11e6-9ccd-d6005beac8b3_story.html

17 "Full transcript: Third 2016 presidential debate." *Politico*. October 20, 2016. https://www.politico.com/story/2016/10/full-transcript-third-2016-presidential-debate-230063

18 Homeland Security. "Joint Statement from the Department Of Homeland Security and Office of the Director of National Intelligence on Election Security." October 7, 2020. https://www.dhs.gov/news/2016/10/07/joint-statement-department-homeland-security-and-office-director-national?_ga=2.238369024.1096939202.1598056945-853520579.1597784546

[19] Kopan, Tal. "Is Trump right? Could a 400-pound couch potato have hacked the DNC?" *CNN.com*. September 28, 2016. https://edition.cnn.com/2016/09/27/politics/dnc-cyberattack-400-pound-hackers/index.html

[20] Windrem, Robert and Arkin, William M. "Trump Told Russia To Blame for Hacks Long Before 2016 Debate." *NBCNews.com*. October 10, 2016. https://www.nbcnews.com/news/us-news/trump-was-told-russia-was-blame-hacks-long-debate-n663686

[21] Parker, Ashley and Helderman, Rosalind S. "In new book, former Trump lawyer Michael Cohen describes alleged episodes of racism and says president likes how Putin runs Russia." *The Washington Post*. September 6, 2020. https://www.washingtonpost.com/politics/cohen-trump-book/2020/09/05/235aa10a-ef96-11ea-ab4e-581edb849379_story.html

[22] Morris, David Z. "Vladimir Putin Is Reportedly Richer Than Bill Gates and Jeff Bezos Combined." *Fortune*. July 29, 2017. https://fortune.com/2017/07/29/vladimir-putin-russia-jeff-bezos-bill-gates-worlds-richest-man/

[23] Ponciano, Jonathan. "Jeff Bezos Becomes The First Person Ever Worth $200 Billion." *Forbes*. August 26, 2020. https://www.forbes.com/sites/jonathanponciano/2020/08/26/worlds-richest-billionaire-jeff-bezos-first-200-billion/?sh=3a6173004db7

[24] United States Senate. "Senate Intelligence Counterintelligence Searchable Volume 5 Report_volume5."

[25] Hettena, Seth. *Trump / Russia: A Definitive History* (p. 89-90). Melville House. Kindle Edition.

[26] Hill, Fiona and Gaddy, Clifford C. *Mr. Putin: Operative in the Kremlin* (pp. 354-355). Brookings Institution Press. Kindle Edition.

[27] Demirjian, Karoun. "Trump praises Putin's response to sanctions, calls Russian leader 'very smart!'" *The Washington Post*. December 30, 2016. https://www.washingtonpost.com/news/powerpost/wp/2016/12/30/trump-praises-putins-response-to-sanctions-calls-russian-leader-very-smart/

[28] Trump, Donald. *Twitter*. December 30, 2016. https://www.thetrumparchive.com/?results=1&searchbox=%22Great+move+on+delay%22

[29] "Michael Flynn transcripts show he discussed sanctions with Russian envoy." *Guardian*. May 30, 2020. https://www.theguardian.com/us-news/2020/may/30/michael-flynn-transcripts-russian-ambassador-senate

[30] Sheth, Sonam. "Grading the Steele dossier 2 years later: what's been corroborated and what's still unclear." *Business Insider*. January 13, 2019. https://www.businessinsider.com/steele-dossier-allegations-trump-russia-mueller-investigation-2019-1?r=US&IR=T

[31] Manchester, Julia. "Watergate prosecutor: Trump, Russia quid pro quo was about dropping of sanctions." *Hill*. February 28, 2018. https://thehill.com/blogs/blog-briefing-room/news/376182-watergate-prosecutor-trump-russia-quid-pro-quo-was-about

[32] Isikoff, Michael. "How the Trump administration's secret efforts to ease Russia sanctions fell short." *Yahoo! News*. June 2, 2017. https://www.yahoo.com/news/trump-administrations-secret-efforts-ease-russia-sanctions-fell-short-231301145.html

[33] Embury-Dennis, Tom. "Trump refuses to impose new Russia sanctions despite law passed by US Congress over election hacking." *Independent*. January 30, 2018. https://www.independent.co.uk/news/world/americas/us-russia-sanctions-trump-no-new-congress-law-election-hacking-intervention-putin-kremlin-a8184866.html

[34] Siemaszko, Corky. "Donald Trump and Vladimir Putin: Timeline of a Bad Bromance." *NBCNews.com*. August 2, 2016. https://www.nbcnews.com/politics/2016-election/donald-trump-vladimir-putin-timeline-bad-bromance-n621131

[35] Forgey, Quint. "'He was outsmarted': Trump mocks Obama on world stage." *Politico*. August 26, 2019. https://www.politico.com/story/2019/08/26/trump-putin-obama-g7-1475439

[36] "Trump sides with Russia against FBI at Helsinki summit." *BBC*. July 16, 2018. https://www.bbc.co.uk/news/world-europe-44852812

[37] Miller, Greg. "Trump has concealed details of his face-to-face encounters with Putin from senior officials in administration." *The Washington Post*. January 13, 2019. https://www.washingtonpost.com/world/national-security/trump-has-concealed-details-of-his-face-to-face-encounters-with-putin-from-senior-officials-in-administration/2019/01/12/65f6686c-1434-11e9-b6ad-9cfd62dbb0a8_story.html

[38] Diamond, Jeremy. "Trump sides with Putin over US intelligence." *CNN.com*. July 16, 2018. https://edition.cnn.com/2018/07/16/politics/donald-trump-putin-helsinki-summit/index.html

[39] "Trump sides with Russia against FBI at Helsinki summit."

[40] Trump, Donald. *Twitter*. July 9, 2017. https://www.thetrumparchive.com/?results=1&searchbox=%22impenetrable+Cyber+Security+unit%22

[41] Geller, Eric. "Trump-Putin meeting rekindles ridiculed cyber plan." *Politico*. July 16, 2018. https://www.politico.com/story/2018/07/16/trump-putin-russia-cybersecurity-689470

[42] Blum, Howard. "Exclusive: What Trump Really Told Kislyak After Comey Was Canned." *Vanity Fair*. November 22, 2017. https://www.vanityfair.com/news/2017/11/trump-intel-slip

[43] Atwood, Kylie. "Trump remains largely silent on reported poisoning of Russian dissident as Europe, US lawmakers offer support." *CNN.com*. August 22, 2020. https://edition.cnn.com/2020/08/21/politics/trump-russia-navalny-silence/index.html

[44] Allassan, Fadel. "U.S. says Russia must investigate poisoning of Putin critic Alexei Navalny." *Axios.com*. August 25, 2020. https://www.axios.com/us-russia-investigation-navalny-poisoning-

72a3ceb5-67c0-4c14-b089-19974148ba8d.html?fbclid=IwAR3_
Uybmgb8cv7YBrA9VFHRfeUy56lX01TwdvG936j3FVVciZ34P_t62hQo

[45] Pompeo, Mike. *Twitter*. August 25, 2020. https://twitter.com/SecPompeo/
status/1298304977996308484?s=20

[46] Savage, Schmitt and Schwirtz. "Russia Secretly Offered Afghan Militants Bounties
to Kill U.S. Troops, Intelligence Says."

[47] Swan, Jonathan and Lawler, Dave. "Exclusive: Trump never raised Russia's Taliban
bounties with Putin." *Axios.com*. July 29, 2020. https://www.axios.com/trump-
russia-bounties-taliban-putin-call-4a0f6110-ab58-41c0-96fc-57b507462af1.html

[48] Eckel, Mike. "A Trump-Putin 'Reset'? Flurry Of Communication Points To
Behind-The-Scenes Diplomacy." *Rferl.org*. April 23, 2020. https://www.rferl.org/a/
russsia-us-trump-putin-reset-flurry-communication-diplomacy/30573019.html

[49] Worldometer. https://www.worldometers.info/coronavirus/country/us/

[50] Barnes et al. "White House Classified Computer System Is Used to Hold
Transcripts of Sensitive Calls."

[51] Brown, Pamela, Sciutto, Jim and Liptak, Kevin. "White House restricted access to
Trump's calls with Putin and Saudi crown prince." *CNN.com*. September 28, 2019.
https://edition.cnn.com/2019/09/27/politics/white-house-restricted-trump-calls-
putin-saudi/index.html

[52] Nechepurenko, Ivan. "Kremlin Says It Hopes Putin's Calls With Trump Won't
Be Made Public." *New York Times*. September 27, 2019. https://www.nytimes.
com/2019/09/27/world/europe/trump-putin-russia-calls.html

[53] Alexander, Farrah. "Melania Trump Summed Up Her Tragic Marriage
In One Response." *Huffington Post*. May 23, 2017. https://www.huffpost.
com/entry/melania-trump-summed-up-her-tragic-marriage-in-
one_b_592444eee4b07617ae4cbfa2

[54] Cohen. *Disloyal: A Memoir* (p. 12).

[55] LaFraniere, Sharon, Weiser, Benjamin and Haberman, Maggie. "Prosecutors Say
Trump Directed Illegal Payments During Campaign." *New York Times*. December 7,
2018. https://www.nytimes.com/2018/12/07/nyregion/michael-cohen-sentence.html

[56] Goldberg, Jeffrey. "Trump: Americans Who Died in War Are 'Losers' and
'Suckers.'" *Atlantic*. September 3, 2020. https://www.theatlantic.com/politics/
archive/2020/09/trump-americans-who-died-at-war-are-losers-and-
suckers/615997/

[57] Steward, Heather. "Theresa May says NATO has 100% support of Donald Trump."
Guardian. January 27, 2017. https://www.theguardian.com/us-news/2017/jan/27/
theresa-may-white-house-visit-donald-trump-nato

[58] "Trump and Britain's Theresa May meet for first time." *MPRNews.org*. January 27,
2017. https://www.mprnews.org/story/2017/01/27/trump-and-britains-theresa-
may-meet-for-first-time

59 Beggin, Riley and Stracqualursi, Veronica. "A timeline of Sally Yates' warnings to the White House about Mike Flynn." *Abcnews.go.com.* May 9, 2017. https://abcnews.go.com/Politics/timeline-sally-yates-warnings-white-house-mike-flynn/story?id=47272979

60 Haberman, Maggie, Schmidt, Michael S. and Shear Michael D. "Trump Says He Fired Michael Flynn 'Because He Lied' to F.B.I." *New York Times.* December 2, 2017. https://www.nytimes.com/2017/12/02/us/politics/trump-michael-flynn.html

61 Estepa, Jessica. "As Trump meets Vladimir Putin, a look at other times the Russian leader met with U.S. presidents." *USA Today News.* July 6, 2017. https://eu.usatoday.com/story/news/politics/onpolitics/2017/07/06/trump-meets-vladimir-putin-look-other-times-russian-leader-met-u-s-presidents/453206001/

62 Crowley, Michael and Goldman, Adam. "Republicans Turn to Rescued Hostages to Highlight Trump Foreign Policy." *New York Times.* August 25, 2020. https://www.nytimes.com/2020/08/25/us/politics/trump-hostages.html

63 Boot, Max. "Opinion: More evidence of Trump's subservience to Putin — and we still don't know why." *The Washington Post.* September 1, 2020. https://www.washingtonpost.com/opinions/2020/09/01/more-evidence-trumps-subservience-putin-we-still-dont-know-why/

64 United States Senate. "Senate Intelligence Counterintelligence Searchable Volume 5 Report_volume5."

65 Barnes, Julian E. and Rosenberg, Matthew. "Charges of Ukrainian Meddling? A Russian Operation, U.S. Intelligence Says." *New York Times.* November 22, 2019 (updated November 26). https://www.nytimes.com/2019/11/22/us/politics/ukraine-russia-interference.html

66 Steinhauser, Paul. "Trump campaign launches ads questioning Biden's mental faculties." *Fox News.* August 18, 2020. https://www.foxnews.com/politics/trump-campaign-launches-ads-questioning-biden-mental-faculties

67 Margolin, Josh et al. "DHS withheld July intelligence bulletin calling out Russian attack on Biden's mental health." *Abcnews.go.com.* September 2, 2020. https://abcnews.go.com/Politics/dhs-withheld-july-intelligence-bulletin-calling-russian-attack/story?id=72747130

68 Margolin, Josh, Bruggeman, Lucien et. Al. "DHS withheld July intelligence bulletin calling out Russian attack on Biden's mental health." ABC News. September 2, 2020. https://abcnews.go.com/Politics/dhs-withheld-july-intelligence-bulletin-calling-russian-attack/story?id=72747130

69 Polantz, Katelyn. "Senate intelligence report warns of repeat of Russian interference in US election." *CNN.com.* August 20, 2020. https://edition.cnn.com/2020/08/19/politics/senate-intelligence-report-russia-2020/index.html

70 Dilanian, Ken. "Trump says he didn't discuss hacked emails with Roger Stone. A bipartisan Senate report says he did." *NBCNews.com.* August 18, 2020. https://

www.nbcnews.com/politics/national-security/bipartisan-senate-report-describes-2016-trump-campaign-eager-accept-help-n1237002

71 Baker, Peter, Haberman, Maggie and LaFraniere, Sharon. "Trump Commutes Sentence of Roger Stone in Case He Long Denounced." *New York Times*. July 10, 2020. https://www.nytimes.com/2020/07/10/us/politics/trump-roger-stone-clemency.html

72 Turak, Natasha. "Trump handing northern Syria to Turkey is a 'gift to Russia, Iran, and ISIS,' former US envoy says." *CNBC.com*. October 7, 2019. https://www.cnbc.com/2019/10/07/trump-handing-syria-to-turkey-is-gift-to-russia-iran-isis-mcgu.html

73 Barnes and Cooper. "Trump Discussed Pulling U.S. From NATO, Aides Say Amid New Concerns Over Russia."

74 Robertson, Nic. "Trump's Germany troops pullout may be his last gift to Putin before the election." *CNN.com*. August 2, 2020. https://edition.cnn.com/2020/08/02/politics/trump-germany-troops-russia-intl/index.html

75 Levin, Bess. "Breaking: Trump Throws Impotent Fit Over 'Rigged' Election for 38th Day Straight." *Vanity Fair*. December 15, 2020. https://www.vanityfair.com/news/2020/12/donald-trump-impotent-fit-2020

76 Chait, Jonathan. "Report: Trump Floated Not Leaving White House on January 20." *New York Magazine*. December 16, 2020. https://nymag.com/intelligencer/2020/12/will-trump-leave-white-house-january-20-inauguration.html

77 Sanger, David E., Perlroth, Nicole and Barnes, Julian E. "Billions Spent on U.S. Defenses Failed to Detect Giant Russian Hack." *New York Times*. December 16, 2020 (updated January 2, 2021). https://www.nytimes.com/2020/12/16/us/politics/russia-hack-putin-trump-biden.html

78 Sanger, David E., Perlroth, Nicole and Schmitt, Eric. "Scope of Russian Hacking Becomes Clear: Multiple U.S. Agencies Were Hit." *New York Times*. December 14, 2020 (updated January 5, 2021). https://www.nytimes.com/2020/12/14/us/politics/russia-hack-nsa-homeland-security-pentagon.html

79 "Putin and Trump discuss arms control issues in phone call." *The Washington Post*. July 23, 2020. https://www.washingtonpost.com/world/national-security/putin-and-trump-discuss-arms-control-issues-in-phone-call/2020/07/23/ab106e18-cd13-11ea-99b0-8426e26d203b_story.html

80 Trump. *Too Much and Never Enough* (p. 146).

Chapter Eight: This Is Their New Hoax

1 Chait, Jonathan. "Trump Binge-Watched Fox News All Night, Woke Up to Watch More Fox." *New York Magazine*. September 10, 2020. https://nymag.com/

intelligencer/2020/09/trump-fox-news-watch-television-binge-woodward-book.html

[2] Chait, Jonathan. "Trump: I Was Unable to Restock PPE for 3 Years Due to Hoaxes." *New York Magazine*. May 6, 2020. https://nymag.com/intelligencer/2020/05/trump-ppe-coronavirus-blame-impeachment-russia.html

[3] Sherman, Amy. "The Obama administration left Trump with a 'stockpile with a cupboard that was bare.'" *Politifact*. April 8, 2020. https://www.politifact.com/factchecks/2020/apr/08/donald-trump/trump-said-obama-admin-left-him-bare-stockpile-wro/

[4] "TRANSCRIPT: ABC News anchor David Muir interviews President Trump in Arizona." *Abcnews.go.com*. May 6, 2020. https://abcnews.go.com/Politics/transcript-abc-news-anchor-david-muir-interviews-president/story?id=70523003

[5] Chait, Jonathan. "Republicans Say Impeachment Distracted Trump From Preparing for Coronavirus." *New York Magazine*. March 31, 2020. https://nymag.com/intelligencer/2020/03/republicans-impeachment-distracted-trump-coronavirus.html

[6] Stieb, Matt. "Read Trump's Letter to Chuck Schumer Blaming Coronavirus in New York on Impeachment." *New York Magazine*. April 2, 2020. https://nymag.com/intelligencer/2020/04/read-trumps-letter-blaming-coronavirus-in-ny-on-impeachment.html

[7] Cook, Nancy, McGraw, Meridith and Cancryn, Adam. "What did Trump know and when did he know it? Inside his Feb. 7 admission." *Politico*. September 10, 2020. https://www.politico.com/news/2020/09/10/trump-coronavirus-bob-woodward-412222

[8] Rieder, Rem. "Trump and the 'New Hoax.'" *Factcheck.org*. March 3, 2020. https://www.factcheck.org/2020/03/trump-and-the-new-hoax/

[9] Wade, Peter. "New Audio: While Trump Defended Sharing 'Fire Fauci' Tweet, He Told Woodward Virus 'Is the Plague.'" *Rolling Stone*. September 15, 2020. https://www.rollingstone.com/politics/politics-news/new-audio-while-trump-shared-fire-fauci-tweet-he-told-woodward-virus-is-plague-1059787/

[10] Subramaniam, Tara and Yan, Holly. "'It affects virtually nobody': Fact-checking Trump's continued efforts to downplay the risks of coronavirus." *CNN.com*. September 22, 2020. https://edition.cnn.com/2020/09/22/politics/trump-covid-19-statement-fact-check/index.html

[11] Breuninger, Kevin. "Herman Cain was on a ventilator before he died from Covid-19, top aide says." *CNBC.com*. August 4, 2020. https://www.cnbc.com/2020/08/04/herman-cain-was-on-a-ventilator-before-he-died-from-covid-19-top-aide-says.html

[12] Karni, Annie. "Trump Defends Indoor Rally, but Aides Express Concern." *New York Times*. September 14, 2020 (updated September 17). https://www.nytimes.com/2020/09/14/us/politics/trump-rally.html

[13] Worldometer. https://www.worldometers.info/coronavirus/country/us/

[14] "More U.S. deaths than World War I and Vietnam: How COVID-19 compares with other deadly events." *Los Angeles Times*. May 1, 2020 (updated September 22). https://www.latimes.com/world-nation/story/2020-05-01/covid-19-death-toll-wars-disasters
After AIDS, the Civil War, the 1918 flu and WWII.

[15] Rupar, Aaron. *Twitter*. September 22, 2020. https://twitter.com/atrupar/status/1308532275697586183

[16] Worldometer. https://www.worldometers.info/coronavirus/country/us/

[17] Cohen, Marshall and Herb, Jeremy. "Breaking down 'Obamagate,' Trump's latest theory about the 'deep state' and Obama's role in the Russia investigation." *CNN.com*. May 13, 2020. https://edition.cnn.com/2020/05/13/politics/trump-obama-obamagate-russia/index.html

[18] Ibid.

[19] Riccardi, Nicholas and Miller, Zeke. "Trump threatens funds for states easing voting in pandemic." *AP News*. May 21, 2020. https://apnews.com/article/61ed35968fb6b0420e463ac65f6ed058

[20] Subramaniam, Tara. "Fact-checking Trump's false claims on unsolicited ballots." *CNN.com*. September 15, 2020. https://edition.cnn.com/2020/09/14/politics/80-million-unsolicited-ballots-fact-check/index.html

[21] McMurry, Evan, Phelps, Jordyn and Lantry, Lauren. "President Donald Trump declines to commit to peaceful transfer of power: 'There won't be a transfer.'" *Abcnews.go.com*. September 24, 2020. https://abcnews.go.com/Politics/president-trump-declines-commit-peaceful-transfer-power/story?id=73205708

[22] Shear, Michael D. "Trump, in Video From White House, Delivers a 46-Minute Diatribe on the 'Rigged' Election." *New York Times*. December 2, 2020. https://www.nytimes.com/2020/12/02/us/politics/trump-election-video.html

[23] Chait. "Report: Trump Floated Not Leaving White House on January 20."

[24] Quinn, Melissa. "The internal watchdogs Trump has fired or replaced." *CBSnews.com*. May 19, 2020. https://www.cbsnews.com/news/trump-inspectors-general-internal-watchdogs-fired-list/

[25] Radcliffe, Shawn and Cassell, Dana K. "Trump Is Taking Hydroxychloroquine: Why Experts Say You Shouldn't." *Healthline*. May 19, 2020. https://www.healthline.com/health-news/trump-is-taking-hydroxychloroquine-why-experts-think-this-is-a-bad-idea

[26] Illing, Sean. "'Flood the zone with shit': How misinformation overwhelmed our democracy." *Vox.com*. February 6, 2020. https://www.vox.com/policy-and-politics/2020/1/16/20991816/impeachment-trial-trump-bannon-misinformation

[27] Paul, Christopher and Matthews, Miriam. "The Russian 'Firehose of Falsehood' Propaganda Model: Why It Might Work and Options to Counter It." *RAND Corporation*. 2016. https://www.rand.org/pubs/perspectives/PE198.html

[28] Saakashvili, Mikheil. "When Russia Invaded Georgia." *Wall Street Journal*. August 7, 2018. https://www.wsj.com/articles/when-russia-invaded-georgia-1533682576

[29] Gearan, Anne and Wagner, John. "Trump national security adviser O'Brien tests positive for coronavirus. He's the highest-ranking administration official known to be infected." *The Washington Post*. July 27, 2020. https://www.washingtonpost.com/politics/trump-national-security-adviser-obrien-tests-positive-for-coronavirus-the-highest-ranking-administration-official-known-to-be-infected/2020/07/27/1590c4dc-d00b-11ea-9038-af089b63ac21_story.html

[30] Woodward, Bob. *Rage* (p. XIII). Simon & Schuster. Kindle Edition.

[31] Kessler, Glenn, Rizzo, Salvador and Kelly, Meg. "President Trump has made more than 20,000 false or misleading claims." *The Washington Post*. July 13, 2020. https://www.washingtonpost.com/politics/2020/07/13/president-trump-has-made-more-than-20000-false-or-misleading-claims/

[32] "In four years, President Trump made 30,573 false or misleading claims." *The Washington Post*. January 20, 2021. https://www.washingtonpost.com/graphics/politics/trump-claims-database/?tid=lk_inline_manual_22&tid=lk_inline_manual_26&tid=lk_inline_manual_31&tid=lk_inline_manual_35&itid=lk_inline_manual_35&itid=lk_inline_manual_42&itid=lk_inline_manual_20&itid=lk_inline_manual_38

[33] Gordon, Devin. "Trump's Favorite TV Network Is Post-parody." *Atlantic*. May 19, 2020. https://www.theatlantic.com/politics/archive/2020/05/trumps-favorite-tv-network-post-parody/611353/

[34] Gursky, Jacob and Woolley, Samuel. "How hate and misinformation go viral: A case study of a Trump retweet." *Brookings TechStream*. September 2, 2020. https://www.brookings.edu/techstream/how-hate-and-misinformation-go-viral-a-case-study-of-a-trump-retweet/

[35] Sanger, David E. and Kanno-Youngs, Zolan. "Russian online trolls often simply retweeted Trump's own tweets." *New York Times*. September 22, 2020 (updated September 25). https://www.nytimes.com/2020/09/22/us/politics/russia-disinformation-election-trump.html

[36] United States Senate. "Russian Active Measures Campaigns and Interference in the 2016 U.S. Election, Volume 2: Russia's Use of Social Media With Additional Views." https://www.intelligence.senate.gov/sites/default/files/documents/Report_Volume2.pdf

[37] Cohen. *Disloyal: A Memoir* (p. 100).

[38] Jacobson, Zachary Jonathan. "Many are worried about the return of the 'Big Lie.' They're worried about the wrong thing." *The Washington Post*. May 21, 2018. https://www.washingtonpost.com/news/made-by-history/wp/2018/05/21/many-are-worried-about-the-return-of-the-big-lie-theyre-worried-about-the-wrong-thing/

[39] Chalfant, Morgan. "Trump talks coronavirus, arms control in phone call with

Putin." *Hill.* July 23, 2020. https://thehill.com/homenews/administration/508720-trump-talks-coronavirus-arms-control-in-phone-call-with-putin

[40] Crowley, Michael. "Trump and Putin Discuss Russia's Attendance at G7, but Allies Are Wary." *New York Times.* June 1, 2020. https://www.nytimes.com/2020/06/01/us/politics/trump-putin-g7.html

[41] "Pandemic, Oil, And Arms Control Dominate Trump, Putin Phone Call." *Rferl.org.* May 7, 2020. https://www.rferl.org/a/pandemic-oil-and-arms-control-dominate-trump-putin-phone-call/30599744.html

[42] Maynes, Charles. "U.S. Sends Ventilators To Russia In $5.6 Million Coronavirus Aid Package." *NPR.org.* May 21, 2020. https://www.npr.org/sections/coronavirus-live-updates/2020/05/21/860143691/u-s-sends-ventilators-to-russia-in-5-6-million-coronavirus-aid-package

[43] Tucker, Emma. "Trump to U.S. Governors: Get Your Own Ventilators." *Daily Beast.* March 16, 2020. https://www.thedailybeast.com/trump-to-us-governors-get-your-own-ventilators

[44] Tétrault-Farber, Gabrielle. "Russian ventilators sent to U.S. made by firm under U.S. sanctions: Russia newspaper." *Reuters.* April 3, 2020. https://www.reuters.com/article/us-health-coronavirus-russia-usa-sanctio/russian-ventilators-sent-to-u-s-made-by-firm-under-u-s-sanctions-russia-newspaper-idUSKBN21L243

[45] Flaherty, Anne et al. "Russia bills US $660K for aid that included gas masks, household cleaning gloves." *Abcnews.go.com.* May 1, 2020. https://abcnews.go.com/Politics/russia-bills-us-660k-aid-included-gas-masks/story?id=70451912

[46] Eckel. "A Trump-Putin 'Reset'? Flurry Of Communication Points To Behind-The-Scenes Diplomacy."

[47] McFaul, Michael. *Twitter.* July 5, 2020. https://twitter.com/mcfaul/status/1279818813882548230?s=11

[48] Nakamura, David, Leonnig, Carol D. and Dawsey, Josh. "Trump flouts coronavirus protocols as security experts warn of need to protect president from a lethal threat." *The Washington Post.* May 9, 2020. https://www.washingtonpost.com/politics/trump-flouts-coronavirus-protocols-as-security-experts-warn-of-need-to-protect-president-from-a-lethal-threat/2020/05/08/3a6a9cec-9136-11ea-a9c0-73b93422d691_story.html

[49] Tsvetkova and Ivanova. "Sharp increase in Moscow pneumonia cases fuels fears over coronavirus statistics."

[50] "Russia Orders Twitter, Facebook to Delete 'Fake' Coronavirus News." *Moscow Times.* March 26, 2020. https://www.themoscowtimes.com/2020/03/26/russia-orders-twitter-facebook-to-delete-fake-coronavirus-news-a69765

[51] Roth, Andrew. "'It's like a normal day': Moscow grapples with virus lockdown." *Guardian.* March 30, 2020. https://www.theguardian.com/world/2020/mar/30/moscow-coronavirus-lockdown-stay-indoors-city

[52] "COVID-19: Moscow Cases 'Likely Three Times Higher' Than Official Toll;

Pakistan To Lift Virus Lockdown." *Rferl.org*. May 7, 2020. https://www.rferl.org/a/covid-19-serbia-lifts-state-emergency-curfew/30598819.html

53 Trump, Donald. *Twitter*. March 9, 2020. https://www.thetrumparchive.com/?results=1&searchbox=%22The+Fake+News+Media+and+their+partner%22&dates=%5B%222020-03-09%22%2C%222020-03-10%22%5D

54 Trump, Donald. *Twitter*. March 18, 2020. https://www.thetrumparchive.com/ ?results=1&searchbox=%22I+always+treated+the+Chinese+Virus+very+seriously%22

55 Eder et al. "430,000 People Have Traveled From China to U.S. Since Coronavirus Surfaced."

56 "The Latest: Russia closing its land border with China." *AP News*. January 30, 2020. https://apnews.com/article/4ab3d1f101c55f376e204727e620afc4

57 Saeed, Saim. "Trump's Europe travel ban explained." *Politico*. March 12, 2020. https://www.politico.eu/article/coronavirus-donald-trump-europe-travel-ban-explained/

58 Worldometer. https://www.worldometers.info/coronavirus/country/us/

59 Miller, Greg, Dawsey, Josh and Davis, Aaron C. "One final viral infusion: Trump's move to block travel from Europe triggered chaos and a surge of passengers from the outbreak's center" *The Washington Post*. May 23, 2020. https://www.washingtonpost.com/world/national-security/one-final-viral-infusion-trumps-move-to-block-travel-from-europe-triggered-chaos-and-a-surge-of-passengers-from-the-outbreaks-center/2020/05/23/64836a00-962b-11ea-82b4-c8db161ff6e5_story.html

60 Ibid.

61 Chappell, Bill. "Coronavirus: Chaos Follows Trump's European Travel Ban; EU Says It Wasn't Warned." *NPR.org*. March 12, 2020. https://www.npr.org/sections/goatsandsoda/2020/03/12/814876173/coronavirus-trump-speech-creates-chaos-eu-says-it-wasnt-warned-of-travel-ban

62 "The Latest: Fauci: US airport crush defeats anti-virus goals." *Wtmj.com*. March 15, 2020. https://wtmj.com/national/2020/03/15/the-latest-fauci-us-airport-crush-defeats-anti-virus-goals/

63 Miller, Dawsey and Davis. "One final viral infusion."

64 Grove, Thomas and Simmons, Ann M. "Three Doctors in Russia Have Fallen Out of Hospital Windows." *Wall Street Journal*. May 7, 2020. https://www.wsj.com/articles/three-doctors-in-russia-have-fallen-out-of-hospital-windows-11588887817

65 Maynes, Charles. "Three Russian Frontline Health Workers Mysteriously Fell Out Of Hospital Windows." *NPR.org*. May 7, 2020. https://www.npr.org/2020/05/07/852319465/three-russian-frontline-health-workers-mysteriously-fell-out-of-hospital-windows

[66] Stewart, Will. "Three more Russian Covid-19 patients fall to their deaths from hospital windows, bringing the number of cases to SEVEN." *Daily Mail.* June 10, 2020. https://www.dailymail.co.uk/news/article-8405487/Three-Russian-Covid-19-patients-fall-deaths-hospital-windows.html

[67] "Russian Scientist Who Worked on Coronavirus Vaccine Stabbed, Falls Out of Window." *Moscow Times.* December 21, 2020. https://www.themoscowtimes.com/2020/12/21/russian-scientist-who-worked-on-coronavirus-vaccine-stabbed-falls-out-of-window-a72427

[68] "St. Petersburg investigators began to doubt the version of the murder of scientist Alexander Kagansky. A polygraph awaits the detained person." *Fontanka.* December 12, 2020. https://www.fontanka.ru/2020/12/21/69645921/

[69] Abutaleb and Dawsey. "New Trump pandemic adviser pushes controversial 'herd immunity' strategy, worrying public health officials."

[70] Mukherjee, Sy. "Trump wants a COVID vaccine before Election Day, but fewer Americans are saying they'll get one." *Fortune.* October 6, 2020. https://fortune.com/2020/10/06/covid-vaccine-update-coronavirus-vaccines-older-americans-herd-immunity/

[71] Milman, Oliver. "US Covid vaccine unlikely to arrive before election following FDA move." *Guardian.* October 6, 2020. https://www.theguardian.com/world/2020/oct/06/coronavirus-vaccine-trump-administration-fda

[72] Allassan, Fadel. "Trump tags FDA chief in 'political hit job' complaint over vaccine rule." *Axios.com.* October 7, 2020. https://www.axios.com/trump-fda-commissioner-political-23de8d63-e1f6-4d2f-89e2-004020377442.html

[73] Khan Burki, Talha. "The Russian vaccine for COVID-19." *Lancet.* November 1, 2020. https://www.thelancet.com/journals/lanres/article/PIIS2213-2600(20)30402-1/fulltext

[74] Ibid.

[75] "Putin says some of his close relatives vaccinated against coronavirus." *TASS Russian News Agency.* October 7, 2020. https://tass.com/world/1209429

[76] Castronuovo, Celine. "Russia reports record number of new coronavirus infections." *Hill.* October 9, 2020. https://thehill.com/policy/international/russia/520380-russia-reports-record-number-of-new-coronavirus-infections

[77] Woodward. *Rage* (p. 286).

[78] Phelps, Jordyn and Gittleson, Ben. "Trump contracts coronavirus after downplaying risk for months. What next?" *Abcnews.go.com.* October 2, 2020. https://abcnews.go.com/Politics/trump-contracts-coronavirus-downplaying-risk-months/story?id=73382906

[79] "Russia's Top Coronavirus Doctor Who Met Putin Tests Positive." *Moscow Times.* April 6, 2020. https://www.themoscowtimes.com/2020/03/31/russias-top-coronavirus-doctor-who-met-putin-tests-positive-a69815

80 Hodge, Nathan and Ilyushina, Mary. "Trump kept a busy schedule during the pandemic. Putin stayed in a bubble." *CNN.com*. October 2, 2020. https://edition.cnn.com/2020/10/02/europe/putin-bubble-trump-covid-intl/index.html

81 Radchenko, Sergey and Rakhmetov, Baurzhan. "Putin Is Ruling Russia Like a Central Asian Dictator." *Foreign Policy*. August 6, 2020. https://foreignpolicy.com/2020/08/06/putin-ruling-russia-like-a-kazakhstan-kyrgyzstan-uzbekistan-tajikistan-belarus-central-asian-dictator/

82 Miller, Christopher. "Putin, Who Has Spent Almost Six Months In Isolation To Avoid The Coronavirus, Sent Trump A Get-Well Note." *BuzzFeed News*. October 2, 2020. https://www.buzzfeednews.com/article/christopherm51/putin-well-wishes-trump-coronavirus-positive-test

Chapter Nine: October Surprise

1 Dale, Daniel. *Twitter*. October 13, 2020. https://twitter.com/ddale8/status/1315794426934046720?s=20

2 Bump, Philip. "Why Donald Trump tweets late at night (and very early in the morning)." *The Washington Post*. September 30, 2016. https://www.washingtonpost.com/news/the-fix/wp/2016/09/30/why-donald-trump-tweets-late-at-night-and-very-early-in-the-morning/

3 "Election 2020 Today: Trump contracts COVID-19, globe reacts." *AP News*. October 2, 2020. https://apnews.com/article/election-2020-virus-outbreak-donald-trump-melania-trump-10-things-to-know-e8019039dd69b2f29473cf4df7f1db1b

4 Trump, Donald. *Twitter*. October 2, 2020. https://www.thetrumparchive.com/ ?results=1&searchbox=%22Tonight%2C+%40FLOTUS+and+I+tested+positive+%22

5 Bender, Michael C. and Ballhaus, Rebecca. "Trump Didn't Disclose First Positive Covid-19 Test While Awaiting a Second Test on Thursday." *Wall Street Journal*. October 4, 2020. https://www.wsj.com/articles/trump-didnt-disclose-first-positive-covid-19-test-while-awaiting-a-second-test-on-thursday-11601844813

6 "Coronavirus Disease 2019 Testing Basics." U.S. Food & Drugs. https://www.fda.gov/consumers/consumer-updates/coronavirus-disease-2019-testing-basics

7 Nuzzi, Olivia. "Donald Trump and Sean Hannity Like to Talk Before Bedtime." *New York Magazine*. May, 2018. https://nymag.com/intelligencer/2018/05/sean-hannity-donald-trump-late-night-calls.html

8 Stolberg, Sheryl Gay and Weiland, Noah. "Study Finds 'Single Largest Driver' of Coronavirus Misinformation: Trump." *New York Times*. September 30, 2020 (updated October 22). https://www.nytimes.com/2020/09/30/us/politics/trump-coronavirus-misinformation.html

[9] D'Ammassa, Algernon. "Trump's doctor may be the first osteopathic physician to serve as president's top healer." *USA Today News.* October 6, 2020. https://eu.usatoday.com/story/news/health/2020/10/06/trump-doctor-sean-conley-do-osteopathic-medicine-vs-allopathic/3636094001/

[10] Hawkins, Derek. "President's blood oxygen levels dropped twice in recent days, doctors say." *The Washington Post.* October 5, 2020. https://www.washingtonpost.com/elections/2020/10/04/trump-covid-live-updates/

[11] Worldometer. https://www.worldometers.info/coronavirus/country/us/

[12] Baker, Peter and Haberman, Maggie. "Trump Leaves Hospital, Minimizing Virus and Urging Americans 'Don't Let It Dominate Your Lives.'" *New York Times.* October 5, 2020 (updated October 7). https://www.nytimes.com/2020/10/05/us/politics/trump-leaves-hospital-coronavirus.html

[13] Applebaum, Anne. "Il Donald." *Atlantic.* October 6, 2020. https://www.theatlantic.com/ideas/archive/2020/10/trump-pays-mussolini-like-attention-his-own-image/616626/

[14] Karni, Annie and Haberman, Maggie. "Trump Makes First Public Appearance Since Leaving Walter Reed." *New York Times.* October 10, 2020 (updated October 12). https://www.nytimes.com/2020/10/10/us/politics/trump-white-house-coronavirus.html

[15] Trump, Donald. *Twitter.* October 5, 2020. https://www.thetrumparchive.com/?results=1&searchbox=%22Don%E2%80%99t+be+afraid+of+Covid%22

[16] "Trump: Don't Let Coronavirus Dominate You" *YouTube.* October 6, 2020. https://www.youtube.com/watch?v=_e55hSFNJOI

[17] Worldometer. https://www.worldometers.info/coronavirus/country/us/

[18] Trump, Donald. *Twitter.* October 5, 2020. https://www.thetrumparchive.com/?results=1&searchbox=%22better+than+I+did+20+years+ago%22

[19] Hogan, Alex. "Watch: Understanding dexamethasone, the steroid used to treat Trump's Covid-19." *Stat News.* October 12, 2020. https://www.statnews.com/2020/10/12/understanding-dexamethasone-the-steroid-used-to-treat-trumps-covid-19/

[20] Sanger, David E. and Broad, William J. "Trump's Virus Treatment Revives Questions About Unchecked Nuclear Authority." *New York Times.* October 11, 2020. https://www.nytimes.com/2020/10/11/us/politics/trump-nuclear-weapons-coronavirus.html

[21] "Detail on Trump's hand fuels speculation after Covid diagnosis." *Yahoo! News.* October 11, 2020. https://au.news.yahoo.com/detail-on-trumps-hand-sparks-speculation-after-covid-diagnosis-040844195.html

[22] "Dexamethasone 3.3 mg/ml Solution for Injection (vial)." EMC. https://www.medicines.org.uk/emc/product/571/smpc#gref

[23] Tillett, Richard L. et al. "Genomic evidence for reinfection with SARS-CoV-2: a

case study." *Lancet*. January 1, 2021. https://www.thelancet.com/journals/laninf/article/PIIS1473-3099(20)30764-7/fulltext

24 Sommer, Will. "Trump Touts Falconer's Benghazi Blood-Sacrifice Conspiracy Theory." *Daily Beast*. October 31, 2020. https://www.thedailybeast.com/trump-touts-falconers-benghazi-blood-sacrifice-conspiracy-theory

25 "Great Barrington Declaration." https://gbdeclaration.org/ (https://gbdeclaration.org/)

26 "Herd immunity letter signed by fake experts including 'Dr Johnny Bananas.'" *Guardian*. October 9, 2020. https://www.theguardian.com/world/2020/oct/09/herd-immunity-letter-signed-fake-experts-dr-johnny-bananas-covid

27 Achenbach, Joel. "Proposal to hasten herd immunity to the coronavirus grabs White House attention but appalls top scientists." *The Washington Post*. October 14, 2020. https://www.washingtonpost.com/health/covid-herd-immunity/2020/10/10/3910251c-0a60-11eb-859b-f9c27abe638d_story.html

28 Ibid.

29 Fiore, Kristina. "The Cost of Herd Immunity in the U.S." *MedPage Today*. September 1, 2020. https://www.medpagetoday.com/infectiousdisease/covid19/88401

30 Gander, Kashmira. "'Overt Lie': White House Adviser Scott Atlas Denies Herd Immunity Strategy Claims." *Newsweek*. September 1, 2020. https://www.newsweek.com/scott-atlas-herd-immunity-deny-strategy-1528827

31 Achenbach. "Proposal to hasten herd immunity to the coronavirus grabs White House attention but appalls top scientists."

32 "President Donald J. Trump Is Protecting Our Nation's Vulnerable Seniors." White House Archives. July 22, 2020. https://trumpwhitehouse.archives.gov/briefings-statements/president-donald-j-trump-is-protecting-our-nations-vulnerable-seniors/ (https://trumpwhitehouse.archives.gov/briefings-statements/president-donald-j-trump-is-protecting-our-nations-vulnerable-seniors/)

33 Washington, Lisa. "Trump Administration Announces New Requirements For Coronavirus Testing In Nursing Homes." *CBS Pittsburgh*. August 26, 2020. https://pittsburgh.cbslocal.com/2020/08/26/nursing-home-covid-testing-requirements/

34 Silver-Greenberg, Jessica and Drucker, Jesse. "Nursing Homes With Safety Problems Deploy Trump-Connected Lobbyists." *New York Times*. August 16, 2020. https://www.nytimes.com/2020/08/16/business/nursing-home-safety-trump.html

35 Relman, Eliza. "Trump wants to reopen the US economy on Easter because he'd like 'packed churches all over our country' despite massive public health risk." *Business Insider*. March 24, 2020. https://www.businessinsider.com/trump-wants-reopen-economy-on-easter-to-have-packed-churches-2020-3?r=US&IR=T

36 Abutaleb, Yasmeen et al. "Trump's den of dissent: Inside the White House task

force as coronavirus surges." *The Washington Post*. October 19, 2020. https://www.washingtonpost.com/politics/trumps-den-of-dissent-inside-the-white-house-task-force-as-coronavirus-surges/2020/10/19/7ff8ee6a-0a6e-11eb-859b-f9c27abe638d_story.html

[37] Pilkington, Ed. "Twitter removes false coronavirus tweet by Trump's favourite health adviser." *Guardian*. October 19, 2020. https://www.theguardian.com/us-news/2020/oct/19/scott-atlas-twitter-removal-false-coronavirus-tweet

[38] "Latest Polls." *FiveThirtyEight.com*. https://projects.fivethirtyeight.com/polls/president-general/national/

[39] Chait, Jonathan. "Trump Determined to Get Vaccine Before Election, Reportedly Overrules FDA Guidelines." *New York Magazine*. October 5, 2020. https://nymag.com/intelligencer/2020/10/trump-vaccine-overrules-fda-election-coronavirus-science.html

[40] Culver, Jordan, Weise, Elizabeth and Weintraub, Karen. "President Donald Trump says COVID-19 vaccines are coming 'momentarily'. Scientists say they're not." *USA Today News*. October 5, 2020. https://eu.usatoday.com/story/news/health/2020/10/05/donald-trump-covid-19-vaccine-momentarily/3632646001/

[41] "Drugmaker Halts Vaccine Trial Because of Sick Volunteer." *New York Times*. January 13, 2021. https://www.nytimes.com/live/2020/10/12/world/coronavirus-covid

[42] Grady, Denise, Wu, Katherine J. and LaFraniere, Sharon. "AstraZeneca, Under Fire for Vaccine Safety, Releases Trial Blueprints." *New York Times*. September 19, 2020 (updated December 30). https://www.nytimes.com/2020/09/19/health/astrazeneca-vaccine-safety-blueprints.html

[43] Morello, Lauren and Cancryn, Adam. "Trump says he might reject stricter FDA vaccine guidelines." *Politico*. September 23, 2020. https://www.politico.com/news/2020/09/23/trump-vaccine-fda-guidelines-420803

[44] Trump, Donald. *Twitter*. October 6, 2020. https://www.thetrumparchive.com/?results=1&searchbox=%22another+political+hit+job%22

[45] Palus, Shannon. "How Much Did COVID Drugs Contribute to Trump's Recovery?" *Slate*. October 19, 2020. https://slate.com/technology/2020/10/donald-trump-covid-19-drugs.html

[46] Dale, Daniel. "Fact check: Trump makes at least 14 false claims in first post-hospital interview on Fox Business." *CNN.com*. October 8, 2020. https://edition.cnn.com/2020/10/08/politics/fact-check-trump-interview-bartiromo-fox-business/index.html

[47] Bump, Philip. "The laughable obviousness of Trump's 'cure' gambit." *The Washington Post*. October 9, 2020. https://www.washingtonpost.com/politics/2020/10/09/laughable-obviousness-trumps-cure-gambit/

[48] Thomas, Katie. "Trump's Antibody 'Cure' Will Be in Short Supply." *New York Times*. October 20, 2020 (updated December 23). https://www.nytimes.

com/2020/10/20/health/covid-antibody-regeneron.html

49 Weise, Elizabeth. "A COVID-19 vaccine by Election Day? Here are the 3 things that would need to happen, and soon." *USA Today News*. October 7, 2020. https://eu.usatoday.com/story/news/health/2020/10/07/covid-19-vaccine-election-day-experts-donald-trump/3637150001/

50 Picchi, Aimee. "Could Trump push a vaccine through before election day?" *CBSNews.com*. September 11, 2020. https://www.cbsnews.com/news/coronavirus-vaccine-process-fda-political-pressure/

51 Westcott, Ben. "September 7 coronavirus news." *CNN.com*. September 7, 2020 (updated September 8). https://edition.cnn.com/world/live-news/coronavirus-pandemic-09-07-20-intl/h_f5e6d11e22a83184e7cce69ec0b36d3c

52 Lybrand, Holmes. "Fact Check: Will there be a coronavirus vaccine by November?" *CNN.com*. August 7, 2020. https://edition.cnn.com/2020/08/07/politics/donald-trump-coronavirus-vaccine-november-fact-check/index.html

53 Herper, Matthew. "Johnson & Johnson Covid-19 vaccine study paused due to unexplained illness in participant." *Stat News*. October 12, 2020. https://www.statnews.com/2020/10/12/johnson-johnson-covid-19-vaccine-study-paused-due-to-unexplained-illness-in-participant/

54 Owermohle, Sarah. "Pfizer delivers final blow to Trump's hope for preelection vaccine." *Politico*. October 16, 2020. https://www.politico.com/news/2020/10/16/pfizer-no-vaccine-trump-election-429843

55 U.S. Northern Command. "About USNORTHCOM." https://www.northcom.mil/About-USNORTHCOM/

56 Murray, Sara and Liptak, Kevin. "Trump has personally pressured drug company CEOs repeatedly to speed vaccine." *CNN.com*. October 7, 2020. https://edition.cnn.com/2020/10/06/politics/trump-pfizer-vaccine/index.html

57 Boehlert, Eric. "Trump's pandemic playbook comes straight from Putin — chaos is the goal." *Press Run*. October 20, 2020. https://pressrun.media/p/trumps-pandemic-playbook-comes-straight (https://pressrun.media/p/trumps-pandemic-playbook-comes-straight)

58 Harding, Luke. "Covering Russia and the west: 'Putin's goal is to make the truth unknowable.'" *Guardian*. July 12, 2020. https://www.theguardian.com/membership/2020/jul/12/covering-russia-and-the-west-putins-goal-is-to-make-the-truth-unknowable

Chapter Ten: Lying In State Media

1 Richards, Kimberley. "Trump's latest speech compared to '1984': 'What you're seeing and what you're reading is not what's happening.'" *Independent*. July 25, 2018. https://www.independent.co.uk/news/world/americas/us-politics/trump-

speech-fake-news-1984-orwell-kansas-a8463471.html

[2] Worldometer. https://www.worldometers.info/coronavirus/country/us/

[3] "National Exit Polls: How Different Groups Voted." *New York Times*. November 3, 2020. https://www.nytimes.com/interactive/2020/11/03/us/elections/exit-polls-president.html

[4] Harcourt, Jennifer et al. "Severe Acute Respiratory Syndrome Coronavirus 2 from Patient with Coronavirus Disease, United States." *Emerg Infect Dis*. June, 2020. https://wwwnc.cdc.gov/eid/article/26/6/20-0516_article (https://wwwnc.cdc.gov/eid/article/26/6/20-0516_article)

[5] Irwin, Neil. "The Pandemic Depression Is Over. The Pandemic Recession Has Just Begun." *New York Times*. October 3, 2020. https://www.nytimes.com/2020/10/03/upshot/pandemic-economy-recession.html

[6] Edwards, Erika. "'Two-way street': CDC report says masks protect wearers and everyone else." *NBCNews.com*. November 10, 2020. https://www.nbcnews.com/health/health-news/two-way-street-cdc-report-says-masks-protect-wearers-everyone-n1247258

[7] Healy, Melissa. "Super-spreading Trump rallies led to more than 700 COVID-19 deaths, study estimates." *Los Angeles Times*. October 31, 2020. https://www.latimes.com/science/story/2020-10-31/super-spreading-trump-rallies-led-to-more-than-700-covid-19-deaths-study

[8] Glasser, Susan B. "Donald Trump's 2020 Superspreader Campaign: A Diary." *New Yorker*. November 3, 2020. https://www.newyorker.com/news/letter-from-trumps-washington/donald-trumps-2020-superspreader-campaign-a-diary

[9] McEvoy, Jemima. "Nevada Gov. In 'Utter Disbelief' Of Trump's 'Callous Disregard' After Two Rallies Defying Covid Rules." *Forbes*. September 16, 2020. https://www.forbes.com/sites/jemimamcevoy/2020/09/16/nevada-gov-in-utter-disbelief-of-trumps-callous-disregard-after-two-rallies-defying-covid-rules/?sh=73074c2db543

[10] Colvin, Jill. "Trump defies coronavirus rules as 'peaceful protest' rallies grow." *Denver Post*. September 15, 2020. https://www.denverpost.com/2020/09/15/trump-rallies-campaign-2020-coronavirus-rules/

[11] Karni. "Trump Defends Indoor Rally, but Aides Express Concern."

[12] Ibid.

[13] Hayes, Chris. *Twitter*. September 14, 2020. https://twitter.com/chrislhayes/status/1305344695007088640?s=20

[14] "Managing the COVID-19 infodemic: Promoting healthy behaviours and mitigating the harm from misinformation and disinformation." World Health Organization. September 23, 2020. https://www.who.int/news/item/23-09-2020-managing-the-covid-19-infodemic-promoting-healthy-behaviours-and-mitigating-the-harm-from-misinformation-and-disinformation

15 Evanega, Sarah et al. "Coronavirus misinformation: quantifying sources and themes in the COVID-19 'infodemic.'" *Cornell Alliance for Science*. July 23, 2020. https://int.nyt.com/data/documenttools/evanega-et-al-coronavirus-misinformation-submitted-07-23-20-1/080839ac0c22bca8/full.pdf

16 Stolberg and Weiland. "Study Finds 'Single Largest Driver' of Coronavirus Misinformation: Trump."

17 Haque, Umair. "Do Americans Understand How Bad Covid in America Really Is?" *Eudaimonia & Co*. November 19, 2020. https://eand.co/do-americans-understand-how-bad-covid-in-america-really-is-207ecfa8e899 (https://eand.co/do-americans-understand-how-bad-covid-in-america-really-is-207ecfa8e899)

18 Ibid.

19 Barnes, Julian E. and Sanger, David E. "Putin Most Likely Directing Election Interference to Aid Trump, C.I.A. Says." *New York Times*. September 22, 2020 (updated October 23). https://www.nytimes.com/2020/09/22/us/politics/cia-russian-election-interference.html

20 Curley, Christopher and Cassell, Dana K. "How Even One Social Gathering Can Quickly Spread COVID-19." *Healthline*. April 1, 2020. https://www.healthline.com/health-news/hone-social-gathering-can-quickly-spread-covid-19

21 Wasserman, David et al. "2020 National Popular Vote Tracker." *Cook Political Report*. https://cookpolitical.com/2020-national-popular-vote-tracker

22 "2020 Election Highlights: With a Record Mail-in Vote and Fears of Postal Delays, a Federal Judge Orders a Sweep for Undelivered Ballots." *New York Times*. November 5, 2020. https://www.nytimes.com/live/2020/11/02/us/trump-vs-biden#with-101-million-votes-cast-early-the-us-heads-toward-its-highest-turnout-in-over-a-century

23 Dale, Daniel. "Fact check: Trump makes series of egregious false claims in Election Night address." *CNN.com*. November 4, 2020. https://edition.cnn.com/2020/11/04/politics/fact-check-trump-election-night-speech/index.html

24 Galeotti. *We Need to Talk About Putin*.

25 Paul and Matthews. "The Russian 'Firehose of Falsehood' Propaganda Model."

26 Tucker, Eric. "FBI official: Russia wants to see US 'tear ourselves apart.'" *AP News*. February 24, 2020. https://apnews.com/article/a55930e0a02d2e21d8ed2be7bc496a6f

27 Boehlert, Eric. "Trump has Covid-19: How Fox News infected America." *Press Run*. October 2, 2020. https://pressrun.media/p/trump-has-covid-19-and-fox-news-made (https://pressrun.media/p/trump-has-covid-19-and-fox-news-made)

28 Stoll, Julia. "Leading cable news networks in the United States in Q4 2020, by number of primetime viewers." *Statista*. January 13, 2021. https://www.statista.com/statistics/373814/cable-news-network-viewership-usa/

29 Hall Jamieson, Kathleen et al. "The Relation between Media Consumption and

Misinformation at the Outset of the SARS-CoV-2 Pandemic in the US." *Harvard Kennedy School Misinformation Review*. April, 2020. https://misinforeview.hks. harvard.edu/wp-content/uploads/2020/04/April19_FORMATTED_COVID-19-Survey.pdf (https://misinforeview.hks.harvard.edu/wp-content/uploads/2020/04/April19_FORMATTED_COVID-19-Survey.pdf)

[30] Savillo, Rob. "Fox News pushed coronavirus misinformation 253 times in just five days." *Media Matters*. July 16, 2020. https://www.mediamatters.org/coronavirus-covid-19/fox-news-pushed-coronavirus-misinformation-253-times-just-five-days

[31] Sollenberger, Roger. "Fox News peddled misinformation about the coronavirus 253 times in five days: study." *Salon*. July 18, 2020. https://www.salon.com/2020/07/17/fox-news-peddled-misinformation-about-the-coronavirus-253-times-in-five-days-study/

[32] Tsipursky, Gleb. "The Deadly Threat of Misinformation About COVID on Fox News, According to Science." *Common Dreams*. September 22, 2020. https://www.commondreams.org/views/2020/09/22/deadly-threat-misinformation-about-covid-fox-news-according-science

[33] Bursztyn, Leonardo et al. "Misinformation During a Pandemic." *National Bureau of Economic Research*. June, 2020 (revised September). https://www.nber.org/papers/w27417

[34] Gabriel, Trip. "Trump May Have Covid, but Many of His Supporters Still Scoff at Masks." *New York Times*. October 6, 2020. https://www.nytimes.com/2020/10/06/us/politics/trump-voters-face-masks.html

[35] Holland and Alper. "Trump advises voluntary mask use against coronavirus but won't wear one himself."

[36] Noack, Rick. "Trump's resistance to face masks, even while he is infected with coronavirus, sets him apart from other world leaders." *The Washington Post*. October 7, 2020. https://www.washingtonpost.com/health/2020/10/07/trump-coronavirus-face-masks-world-leaders/

[37] Peeples, Lynne. "Face masks: what the data say." *Nature*. October 6, 2020. https://www.nature.com/articles/d41586-020-02801-8

[38] Boodman, Eric. "Universal mask use could save 130,000 U.S. lives by the end of February, new study estimates." *Stat News*. October 23, 2020. https://www.statnews.com/2020/10/23/universal-mask-use-could-save-130000-lives-by-the-end-of-february-new-modeling-study-says/

[39] Jackson, Brooks. "FactChecking Trump's Town Hall." *Factcheck.org*. October 16, 2020. https://www.factcheck.org/2020/10/factchecking-trumps-town-hall/

[40] Gallucci, Nicole. "8 Karens and Kens who threw huge tantrums instead of putting on masks." *Mashable UK*. June 29, 2020. https://mashable.com/article/karen-no-mask-videos-tantrums-coronavirus/?europe=true

[41] Peeples. "Face masks: what the data say."

[42] Andone, Dakin. "Protests are popping up across the US over stay-at-home

restrictions." *CNN.com*. April 17, 2020. https://edition.cnn.com/2020/04/16/us/protests-coronavirus-stay-home-orders/index.html

43 Gallaway, M. Shayne et al. "Trends in COVID-19 Incidence After Implementation of Mitigation Measures — Arizona, January 22–August 7, 2020." Centers for Disease Control and Prevention. October 9, 2020. https://www.cdc.gov/mmwr/volumes/69/wr/mm6940e3.htm

44 Brauner, Jan M. et al. "The effectiveness of eight nonpharmaceutical interventions against COVID-19 in 41 countries." *MedRxiv*. October 14, 2020. https://www.medrxiv.org/content/10.1101/2020.05.28.20116129v4

45 Gabbatt, Adam. "Thousands of Americans backed by rightwing donors gear up for protests." *Guardian*. April 18, 2020. https://www.theguardian.com/us-news/2020/apr/18/coronavirus-americans-protest-stay-at-home

46 Forgey, Quint et al. "'I'd love to have it open by Easter': Trump says he wants to restart economy by mid-April." *Politico*. March 24, 2020. https://www.politico.com/news/2020/03/24/trump-wants-to-restart-economy-by-mid-april-146398

47 Moreland, Amanda et al. "Timing of State and Territorial COVID-19 Stay-at-Home Orders and Changes in Population Movement — United States, March 1–May 31, 2020." Centers for Disease Control and Prevention. September 4, 2020. https://www.cdc.gov/mmwr/volumes/69/wr/mm6935a2.htm

48 Forgey et al. "I'd love to have it open by Easter."

49 Gangel, Herb and Stuart. "'Play it down': Trump admits to concealing the true threat of coronavirus in new Woodward book."

50 Beer, Tommy. "All The Times Trump Compared Covid-19 To The Flu, Even After He Knew Covid-19 Was Far More Deadly." *Forbes*. September 10, 2020. https://www.forbes.com/sites/tommybeer/2020/09/10/all-the-times-trump-compared-covid-19-to-the-flu-even-after-he-knew-covid-19-was-far-more-deadly/?sh=3394bc8bf9d2

51 Gangel, Herb and Stuart. "'Play it down': Trump admits to concealing the true threat of coronavirus in new Woodward book."

52 "No, COVID-19 Is Not the Flu." *John Hopkins Bloomberg School of Public Health*. October 20, 2020. https://www.jhsph.edu/covid-19/articles/no-covid-19-is-not-the-flu.html

53 Trump, Donald. *Twitter*. October 6, 2020. https://www.thetrumparchive.com/?results=1&searchbox=%22Flu+season+is+coming+up%21%22

54 "Past Seasons Estimated Influenza Disease Burden." Centers for Disease Control and Prevention. https://www.cdc.gov/flu/about/burden/past-seasons.html

55 Worldometer. https://www.worldometers.info/coronavirus/country/us/

56 Cohen, Max. "Kellyanne Conway reacts to Trump's use of 'kung flu,' months after calling term 'highly offensive.'" *Politico*. June 24, 2020. https://www.politico.com/news/2020/06/24/kellyanne-conway-trump-kung-flu-coronavirus-337682

[57] Worldometer. https://www.worldometers.info/coronavirus/

[58] Worldometer. https://www.worldometers.info/coronavirus/country/us/

[59] Trump, Donald. *Twitter*. August 30, 2020. https://www.thetrumparchive.com/?dates=%5B%222020-08-01%22%2C%222020-08-31%22%5D&retweet=%22true%22&results=1&searchbox=%22CDC%22

[60] Sullivan, Peter. "GOP uses debunked theory to downplay COVID-19 death toll." *Hill*. September 6, 2020. https://thehill.com/policy/healthcare/515227-gop-uses-debunked-theory-to-downplay-covid-19-death-toll

[61] Aschwanden, Christie. "Debunking the False Claim That COVID Death Counts Are Inflated." *Scientific American*. October 20, 2020. https://www.scientificamerican.com/article/debunking-the-false-claim-that-covid-death-counts-are-inflated1/

[62] Ibid.

[63] Fichera, Angelo. "Trump Baselessly Suggests COVID-19 Deaths Inflated for Profit." *Factcheck.org*. October 29, 2020. https://www.factcheck.org/2020/10/trump-baselessly-suggests-covid-19-deaths-inflated-for-profit/

[64] "Speech: Donald Trump Holds a Campaign Rally in Waukesha, Wisconsin - October 24, 2020." *Factbase*. October 24, 2020. https://factba.se/transcript/donald-trump-speech-campaign-rally-waukesha-wisconsin-october-24-2020 (https://factba.se/transcript/donald-trump-speech-campaign-rally-waukesha-wisconsin-october-24-2020)

[65] Collins. "Trump could help solve the mask problem."

[66] Dale, Daniel. *Twitter*. March 29, 2020. https://twitter.com/ddale8/status/1244383303802793987?s=20

[67] Karni, Annie and Haberman, Maggie. "A White House Long in Denial Confronts Reality." *New York Times*. October 3, 2020 (updated October 6). https://www.nytimes.com/2020/10/03/us/politics/white-house-coronavirus.html

[68] Behrmann, Savannah. "'Politically correct': Trump pokes Fox News Host Laura Ingraham for wearing a mask." *USA Today News*. October 30, 2020. https://eu.usatoday.com/story/news/politics/elections/2020/10/30/trump-fox-news-laura-ingraham-politically-correct-wearing-mask/6094042002/

[69] Neuman, Scott. "'Maybe I'm Immune': Trump Returns To White House, Removes Mask Despite Infection." *NPR.org*. October 6, 2020. https://www.npr.org/sections/latest-updates-trump-covid-19-results/2020/10/06/920625432/maybe-i-m-immune-trump-returns-to-white-house-removes-mask-after-covid-treatment

[70] Tillett et al. "Genomic evidence for reinfection with SARS-CoV-2."

[71] "'I'll kiss everyone': Trump claims he has immunity at first rally since Covid diagnosis – video." *Guardian*. October 13, 2020. https://www.theguardian.com/global/video/2020/oct/12/ill-kiss-everyone-trump-claims-he-has-immunity-at-first-rally-since-covid-diagnosis-video

[72] "The Great Lockdown: Worst Economic Downturn Since the Great Depression." *International Monetary Fund.* March 23, 2020. https://www.imf.org/en/News/Articles/2020/03/23/pr2098-imf-managing-director-statement-following-a-g20-ministerial-call-on-the-coronavirus-emergency

[73] Samuels, Alex. "Dan Patrick says 'there are more important things than living and that's saving this country.'" *Texas Tribune.* April 21, 2020. https://www.texastribune.org/2020/04/21/texas-dan-patrick-economy-coronavirus/

[74] Surowiecki, James. "Forget Shutdowns. It's 'Demand Shock' That's Killing Our Economy." *Marker.* October 15, 2020. https://marker.medium.com/forget-shutdowns-its-demand-shock-that-s-killing-our-economy-3062e94c122e

[75] Worldometer. https://www.worldometers.info/coronavirus/country/us/

Conclusion

[1] Rupar, Aaron. *Twitter.* October 26, 2020. https://twitter.com/atrupar/status/1320748839331135489

[2] Specter, Michael. "After Ebola." *New Yorker.* August 1, 2014. https://www.newyorker.com/news/daily-comment/whats-ebola

[3] Hiltzik, Michael. "Column: Has Trump even read his own 'Coronavirus Guidelines for America?'" *Los Angeles Times.* March 24, 2020. https://www.latimes.com/business/story/2020-03-24/trump-guidelines-for-america

[4] Fritze, John. "Coronavirus postcard that featured Trump's name cost struggling Postal Service $28 million." *USA Today News.* May 28, 2020. https://eu.usatoday.com/story/news/politics/2020/05/28/coronavirus-post-card-trump-cost-post-office-28-million/5274034002/

[5] Wasserman et al. "2020 National Popular Vote Tracker."

[6] Noland, Marcus and Yiwen Zhang, Eva. "COVID-19 and the 2020 US Presidential Election." Peterson Institute for International Economics. March, 2021. https://www.piie.com/sites/default/files/documents/wp21-3.pdf

[7] Jacobs, Ben. "Is Trump's Coup a 'Dress Rehearsal?'" *New York Magazine.* December 27, 2020. https://nymag.com/intelligencer/2020/12/historians-fear-trumps-failed-coup-is-a-dress-rehearsal.html

[8] Dolan, Eric W. "Trump perceived as abnormally sadistic and narcissistic by both conservatives and liberals, study finds." *PsyPost.* April 29, 2020. https://www.psypost.org/2020/04/trump-perceived-as-abnormally-sadistic-and-narcissistic-by-both-conservatives-and-liberals-study-finds-56646

[9] United States Senate. "Russian Active Measures Campaigns and Interference in the 2016 U.S. Election."

[10] Rupar, Aaron. Twitter. March 25, 2021. https://twitter.com/atrupar/status/1375286080530866191?s=20

[11] Cole, Devan. "White House chief of staff: 'We are not going to control the pandemic.'" *CNN.com*. October 26, 2020. https://edition.cnn.com/2020/10/25/politics/mark-meadows-controlling-coronavirus-pandemic-cnntv/index.html

[12] Murphy, Joe and Siemaszko, Corky. "Operation Warp Speed at a crawl: Adequately vaccinating Americans will take 10 years at current pace." *NBCNews.com*. December 29, 2020 (updated December 30). https://www.nbcnews.com/news/us-news/current-rate-it-ll-be-10-years-americans-adequately-vaccinated-n1252486

[13] Trump, Donald. *Twitter*. December 30, 2020. https://www.thetrumparchive.com/?results=1&searchbox=%22The+Federal+Government+has+distributed%22

[14] Burns, Robert. "AP FACT CHECK: Trump distorts military role in vaccines." *AP News*. November 28, 2020. https://apnews.com/article/donald-trump-politics-coronavirus-pandemic-4f0591ffa6ec392e884652f5fda75194

[15] Florko, Nicholas. "New document reveals scope and structure of Operation Warp Speed and underscores vast military involvement." *Stat News*. September 28, 2020. https://www.statnews.com/2020/09/28/operation-warp-speed-vast-military-involvement/

[16] LaFraniere, Sharon, Thomas, Katie and Weiland, Noah. "Trump Administration Passed on Chance to Secure More of Pfizer Vaccine." *New York Times*. December 7, 2020 (updated December 11). https://www.nytimes.com/2020/12/07/us/politics/trump-pfizer-coronavirus-vaccine.html

[17] Lee, MJ. "Biden inheriting nonexistent coronavirus vaccine distribution plan and must start 'from scratch,' sources say." *CNN.com*. January 21, 2021. https://www.cnn.com/2021/01/21/politics/biden-covid-vaccination-trump/index.html

[18] Florko, Nicholas. "Trump officials actively lobbied to deny states money for vaccine rollout last fall." *Stat News*. January 31, 2021. https://www.statnews.com/2021/01/31/trump-officials-lobbied-to-deny-states-money-for-vaccine-rollout/

[19] Sammon, Alexander. "Prosecuting Trump Is the Only Way to Heal the Nation." *American Prospect*. November 25, 2020. https://prospect.org/justice/prosecuting-trump-is-the-only-way-to-heal-the-nation/ (https://prospect.org/justice/prosecuting-trump-is-the-only-way-to-heal-the-nation/)

[20] Budryk, Zack. "Clyburn: We may need a 9/11-like commission on COVID-19 response." *Hill*. December 17, 2020. https://thehill.com/homenews/house/530707-clyburn-to-chuck-todd-we-may-need-a-9-11-like-commission-on-covid-response

[21] Garger, Kenneth. "Trump says US 'probably' would never have COVID-19 vaccine if he wasn't president." *New York Post*. March 10, 2021, 2020. https://nypost.com/2021/03/10/trump-says-us-probably-wouldnt-have-covid-19-vaccine-if-not-for-him/

Postscript: The Pandemic Putsch

[1] Baker, Peter, Haberman, Maggie and Karni, Annie. "Pence Reached His Limit With Trump. It Wasn't Pretty." *New York Times*. January 12, 2020 (updated January 13). https://www.nytimes.com/2021/01/12/us/politics/mike-pence-trump.html

[2] "These 10 House Republicans voted to impeach Trump on Wednesday." *CNN. com*. January 13, 2020. https://edition.cnn.com/2021/01/13/politics/house-republicans-vote-yes-impeachment/index.html

[3] Goodman, Dugas and Tonckens. "Incitement Timeline: Year of Trump's Actions Leading to the Attack on the Capitol."

[4] Clement, Scott, Guskin, Emily and Balz, Dan. "Post-ABC poll: Overwhelming opposition to Capitol attacks, majority support for preventing Trump from serving again." *The Washington Post*. January 15, 2021. https://www.washingtonpost.com/politics/trump-poll-post-abc/2021/01/14/aeac7b96-5690-11eb-a817-e5e7f8a406d6_story.html

[5] "Covid pandemic turned 2020 into deadliest year in U.S. history, CDC finds." *NBCNews.com*. December 22, 2020. https://www.nbcnews.com/health/health-news/covid-pandemic-turned-2020-deadliest-year-u-s-history-cdc-n1252078

[6] Rizzo, Salvador. "Trump's fusillade of falsehoods on mail voting." *The Washington Post*. September 11, 2020. https://www.washingtonpost.com/politics/2020/09/11/trumps-fusillade-falsehoods-mail-voting/

[7] Swan and Basu. "Episode 1: A premeditated lie lit the fire."

[8] Dale, Daniel. "Fact check: Trump delivers the most dishonest speech of his presidency as Biden closes in on victory." *CNN.com*. November 6, 2020. https://edition.cnn.com/2020/11/05/politics/fact-check-trump-speech-thursday-election-rigged-stolen/index.html

[9] Gardner, Amy. "'I just want to find 11,780 votes': In extraordinary hour-long call, Trump pressures Georgia secretary of state to recalculate the vote in his favor." *The Washington Post*. January 4, 2020. https://www.washingtonpost.com/politics/trump-raffensperger-call-georgia-vote/2021/01/03/d45acb92-4dc4-11eb-bda4-615aaefd0555_story.html

[10] Lockhart, Joe. "Call out Trump's big lie." *CNN.com*. January 15, 2021. https://edition.cnn.com/2021/01/14/opinions/trumps-big-lie-impeachment-lockhart/index.html

[11] Wasserman et al. "2020 National Popular Vote Tracker."

[12] "Capitol riots: Did Trump's words at rally incite violence?" *BBC*. January 13, 2021. https://www.bbc.co.uk/news/world-us-canada-55640437

[13] "What Trump Said to Supporters on Jan. 6 Before Their Capitol Riot." *Wall Street Journal*. January 12, 2021. https://www.wsj.com/articles/what-trump-said-to-supporters-on-jan-6-before-their-capitol-riot-11610498173

Made in the USA
Monee, IL
19 June 2021